SIOUX CITY
A PICTORIAL HISTORY

Sioux City was known as the Steamboat Capital of the Upper Missouri River from 1868 until 1873. This rare photo, taken from a third-floor window of the Sawyers Block at the northwest corner of Second and Pearl streets, shows Sioux City's levee about 1870. The two nearest steamboats are the North Alabama (left) and the Zephyr (right). Photo courtesy of Sioux City Public Museum

SIOUX CITY
A PICTORIAL HISTORY

Scott Sorensen and B. Paul Chicoine

Design by Jamie Backus Raynor
Donning Company/Publishers
Norfolk/Virginia Beach

To Diane and Rosie

Library of Congress Cataloging in Publication Data

Sorensen, Scott, 1952-
    Sioux City: a pictorial history

    Bibliography: p.
    Includes index.
    1. Sioux City (Iowa)—History—Pictorial
works.   2. Sioux City (Iowa)—Description—
Views.   I. Chicoine, B. Paul, 1951-
II. Title.
F629.S6S87   1982   977.7'41   82-17723
ISBN 0-89865-276-6

Printed in the United States of America.

Contents

Foreword

Walt Whitman, who heard America singing in every locale and many voices, never lived in Sioux City nor the region around it which has come to be known as Siouxland. Yet Whitman's sense of the area provides a key to reading this book and discovering its riches of depiction. Listen to Walt as you begin . . .

"Others may praise what they like:

But I, from the banks of the running Missouri, praise nothing in art or aught else,

Till it has well inhaled the atmosphere of this river, also the western prairie-scent,

And exudes it all again . . . ."

The writers and collators of this book have gained in relative youth the perspective of the centuries in which human beings have moved around Siouxland. Their talent for finding, understanding, and relating resources of actualities contributes to their unusual ability to turn those scenes and happenings into that rare commodity, reality. The blending style comes from their inhaling the atmosphere, as Whitman required; and as they "exude it all again," the addition emerges from their genuine interest in the seasons and people of this place. They pay proper respect to predecessor keepers of the words and pictures, but they merit special thanks for making this the first sensible venture in putting the Sioux City story into a genuine narrative and photographic coherence. It is a salutary work for a vital chronicle, and their sensitive labors will light the next eras and persons of this place where three rivers meet and represent the flow of history.

Prepare to participate in the experience. The authors are positive in their attitudes but will let you know the darker undercurrents. Their praise of the events and actors in the Siouxland drama is invested with the tension involved in Carl Sandburg's questions which the people always ask: "Where to? What next?"

—Carrol McLaughlin

Preface

"A new gateway to the West" was one nineteenth-century journalist's memorable metaphor for Sioux City, then a rough-and-tumble Iowa border town whose sheltering bluffs and broad crescent riverfront led, in succession, early Missouri River fur traders, steamboatmen, and railroad builders to brand it as a strategic crossroad for exploration and commerce onto America's northern plains.

For generations untold, the confluence of the Big Sioux, Floyd, and Missouri rivers where Sioux City now stands, has witnessed and influenced the comings and goings of mankind. To its earliest native inhabitants it was a haven for hunting, fishing, and camping, as well as a refuge from the prairie's winter fury. It excited the imaginations of nineteenth-century explorers and artists who passed its shores. Only later would it give birth to a community which at various times would be regaled as Iowa's capital city of commerce—a meatpacking, transportation, and marketing center superseded only by St. Louis and Chicago!

Sioux City's history has been a colorful saga. But through it all, through its triumphs and tragedies, it has remained foremost a city of people. The land speculator seeking fortune on the edge of the wilderness, the farmer drawn by the promise of fertile soil, the immigrant pursuing a better life for self and loved ones—all were people with dreams who were willing to work, and work hard, to make their dreams come true. Their determination and courage has transcended all aspects of Siouxland's history from settlement to present, to become the foundation for Sioux City's future.

The authors wish to acknowledge those persons and institutions who have made this account possible and who have contributed immeasurably to its worth. Those who research and write about Sioux City, of course, owe a great debt to the early compilers of city history. Four of these pioneer historians deserve a special tribute: O. B. Talley (1860-1925), an abstractor by profession, whose detailed researching of government records and newspapers has made the study of transportation and land development in the Siouxland area anything but abstract; Constant R. Marks (1841-1932), a Sioux City attorney for over sixty years, who chronicled the lives of many of the community's pioneers; Gertrude Brown Henderson (1883-1954), whose overwhelming love of local history led her to research and write extensively on a wide variety of subjects; and Alice Spalding (1876-1967), who meticulously indexed years of early Sioux City newspapers.

The contributions of these past pioneers and of countless others were made available to the authors through the courtesy of the Sioux City Public Museum, an institution without whose immense resources and cooperation the writing of this book would have been impossible. The museum, a collector of documentary history for decades, is to be especially commended for the substantial upgrading of its archival services from 1979 through 1981 as a result of an archival program funded jointly by the National Historical Publications and Records Commission and the Sioux City Museum and Historical Association. During this project, archival staff under the direction of John L. LeDoux organized, cataloged, and stored thousands of photographs and other important collections, an effort which made the authors' subsequent research efforts more gratifying and more successful. Credit must also go to the museum's Siouxland Oral History Program for providing the transcribed insights of more than 400 individuals, whose personal memories helped supply the participatory aspect vital to the text and many of the captions. Last but certainly not least, special thanks are extended to museum director B. R. Diamond, registrar Sadie Taxer, and other museum staff members for their unfailing moral support and research cooperation, and for keeping us supplied with those ever-vital pots of coffee during the many long evenings of research and writing.

The majority of photographs displayed in this book are from the archival collections of the Sioux City Public Museum. The authors are also grateful to the many other individuals and institutions who lent photographs for reproduction, as well as those who shared pictures with us which for one reason or another could not be used. Mary Bennett, photo archivist for the Division of the State Historical Society of Iowa, John Carter, curator of photographs for the Nebraska State Historical Society, Christie Dailey, editor of *The Annals of Iowa,* and the staff of the Sioux City Public Library also were very helpful. Paul Fleckenstein, of Woodworth Commercial Photos, provided the excellent photographic reproductions for the publisher.

Experts in specific fields of Sioux City history greatly benefitted the book's content and style. Richard L. Poole, chairman of the Speech and Theatre Department at Briar Cliff College and an authority on Sioux City theater history, graciously reviewed chapters 3, 4, and 5 and contributed many additional details beyond the authors' knowledge to those sections relating to the Academy of Music and the Peavey Grand Opera House. Roy and Jean Raney of Denver, Colorado, whose combined interests in Sioux City history from 1875 and 1885 are matchless in this day, generously volunteered many hours to review and edit all chapter texts and many of the captions. Together they aided the authors immeasurably, not only in identifying historical weaknesses, but also in improving writing style. Cognizant of the important contributions made by these very special individuals, however, the authors assume all responsibility for errors or misinterpretations.

And, for bearing with our efforts, our absences, and the burdens entailed in writing a book, our thanks to our wives Diane and Rosie, without whose support we could never have finished this work.

Prologue

Recording Exploits on a Buffalo Hide.
*Drawing by Chuck Raymond; courtesy of
Sioux City Public Museum*

*For nearly 100 years the Missouri and Big
Sioux rivers marked the juncture of
customs—and languages—between Sioux-
land's Plains and Woodland peoples.
Drawing by Chuck Raymond; courtesy of
Sioux City Public Museum*

*The westward push of white colonialism
throughout this nation's early centuries
forced America's native inhabitants to
crowd ever westward. The Dakota nation,
pressed by their ancient Ojibway enemies in
the Great Lakes region, migrated into
Minnesota, northwestern Iowa, and the
Dakotas by 1800—a domain which included
present-day Sioux City. Drawing by Chuck
Raymond; courtesy of Sioux City Public
Museum*

Sioux City shares with much of the Great Plains a geological and biological heritage of dramatic and sometimes violent change. The chapters of that past, written over millions of years by nature, are preserved for all to see in the rugged bluffs and winding river bottoms of our community, and in the folklore of its native people.

During certain periods of its past, Sioux City has been covered with molten lava and Arctic ice. It has also been a swamp, a jungle, a desert, and a prairie. Each of these transitions has helped to shape this community's destiny and left a special mark on Siouxland, a term coined in the late 1940s by noted northwest Iowa author Frederick Manfred.

Exposures of limestone and shale, the oldest native geological material visible in western Woodbury County, can be seen in certain road cuts, creek bottoms, and river bluffs near Sioux City and Stone Park. These deposits range from 20 to 200 feet deep at points, and contain the fossil remains of sea mollusks, fish, and other marine creatures which thrived in the Midwest's last great inland seas of the Cretaceous Period over 60 million years ago.

Following the upheaval of the Rocky Mountains and the withdrawal of the seas, these fossil deposits were carved and battered by wind and stream erosion to create a surface terrain more like that of western South Dakota than of the rolling bluffs we know today. The Missouri River, which was created during this period to drain the new plateau, staged an abrupt about-face from its northward passage 45 million years later, to be thrown against this rock, thus defining the contour of Sioux City's Missouri River Valley.

Finally, between 1 and 2 million years ago, a cataclysmic series of events took place that would become important to Sioux City geologically as well as commercially. Four gigantic glaciers, each thousands of miles wide and up to ten thousand feet thick, came creeping at intervals out of the frozen Arctic to cover much of what is now the northern United States and Canada. Two of these glaciers plunged their icy fingers across Siouxland, triggering the disappearance of the region's early plains-era wildlife, including the mastodon, horse, and camel. These glaciers' scouring and filling action gouged out lakebeds and heaped plain and valley alike with a moonscape of Ice Age debris, called till. Quartz boulders, deposits of gravel and sand, and the blue clays which line Siouxland's streams and riverbeds are a few of that era's most visible legacies.

Even the hot, dry periods between the glaciers worked to Siouxland's advantage. Great, raging winds from the south and west pulverized the unglaciated plains west of the Missouri River, depositing a rich mantle of yellow dust as much as 300 feet deep to either side of the Missouri River. Called loess, it is, with proper moisture and humus conditions, an unusually fertile soil, as well as an excellent raw material for brick.

The Missouri River, the Big Sioux, the Floyd River, and Perry Creek—once swollen meltwater streams—returned in time to their narrow channels to lazily carve out the generous valleys which we know today. Conditions became ideal for grazing and browsing animals. The bison, elk, and deer returned. The Missouri River once again teemed with fish, the woods with nuts and berries. The time was then ripe for a new arrival to Siouxland's environment—this time in the form of man.

The questions of who the first Sioux Cityans were, where they came from, and when they arrived has baffled both white men and native Americans in western Woodbury County throughout much of our recorded history. Most anthropologists agree, however, that Siouxland's earliest inhabitants were direct descendants of Stone-Age Asian hunters who crossed the Bering Strait land bridges in search of big game at least 12,000 to 15,000 years ago. Evidence unearthed in nearby Cherokee County and discovered along the streambeds and lowlands of Woodbury County points to the presence of scattered tribes of elk and bison hunters as far back as 10,000 years ago. What became of these people is not fully known, but they were probably the victims of a great drought that began about 5000 B.C. and lasted until about 4,500 years ago. The discovery of Folsom-type projectile points, skin-working tools, butchered bison bones, and caches of seeds, roots, and wild plant foods shows the existence of a small, bison-hunting and seed-gathering culture through the entire period of drought.

The drought hardly had ended when once again native man—tribes from a group of nations known collectively as the Plains Woodland Culture—moved into the Missouri Valley from the east. The most visible of these tribes are known as the Mill Creek Culture and existed in the Sioux City area between 500 B.C. and A.D. 1000, with a major village site situated on Broken Kettle Creek, just north of today's city limits. Unlike the nomadic tribes which preceded and followed them, the Mill Creek tribes occupied the same village sites for generations, often building new rectangular mud, grass, and timber lodges over the old, resulting in the formation of mounds. They cultivated crops such as pumpkins, corn, melons, and herbs to serve with wildfowl and meat. They were highly skilled in fashioning bone tools such as bison-shoulder-blade hoes, fish hooks, awls, and soup ladles, and in the production of decorative pottery bowls and jars. Owing to changing climate or, perhaps, pressure from the nearby Oneota tribes, the Mill Creek tribes had vanished from the Big Sioux Valley by 1400. No one knows where they went.

By the time the white man reached western Woodbury County in the mid-1700s, two distinct Siouan-speaking subcultures appeared on the Missouri's riverbanks to greet him. The first group, made up of the Otos, Omahas, Iowas, and Poncas, dwelled in the river bottoms of the Missouri River and its tributaries from Omaha to what is now the state of South Dakota.

Their village life was largely uncomplicated. Women tended crops of corn, squash, and beans, while men hunted among the wooded bluffs and plains and defended their families from outside attack. Their clothing, fashioned from skins, was often highly elaborate and skillfully ornamented with quills.

Sioux City took its name from the Big Sioux River—known to early native inhabitants as the Tchan-kas-an-data ("the pipe of peace")—and from the Dakota Sioux nation, the second largest and most powerful of the Midwest's Siouan-speaking tribes. The name "Sioux," a French-Canadian derivative of *Nadowessioux,* is from an Ojibway name for their old enemies and signifies "snake," or by metaphor, "enemy." The term has since identified the proud, fierce nation of nomads who, when pressed from their ancestral home in Wisconsin by white encroachment, migrated to northwest Iowa, Minnesota, and the Dakotas during the 1700s. Skilled on horseback and brave in character, the Dakota dominated the Iowa and Dakota shores of the Big Sioux River and lands north of the Floyd well into the early 1800s. They hunted and fished along the Big Sioux Valley, wintered beneath its bluffs, and buried their dead on its hills.

Yet life in the middle-1700s was nearing its eclipse for the Dakota and their Siouan neighbors. Blue beads, traded northward from tribe to tribe along the Missouri, were rumored to come from strange men "with skins the color of corn." Honey bees, then foreign to Siouxland's native peoples, also were observed by Ponca and Omaha medicine men as harbingers of impending change. They would not have long to wait.

11

On May 14, 1804, President Thomas Jefferson dispatched young U.S. Army Captains Meriwether Lewis and William Clark on what was to become a 5,000-mile, three-year expedition of discovery across the newly-purchased French territory of Louisiana. Nearly fifty men—soldiers, hunters, scouts, and professional Missouri River boatmen—comprised the handpicked company. A fifty-foot keelboat escorted by two log pirogues carried the expedition's supplies, which included, among numerous necessary items, hundreds of peace medals, trinkets, mirrors, and blankets to placate the various Indian tribes along the route.

By late August, the explorers had poled, paddled, pushed, and pulled their way up the Missouri River to the shores of what is now northern Woodbury County, where, on August 20, 1804, Sergeant Charles Floyd, a Kentucky native, suddenly sickened and died.

Floyd's burial atop the river bluff which now bears his name marked the first interment of a United States soldier west of the Mississippi River. Painting by Dean Cornwell; courtesy of New York Life Insurance Company

Chapter 1

Strangers at the Bluff

1764-1853

"We Set out under a gentle breeze from the South-East," wrote a bone-weary and saddened Captain Meriwether Lewis, as he squinted at his diary by firelight. "Passed two islands on the South Side and at the first Bluff on the South Side Sergeant Floyd died with a great deal of composure.... We buried him on the top of the bluff ½ Mile below a Small river to which we gave his name.... A Seeder post with the name Sergt. C. Floyd died here 20th of august 1804 was fixed at the head of his grave."

Such episodes as the death of Charles Floyd, a soldier in the service of the United States Army, were not new to this corner of America's yet-unconquered West by this summer's eve of August 20, 1804; but the writer was logging a milestone in history far more momentous than he could have imagined. Lewis, then just twenty-nine, was an explorer—a co-commander (with fellow Captain William Clark) on this fledgling nation's first expedition of discovery across the American continent. His pained description of the journey's first and only casualty was to give the world its first written description of the landmarks that would become Sioux City.

Lewis and Clark, however, were not the first white-skinned visitors to lay eyes on Sioux City's distinctive headlands. Commencing forty years earlier, French and Spanish fur traders, some from as far south as St. Louis and New Orleans, were regularly paddling their dugout canoes and keelboats past the future townsite on the Missouri River, enroute for the fur-rich Northern Plains.

One of these daring *voyageurs,* a Frenchman named Boyer, is believed to have been the first white man to visit this corner of northwest Iowa, leading a small band of St. Louis fur trappers up the treacherous Missouri as early as 1764. Another bold adventurer, Charles LeRaye, the son of a French nobleman and Revolutionary War hero, is known to have spent the winter of 1801-1802 near the mouth of the Big Sioux

Meriwether Lewis and William Clark were commanders of the 1804-1806 Louisiana Expedition up the Missouri. Photo courtesy of Sioux City Public Museum

River as captive of a Sioux Indian war party. LeRaye's memoirs, published years after his ransom by fellow fur trappers in 1803, tell of intense suffering endured by captive and captor alike at the Big Sioux camp. They also give the region's first weather report.

Despite the nearly half-century of river traffic that followed Boyer and LeRaye up the "Big Muddy"—a migration which included such visitors as naturalist John James Audubon and artists George Catlin and Karl Bodmer—the area we regard today as Sioux City was not formally settled until 1848. In that year William Thompson, a Mexican War veteran and widower from Morgan County, Illinois, constructed a log trading post at the base of Floyd's Bluff and subsequently staked out a townsite. While a handful of French squatters are believed to have preceded him into the neighborhood, Thompson is today regarded as Woodbury County's first registered settler. His townsite, however, was doomed to fail. Platted as Floyd's Bluff City, it withered due to an inhospitable hillside location—a factor further compounded by Thompson's entanglement in Woodbury County's first recorded murder. Despite the fact that the Iowa legislature designated it as the seat of government for Woodbury County, Floyd's Bluff City never progressed beyond its single trading-post cabin.

It remained for Theophile Bruguier, a Canadian, in 1849, to sow the first viable seed of Sioux City settlement. A native of L'Assumpcion, near Montreal, Bruguier was already a hardened fourteen-year veteran of the upper Missouri River fur trade when he arrived with his two Indian wives and father-in-law, an aged Asanti chief named War Eagle, to establish an independent fur trading depot near the mouth of the Big Sioux River.

J. C. C. Hoskins, a pioneer Sioux Cityan and later first city engineer, describes Bruguier's trading post as "a community of log cabins...a large log house [standing apart from] a half a dozen smaller cabins or stables." Bruguier constructed these additional cabins, history recalls, to shelter his numerous Yankton Sioux relatives who regularly journeyed overland from as far north as Fort Pierre and the Sissiton region in the Dakotas to trade at the Big Sioux post.

Bruguier's sprawling trading post and farm holdings during this period encompassed much of what is now South Riverside and Riverside Park, and extended as far as Prospect Hill. He also claimed "squatter's rights" to a 160-acre parcel of swampy flatland on the east bank of Perry Creek. This piece of land, which he later sold to fellow fur trader Joseph Leonnais, constitutes much of what is today's downtown district. Some other settlers claiming land in the vicinity at this time included August Traversier, a rival American Fur Company trader, Gustave Pecaut, Charles Rouleaux (Rulo), Louis Letellier, Leander L'Cartier (Kirke), Henry Angie, and Louis Menard.

Existence for residents of this yet-unnamed French-Anglo colony at The Bluffs hinged on the fortunes of the fur trade and the cycles of the land which surrounded it. Cut off from civilization by a thousand miles of frozen river in winter and sun-scorched prairie in summer, Sioux City's first white families focused by necessity on the simple exigencies of survival: sickness and health, birth and death, how to trade peacefully with tribal patrons often at war with each other, and succeeding in that, the provision of adequate food, clothing, and shelter.

This 1833 watercolor by Karl Bodmer shows the crew of the steamboat Yellowstone, *caught on a Missouri River sandbar, struggling to lighten their ship's cargo. The* Yellowstone, *built and operated by the American Fur Company, was the first steamboat to visit the future site of Sioux City, passing the location six times between 1831 and 1833. Photo courtesy of the InterNorth Art Foundation, Joslyn Art Museum, Omaha, Nebraska*

Floyd's Grave, Where Lewis and Clark Buried Sergeant Floyd, *by George Catlin, 1832. Photo of watercolor courtesy of National Museum of American Art, Smithsonian Institution; gift of Mrs. Sarah Harrison*

View from Floyd's Grave, 1,300 Miles
Above St. Louis *was painted by George
Catlin.*

*Many distinguished travelers over the
decades have described the beauty of
Charles Floyd's burial place. Artist George
Catlin, returning by canoe from the 1832
Yellowstone expedition up the Missouri,
was moved to rhapsody, writing:*

> *I landed my canoe in front of this grass
> covered mound, and all hands being
> fatigued, we camped a couple of days at
> its base. I several times ascended it and
> sat upon his grave, overgrown with
> grass and the most delicate wild
> flowers, where I sat and contemplated
> the solitude and stillness of this
> tenanted mound; and beheld from its
> top the windings infinite of the
> Missouri . . . its thousand hills and
> domes of green vanishing into blue in
> the distance . . . and looked upon the
> valley below me, both up and down the
> river, and contemplated the thousand
> hills and dales that are now carpeted
> with green, streaked as they will
> someday be, with the plow and yellow
> with the harvest sheaf; spotted with
> lowing kine, with houses and fences,
> and groups of hamlets and villas.
> (Catlin,* North American Indians).

*This written description and the
accompanying Catlin views are the earliest
known illustrations of Sioux City in
existence. Photo of watercolor courtesy of
National Museum of American Art, Smithsonian Institution; gift of Mrs. Sarah
Harrison*

Karl Bodmer and Prince Maximilian are shown meeting with the Indians. This is one of over 400 subjects Bodmer rendered in watercolors as the official artist of German naturalist-prince Alexander Philip Maximilian von Wied's epic American expedition of 1832-34. Bodmer's paints and sketchbooks, kept close-at-hand in the large pouch seen in this artist's self portrait, provided the curious world with an invaluable source of information on the then-unconquered upper Missouri River country.

Shown right to left: Karl Bodmer, Prince Maximilian, and interpreter Touissant Charboneau, former scout for the Lewis and Clark Expedition. Photo of Bodmer watercolor courtesy of the InterNorth Art Foundation, Joslyn Art Museum, Omaha, Nebraska

Mouth of the Big Sioux River, May 8, 1833. Swiss artist Karl Bodmer, Prince Maximilian, and their fellow passengers aboard the steamboat Yellowstone enjoyed much the same view of Sioux City's Riverside bluffs as do today's travelers along Interstate 29. Painted from the Yellowstone's deck at what is now dry land near Sioux Point—then mid-channel on the Missouri River—Bodmer's artistry captured the marriage of Siouxland's two largest rivers. Photo of Bodmer watercolor courtesy of InterNorth Art Foundation, Joslyn Art Museum, Omaha, Nebraska

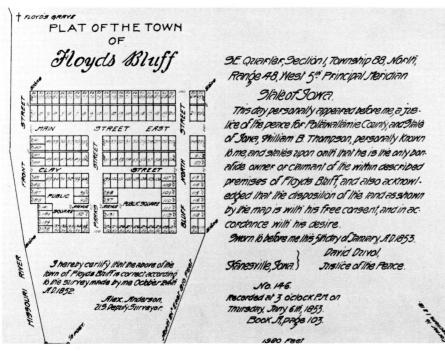

PLAT OF THE TOWN
OF
Floyds Bluff

SE Quarter, Section 1, Township 88, North, Range 48, West 5th Principal Meridian

State of Iowa.

This day personally appeared before me, a justice of the peace for Pottawattamie County and State of Iowa, William B Thompson, personally known to me, and states upon oath that he is the only bonafide owner or claimant of the within described premises of Floyds Bluff, and also acknowledged that the disposition of the land as shown by the map is with his free consent, and in accordance with his desire.

Sworn to before me this 5th day of January, A.D. 1853.

David Davol,
Kanesville, Iowa.} Justice of the Peace.

No. 146.
Recorded at 3 o'clock P.M. on Thursday, Jany 6th, 1853. Book A, page 103.

I hereby certify that the above plat of the town of Floyds Bluff is correct according to the survey made by me October 24th A.D. 1852.

Alex. Anderson,
U.S. Deputy Surveyor.

Floyd's Bluff City—recorded in 1853 and known also as Floyd City, Thompsonville, and Thompsonstown—preceded Sioux City in actual platting by only two years. William Thompson's combined trading post and cabin home on the site was an important stopping place for land travelers on the oxcart trail from Council Bluffs. Loss of county seat status to nearby Sioux City combined with other factors to doom the settlement. Interstate Highway 29 and the Missouri River today cover the area. Photo courtesy of Sioux City Public Museum

Theophile Bruguier (1813-1896), a former student of law from the village of L'Assumpcion near Montreal, left Canada at the age of twenty-one following the death of his fiancee to join the St. Louis-based American Fur Company as a post clerk and trader.

Bruguier's legendary impatience with restraints caused him to break with American Fur during the late 1830s and assume fellowship with a tribe of Yankton Sioux Indians, a trading relationship which culminated in his marriage to all three daughters of a Yankton Sioux tribal elder, War Eagle, and the establishment of an independent trading post near the mouth of the Big Sioux River in 1849. He was instrumental in convincing Council Bluffs (then Kanesville) fur trade outfitter James A. Jackson to establish a townsite at Sioux City.

Bruguier served as an Indian commissioner, contract army wagon freighter, and one-term clerk of courts for Woodbury County before retiring to a farm near Salix, Iowa. Lithograph courtesy of Sioux City Public Museum

Amelia Menard Rulo was an early resident of the Floyd's Bluff French community of the 1850s. One of three half-Indian daughters of fur trader Louis Menard, Amelia was approaching adulthood in 1848 when William Thompson staked out his townsite along the cart trail. It was over the attentions of Amelia's sister, Sophia Menard, that William Thompson murdered U.S. Indian agent James Norwood during a dance at a nearby cabin in September 1852.

Amelia, shown here in an 1860 photo, later married trader Charles Rouleaux (Rulo) and went on to help establish the community of Rulo, Nebraska. Photo courtesy of Sioux City Public Museum

Bruguier's cabin, constructed of local cottonwood in 1849, was only one of a small cluster of cabins and fur storage sheds erected near the mouth of the Big Sioux River. Shown here reduced in height from its original one-and-one-half floors, this structure is believed to be only half of a "double-log" cabin, meaning that it and a similar adjoining structure shared a common roof. Its logs were squared with an adze, dovetailed, and pegged at the corners in a construction style typical of early French Canada.

The cabin was home to the Bruguier family until 1869, when it was sold to William Tredway. Its existence, however, was largely forgotten until 1933, when a Wall Street Mission work relief crew under the direction of Reverend John Hantla, Sr., discovered it beneath a facade of newer siding. With the help of federal work-relief funds, it was dismantled and reassembled piece-by-piece at its current site in Riverside Park, where it serves as a club house for the Girls of 68, a women's organization of pioneer descendants. Photo courtesy of Sioux City Public Museum

Among a party of 100 trappers, traders, and seekers-of-fortune to depart St. Louis for the upper Missouri River country in 1839 was sixteen-year-old Joseph Leonnais, a young runaway from lower Canada.

Leonnais, pictured here in his later years, spent his next thirteen years working side-by-side with such frontier notables as keelboatmen Mike Fink and Joseph LaBarge before settling on a 160-acre claim purchased from Theophile Bruguier in 1852. His farm, which he later sold to Dr. John Cook as an "orchard site," included much of today's downtown area. Mrs. Mary Ann Lapore, a widowed sister living with him at the time, later became the first white woman to be married in Sioux City. Photo courtesy of Sioux City Public Museum

Throughout much of this century, popular tradition held this giant oak in Riverside Park to be the Council Oak tree, beneath which Captains Lewis and Clark met with local Indians, and Yankton Sioux leader War Eagle, Theophile Bruguier's father-in-law, presided over tribal councils. Consequently, a storm of controversy erupted when a local contractor bulldozed the crumbling stump—all that remained of the tree in 1971—into the nearby Big Sioux River.

While it is true that the Council Oak was already fully grown at the time of Lewis and Clark's visit and was familiar to later settlers, no historical evidence has yet come to light of such activities beneath its bows. Lewis and Clark recorded no parleys with Indians during their brief encampment on the Big Sioux, and Mrs. Julia Conger, Bruguier's daughter and War Eagle's granddaughter, denied in 1922 that she had ever heard of the tree spoken of by Indians or early white men.

Pioneer historian Constant R. Marks, furthermore, documented the legend to be one of Sioux City's earliest real estate promotion schemes, in which developers M. B. Davis, L. S. Fawcett, and other local landowners arranged with the Sioux City Journal in the 1880s to devise an advertising campaign focusing on the park's oldest tree. Fact or fiction, the Council Oak remained one of Riverside Park's most revered attractions for nearly a century. A granite monument today marks its passing. Photo by Philip C. Waltermire; courtesy of Sioux City Public Museum

Chapter 2

Setting Down Stakes

1853 – 1868

Speculation and townsite mania raged rampant across Iowa's western frontier in the 1850s, bringing with it the bloom of cityhood for The Bluffs.

In the early 1850s, following the lead established by William Thompson and other nearby townsite promoters, pioneer settler Theophile Bruguier reportedly convinced Council Bluffs merchant James A. Jackson and Jackson's step-father-in-law, Dr. John K. Cook, a government surveyor, that the fertile bluff bottoms between the Big Sioux and Floyd rivers held vast profit potential as a townsite development.

The Sioux City Townsite Company, as a result, was organized in 1854 and included the following members: Dr. Cook; Jackson; Iowa territorial official Jesse Williams; banker Daniel Rider; Congressman Bernhart Henn; and Iowa's two senators, George W. Jones and A. C. Dodge. The abilities of each of these shareholders helped to insure the townsite project's success. Representative Henn and Senators Jones and Dodge lobbied for the company's varied interests in Congress, Rider and Jackson supplied financial backing, and Jesse Williams supervised the promotion and sale of town lots through Iowa's largest real estate firm, Henn, Williams and Company.

Sioux City's first streets were staked out by resident townsite agent Dr. Cook and fellow surveyor George Chamberlin in the winter of 1854-55. Cook and Chamberlin boarded with trapper Joseph Leonnais and his sister, Mrs. Mary Ann Lapore, at their cabin near Perry Creek. The town was to be a model frontier community, complete with a central public square, a central business district, and a residential neighborhood—all, according to Cook's precise plan, to be located west of Perry Creek. Realization that the settlement's success depended upon good river access, however, led Dr. Cook and Daniel Rider to purchase Joe Leonnais' pre-emptive rights to an additional 160 acres of Missouri riverfront. This farm, which Leonnais sold for $3,000 despite the warnings of his sister, became

Woodbury Sanborn, Charles Claypoole, and Edmund Pendleton (left to right) are standing near the window of the Sherwin Land Office School in the early 1880s. This building has been part of Sioux City's history since 1857. Carried in sections from St. Louis by steamboat and assembled at the southeast corner of Seventh and Douglas streets, it was used by G. W. F. Sherwin as his real estate office. Later it served as temporary homes for both the Congregational and Methodist Episcopal churches. In 1870 the school board rented it as an intermediate school for $150 annually, hence the name of Sherwin Land Office School. In the early 1880s, when this photograph was taken, the school system retired the building. For years it stood behind the John P. Allison home. Finally, in 1908, the Boys of '68 acquired the historic structure for their clubhouse and moved it to Stone Park, where it still stands today. Photo courtesy of Sioux City Public Museum

Sioux City's downtown East Addition.

From that time on, Sioux City began to look like a town rather than a mere bend in the river. Cabins sprouted from the muddy riverbank. A bank, hotels, and a government land office opened for business in 1855, as did the city's first post office. These last two government offices, headed by Dr. S. P. Yeomans and Dr. Cook, respectively, reflected the power wielded by the company's political members, since such offices in those times were granted only by government favor. Legislators Henn, Jones, and Dodge succeeded in pushing through Congress a land grant in 1856 to assist construction of a railroad from Dubuque. Little did it matter to Sioux City's promoters that Dubuque, 300 miles to the east, had only recently acquired its own railroad. Sioux City, its supporters proclaimed, was certain to be next in line!

In an 1856 county election, Sioux City succeeded nearby Floyd's Bluff—with its solitary resident—and Sergeant's Bluff's City (now Sergeant Bluff) as Woodbury County's official and final county seat. The next year, in a unique twist of events, Iowa's legislature officially incorporated Sioux City as a town. In doing so, the state officials stipulated that the new river hamlet adopt the ward system of local government, with the First Ward encompassing all land west of Perry Creek, and Jones Street dividing the Second and Third wards.

Sioux City's early elections based on this system were highly competitive affairs, with voting outcomes often hinging upon quick wit and pugilistic prowess, as each ward vied for political and economic favors. At the city's first election, held on August 3, 1857, Dr. Cook himself nearly created a city-wide riot when, in his capacity of county judge, he declared invalid the Third Ward's ballots in order to elect a mayor of his own choice. Not until eight months later would Sioux City properly elect its own first mayor. Grading streets, bridging Perry Creek, and controlling stray hogs and cattle on the streets were among the concerns of the community's early mayors and councils.

Because of the highly speculative nature of its founding, Sioux City's population during its first years was dominated largely by non-laboring investors—doctors, bankers, lawyers, merchants, and land agents—who had come out by horseback and steamboat, intending to "strike it rich" in townsite land. This scramble for land made the U.S. Land Office on Pearl Street the nucleus of Sioux City's economic, political, and social life, for a time surpassing even the riverfront in activity. Town lots, selling for as much as $1,000 in early 1857, changed hands on nearly a day-to-day basis.

The high cost of land and the shortage of farmers caused agriculture to lag behind for several years. The city, for the only time in its agricultural history, was required to import the bulk of its food. The Missouri River thus became Sioux City's life line—supplying the town with food, tools, lumber, and manufactured goods, along with an ever-steady stream of hopeful settlers and home buyers. In 1856 only six steamboats docked at Sioux City's First Street levee. By 1857 the number of arrivals had mushroomed to more than fifty vessels. Mary E. Wilkins, the town's first schoolteacher, and Seth W. Swiggett, founder of the village's first newspaper, the *Sioux City Eagle,* were two of that flotilla's most noted early passengers.

Late in 1857, however, a financial depression, called a "panic," put a damper on Sioux City's town lot mania. Property values plummeted. The "paper fortunes" of many investors vanished. Postponement of rail construction and a restriction of local government funds, never large to begin with, added to the city's woes. By August 1860 the city government teetered on the brink of bankruptcy.

The panic of 1857, a financial disaster to many early Sioux Cityans, wrought major changes in the city's social development. By the late fall of 1857, many of the town's early boosters had abandoned the scene of their misfortunes; others had simply returned East for the winter. Those hardy pioneers who remained, though, rallied against the prevailing gloom by organizing a community-wide Thanksgiving celebration in much the same fashion as the Pilgrims' first Thanksgiving.

Another significant diversion initiated for benefit of the winter-bound populace was the creation of the Sioux City Lyceum, a debating society of prominent Sioux City businessmen. At weekly meetings they listened to lectures and argued such important issues of the day as "Resolved, that the United States should acquire Cuba—peaceably if she can, forcibly if she must" and "Should women enjoy the same rights of property and franchise as men?" Through these public exercises, Sioux City's pioneer men sharpened their skills in public discourse while honing their promotional talents for the good times "just around the bend."

Two other benefits resulted from the panic of 1857. First, Sioux City's artificially high real estate values stabilized, allowing the town to renew its growth at a slower and more orderly pace. The same reduction in land prices attracted a migration of farmers, thereby ending the community's long reliance on expensive imported foods. The rich soil of the area, largely ignored prior to 1860, thus made agriculture a major factor in Sioux City's economy.

The outbreak of the Civil War in 1861, however, interrupted minor economic gains locally and once again shelved the community's hopes for its long-promised railroad. The war's Eastern battles caused great concern, but an outbreak of widespread Indian/white violence in northern Iowa and southern Minnesota brought the reality of bloodshed much closer to Sioux City's door. The Indians' apparent murder of two local farmers, Thomas Roberts and Henry Cordua, in July 1861, resulted in the formation of the Sioux City Home Guard, a volunteer militia company, to patrol against Indian attack. Reorganized as the Sioux City Cavalry, and later as Company I of the Seventh Iowa Cavalry, the unit served with distinction throughout the 1862-1863 Dakota Indian campaigns.

Sioux City's selection by the U.S. Army as the marshaling point for these campaigns, combined with a new boom in steamboat traffic created by gold strikes in western Montana Territory, doubled the town's size in 1862 and eased its citizens' fears of vulnerability. Early banker George Weare mirrored this feeling of jubilation in June 1863, writing to a friend, "Four boats are now at the landing loaded with mules, horses, forage, stores and 400 of the 30th Wisconsin Infantry Regiment.... Sioux City never saw such times as these. Streets jam full all the time and every buddy making money."

At the Civil War's close in 1865, Sioux City promoters once again turned their attention toward securing a railroad; their goal was to make Sioux City a major outfitting location for post-war Dakota- and Montana-bound travel. Sioux City merchant-wagonmaster Colonel James A. Sawyers and other supporters tried to open an overland wagon freighting route to those regions but failed. The failure, however, fueled the city's railroad endeavors.

On October 20, 1866, a capacity crowd of local businessmen, financiers, and speculators swarmed into lantern-lit Casady's Hall to decide Sioux City's railroad future. W. W. Walker, representing Eastern railroad magnate John I. Blair, informed the assembly of Blair's plans to build the Sioux City and Pacific Railroad, which would ultimately link Sioux City, via Missouri Valley, Iowa, with Chicago and the industrial East. In return, the community was required to provide county land and depot grounds on the city's levee, as well as free right-of-way into the city.

County voters approved the land donation on February 11, 1867. Thirteen months later, on March 9, 1868, the first scheduled passenger train of the Sioux City and Pacific clattered across the Floyd River onto First Street. Its arrival in a cloud of smoke and steam marshaled a spirit of rejoicing in the bluff city, a spirit mirrored in the *Sioux City Journal*'s headline of the day: "SAVED AT LAST!"

English-born physician-turned-surveyor John K. Cook was the founder of Sioux City. Convinced of the potential of the region, he personally supervised the city's first survey work during the winter of 1854-55, later serving as resident townsite promoter. He also helped organize the Sioux City Claims Association to ensure squatter's rights of pre-emption.

Dr. Cook maintained a limited medical practice, as well as serving as first postmaster (1855-57), county judge (1856-57), and two-term mayor of the town from 1861 through 1862. He resided in Sioux City until 1879, when he moved with his family to St. Louis. Upon his death, on November 14, 1885, pioneer banker John P. Allison stated of Cook, "He was a power in this section, and the number of his friends was only limited by the number of the population." Photo courtesy of Sioux City Public Museum

Dr. Cook's second plat of Sioux City shows the Sioux City Townsite Company's original location (left) west of Perry Creek, and Sioux City East Addition, which he staked out in 1855 after having purchased the claim of local fur trader Joseph Leonnais for $3,000. Because the original townsite included only a small stretch of riverfront below Prospect Hill. Dr. Cook considered it inadequate for proper development of a city. His acquisition of Leonnais' property, which included the major portion of the present-day business district, helped avert what might have become a major economic handicap. This plat was filed before county recorder Samuel H. Casady at 1 p.m. September 16, 1856. Map courtesy of Woodbury County Recorder's Office; photo by B. Paul Chicoine

Victoria Angie, known as "the prairie flower," was a central figure in an early local conflict known as Angie's War, a dispute involving local white relations with the French and Indians, vigilante justice, romance, and land.

Before the Sioux City Land Office opened for filing in 1856, the Sioux City Townsite Company sold pre-emptive rights to land only, not the land itself. While up to 160 acres could be secured legally in this fashion, Sioux City's early squatters organized a claims club to enforce their attempts to gain larger acreages. The Angie War began when Richard Rowe, a white man, allowed Canadian-born Henry Angie and his half-Indian family to reside in his house, located along the Floyd River, during the winter of 1855-56. Legend states that Rowe was infatuated with Angie's daughter Victoria, although "the prairie flower" later repudiated this theory. On Rowe's return the following spring, however, he discovered that Henry Angie was claiming ownership of the house and land. When Angie refused to leave, Sioux City's American settlers sided with Rowe, at one point laying siege to the cabin with gunfire. Ultimately, Angie accepted the $100 offered by the claims club and left town. Photo courtesy of Sioux City Public Museum

26

This 1854 drawing depicts the steamboat *Omaha* at Florence, Nebraska; it was the first steamboat to carry a cargo destined exclusively for Sioux City. James A. Jackson, a Council Bluffs merchant and shareholder in the Sioux City Townsite Company, chartered the 300-ton sidewheeler in St. Louis, and the entire infant community of Sioux City welcomed the *Omaha's* arrival in June 1856. Its $70,000 manifest included, among other items, boilers, engines, and saws for the town's first lumbermill, and a number of prefabricated store and office buildings. Prior to the *Omaha's* historic trip, Sioux City had been only a stopover port for fur company and military steamers traveling into the Western reaches. Sketch by George Simons; courtesy of Nebraska State Historical Society

Included in the cargo of steamboat *Omaha* during its premier voyage to Sioux City in 1856 were the boilers and machinery for his sawmill, built by James A. Jackson and Milton Tootle near the mouth of Perry Creek, now 223 Water Street. The mill was sold in 1857 to former mill manager Luther Sanborn and partner Judson Follett, and it supplied most of the lumber, shingles, and, in later years, the finished materials for many of Sioux City's pioneer homes and businesses. The Sanborn and Follett Mill remained in operation until 1893. Photo courtesy of Sioux City Public Museum

The Tootle and Jackson store, at the northeast corner of Second and Pearl streets, was one of the most successful general stores in the region. It was also Sioux City's first prefabricated business building, arriving in sections from St. Louis on board the steamboat Omaha *during the vessel's historic journey in 1856. Tootle and Jackson, owned by Milton Tootle of St. Joseph, Missouri, and James A. Jackson of Council Bluffs, claimed to be the outfitting depot for the upper Missouri Valley. The store's stock of merchandise, sold both wholesale and retail at the "sign of the elephant," included dry goods, carpets, boots and shoes, saddlery, groceries, Queensware, hardware, iron, steel, and furniture.*

Milton Tootle, the firm's senior partner, became sole proprietor in July 1859. This business flourished and remained an influential enterprise in Sioux City for many years after. Photo courtesy of Sioux City Public Museum

Seth W. Swiggett was Sioux City's first newspaper publisher. After managing papers in Cincinnati and Des Moines, Swiggett moved to the frontier village of Sioux City, where he printed the first issue of the Sioux City Eagle on July 4, 1857. From its headquarters at the northwest corner of Third and Pearl streets, the Eagle was a constant promoter of Sioux City's interests. Swiggett published the Eagle until October 15, 1859, when it was consolidated with the Sioux City Register. Later, in March 1860, Swiggett and Isaac Pendleton created a short-lived paper called the Sioux City Times. The Oracle, another Swiggett paper, was published from 1894 to 1895. Photo courtesy of Sioux City Public Museum*

Robert Means was Sioux City's first mayor. Voters showed keen interest in early Sioux City ward system elections, each ward hoping to reap benefits for its area. As the Sioux City Eagle observed, "Our otherwise friendly citizenry are arrayed against each other."*

At the first city election, August 3, 1857, voters from all three wards cast their ballots for mayor. While the vote totals clearly showed Third Ward candidate Ezra Millard to be the winner, County Judge John Cook, a major First Ward landowner, unceremoniously threw out the votes of the Third Ward, thereby "electing" his own ward's candidate, J. B. S. Todd. The turmoil and confusion which resulted became even more acute when Todd, a relative of Mary Todd Lincoln, declined the post, believing that Millard was the rightful winner.

Sioux City functioned without a mayor for eight months after the ruckus. Finally, in the town's second election, on April 3, 1858, Democrat and former customs officer Robert Means outpolled Citizens' party candidate Dr. Justus Townsend 122 to 96 to become Sioux City's first official—albeit belated—mayor. Photo courtesy of Sioux City Public Museum

Woodbury Sanborn, Charles Claypoole, and Edmund Pendleton (left to right) are standing near the window of the Sherwin Land Office School in the early 1880s. This building has been part of Sioux City's history since 1857. Carried in sections from St. Louis by steamboat and assembled at the southeast corner of Seventh and Douglas streets, it was used by G. W. F. Sherwin as his real estate office. Later it served as temporary homes for both the Congregational and Methodist Episcopal churches. In 1870 the school board rented it as an intermediate school for $150 annually, hence the name of Sherwin Land Office School. In the early 1880s, when this photograph was taken, the school system retired the building. For years it stood behind the John P. Allison home. Finally, in 1908, the Boys of '68 acquired the historic structure for their clubhouse and moved it to Stone Park, where it still stands today. Photo courtesy of Sioux City Public Museum

Isaac Pendleton—attorney, border brigade volunteer, and judge—was a driving force in the formation of Sioux City's Republican party. Upon his arrival in Sioux City in 1858, Pendleton joined A. W. Hubbard and others in popularizing the newly-created political organization in what was, at its outset, a predominantly Democratic community. During the 1860 Lincoln campaign, Pendleton teamed up with former Sioux City Eagle editor Seth Swiggett to create the Republican-oriented Sioux City Times. Pendleton proved to be a forceful writer and a strong local proponent of Lincoln's cause. Following a term in the state legislature, Pendleton succeeded Hubbard as district court judge, holding the position until 1866. In later years the district court nearly became a family position, with brother-in-law George W. Wakefield, nephew A. O. Wakefield, and grandson Donald M. Pendleton later serving on the bench. Photo courtesy of Sioux City Public Museum

John Church Cushing Hoskins (1820-1909) served as Sioux City's city engineer from 1858 to 1878 and as postmaster from 1861 to 1878. A leader in civic improvement, Hoskins in later years became the first president and leading spirit of the Sioux City Scientific Association and the Academy of Science and Letters, as well as a staunch booster of the Floyd Monument project. In this photograph, taken in December 1908, J. C. C. Hoskins looks back fondly over his fifty-one years in Sioux City. Photo by Genelli; courtesy of Sioux City Public Museum

William H. Bigelow, pioneer real estate dealer and banker, arrived in Sioux City in 1857. By July of that year he had built a frame house at the far north end of Sioux City, at the southeast corner of Ninth and Nebraska streets.

Bigelow was elected mayor by a convincing margin in 1859, beginning a term of office marked by his concentrated efforts at improving the city as a whole, rather than promoting any particular ward.

Mayor Bigelow recognized the importance of the Missouri River and local agriculture in his inaugural address, stating, "The Big Muddy now brings us cash instead of corn, and takes from us corn instead of cash. Our market is our levee." Photo courtesy of Sioux City Public Museum

John P. Allison (left) and George Weare
stood in front of their new bank building at
405 Pearl Street in 1878. George Weare
arrived by stage on December 26, 1855, and
opened the Sioux City branch of the noted
Cedar Rapids bank of Greene, Weare,
Graves and Company the following day.
The bank, first located in the attic of the
U.S. Land Office building, had only a tin box
for a safe and a dry goods case for a counter.
When the panic of 1857 swept away the
parent bank, Weare began a private concern, providing substantial economic
support to the fledgling community.

John Allison studied law in New Hamp-
shire under Horace C. Bacon and came to
Sioux City in the spring of 1857 as clerk for
the banking and real estate firm of Henn,
Williams, Cook and Company. Later that
year, he was admitted to the bar. For three
years, beginning on August 19, 1857, he was

a partner in the banking firm of Means,
Allison and Company.

Weare and Allison formed a new partnership on September 6, 1860, with the Bank
of Weare and Allison remaining a prominent
institution until Allison's retirement in
1901. Weare consolidated the bank with the
Iowa State National Bank that same year.
At the time of the merger, Weare and
Allison was the oldest Iowa financial
institution to be run by its original partners.

The number of public offices occupied by
these bankers attest to the high esteem in
which they were held by fellow Sioux
Cityans. Weare was a member of the first
city council and was mayor in 1866. Allison
held the important posts of county judge
(1859-61), county treasurer (1879-85), and
director of the school board (1869-72 and
1876-84). Photo courtesy of Sioux City
Public Museum

This photograph looks west from Eighth and Jackson over the northern part of Sioux City, circa 1863. In the foreground, young Edgar Stone (left) and Charlie Chamberlin play on a warm summer's day.

Edgar was the son of T. J. Stone, who in 1870 founded the First National Bank along with A. W. Hubbard. Charlie's father was George Chamberlin, who helped Dr. Cook survey Sioux City in 1854-55. Both of these boys later were employed at the First National Bank. Chamberlin left the bank after five years and in 1883, at age twenty-five, was proudly listing his occupation as "speculator." Stone later became vice-president of First National. His widow, Lucia Stone, donated one-half of present-day Stone Park to the city in 1912; the city purchased the rest soon after. Photo courtesy of Sioux City Public Museum

Brigadier General John Cook, a volunteer officer from Springfield, Illinois, was dispatched by the U.S. War Department to Sioux City in the fall of 1862 to organize the army's planned 1863 Dakota expeditions against warring Sioux nations. He was not the same man who laid out the town. Cook transformed Sioux City into a massive military camp during the winter of 1862-63, with large stables, warehouses, and barracks being erected between Fourth Street and the levee. Many other existing buildings, including the Methodist Episcopal Church at 815 Douglas Street, were also pressed into service as temporary quarters for the over 1,200 cavalrymen and 300 infantry men who wintered here. Photo courtesy of Sioux City Public Museum

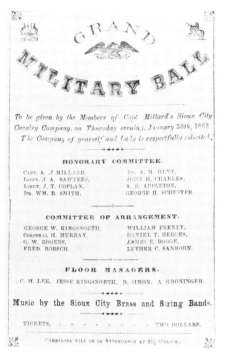

The Grand Military Ball, held the evening of January 30, 1862, at the Central House, served both recreational and military purposes. Entertainment was scarce in the frontier community, and the prospect of assisting the Sioux City Cavalry Company while having a good time was undoubtedly enticing.

With the outbreak of the Civil War, the U.S. Army diminished its defense of the Western regions. Still, tenuous relations existed between whites and native Americans. In the spring of 1861, residents formed a home guard to provide protection for Sioux City and the surrounding area against possible Indian attack. Iowa Governor Samuel Kirkwood offered state assistance and changed the unit's name to Frontier Guard. Conditions became more volatile after the killing of local farmers Henry Cordua and Thomas Roberts on July 9, 1861.

The Sioux City Cavalry replaced the Frontier Guard in September 1861, with Captain Andrew J. Millard, First Lieutenant James A. Sawyers, and Second Lieutenant J. T. Coplan leading the company. When General Alfred Sully directed his troops against the Sioux nation in 1863, he chose the Sioux City unit to act as his bodyguard, later remarking, "A better drilled or disciplined company than the Sioux City Cavalry cannot be found in the regular or volunteer service of the United States." The Sioux City Cavalry Company later became Company I of the Seventh Iowa Cavalry. Ball invitation courtesy of Sioux City Public Museum

In June of 1863, General Alfred Sully, a brilliant Indian fighter and skilled tactician, replaced Cook in command of the Dakota campaigns. Sully's subseqeunt leadership at the Battle of Whitestone Hills (in present-day North Dakota) on September 3, 1863, ended once and for all the Indian threat against northwest Iowa and Minnesota. Photo courtesy of Sioux City Public Museum

James M. Bacon was one of three Bacon brothers associated with early Sioux City history. Horace C. Bacon, who was one of the town's first attorneys, came in 1855 and assisted Dr. Cook in the local management of the Sioux City Townsite Company. Moses W. Bacon, also arriving in 1855, resided here until his death in 1859. James M. Bacon (shown here) arrived in 1859 and immediately opened a wholesale and retail hardware store on Pearl Street. He became one of the city's most successful businessmen. Bacon joined the Dakota Cavalry when the Civil War broke out and was quartermaster under Generals Cook and Sully for three years. A staunch Democrat, he served as alderman for one term and was mayor in 1867. Photo courtesy of Sioux City Public Museum

Two-year-old Mary Davis (left) and four-year-old Stella Davis posed circa 1863. These daughters of Sioux City pioneers S. T. and Jane A. Davis made names for themselves during their many years as residents. Stella possessed a keen business mind and worked in her father's real estate office. She later married William Gordon, a promoter during the 1880s through the 1930s.

Mary Davis, who married banker Henry M. Bailey, was an avid student of the environment. She led multitudes of Sioux City school children on nature hikes, earning the nickname of "Sioux City's Bird Woman." Photo courtesy of Ruth Bailey Iseminger, Spokane, Washington

The Dr. William Remsen Smith farm, in the western portion of Sioux City, was photographed circa 1865.

Doctor Smith (1828-94) was one of the area's most distinguished pioneer doctors, governmental officials, and businessmen. Arriving in the spring of 1856, he immediately established a vast medical practice which extended into the far reaches of Siouxland. In the 1860s he was a member of the Home Guard and a surgeon for the Union army. He served as city mayor in 1863 and 1881. He was also receiver for the Land Office from 1865 to 1878, except for a brief respite during President Andrew Johnson's administration.

During this period Smith wrote Congressman Hubbard:

> *The office is a very nice little thing and of course its continuance would be quite desirable. What I realize from it is stated and regular and has a great advantage in that respect over what I get from my practice....I have no idea of giving place to a Copperhead if I can help it. But if the President insists that the office depends upon my separation from the great Republican and Union party of the nation, I shall stick exclusively to Pills and let the Office go to the dogs.*

Smith's farm (shown here) was the family home from the 1860s through the 1880s, at which time he subdivided his 160 acres and created Smith's Villa Addition. Rebecca Osborn Smith, wife of Doctor Smith, wrote the following on the back of this photograph: "Old Homestead on the farm where Stone Home now stands. Remmi, Burt, Dannie, and Arthur were born in this home." Photo courtesy of Sioux City Public Museum

Pearl Street was Sioux City's main avenue of commerce when this view was taken in 1866. E. R. Kirk and Company occupied the building on the left, at the northwest corner of Second and Pearl streets. On the east side of the street was W. H. Livingston and Company, Clothing and Dry Goods. Other businesses along this thoroughfare included saloons, drugstores, and hardware suppliers. Prior to the railroad's arrival, Sioux City might have passed for any other western Iowa prairie town. Photo courtesy of Sioux City Public Museum

The businesses located on the north side of Second Street west of Pearl Street were associated with the river trade in the 1860s. Charles E. and Daniel T. Hedges hatched many of the ideas for their widespread enterprises in the building on the right. Hedges and Company bought furs which were being sent downriver, and traders no doubt watched carefully as their goods were weighed on the Fairbanks scale situated immediately in front of the store.

In the center is an early hotel, called the Hagy House from 1858 to 1865. On the left, steam is seen rising from the Sanborn and Follett mill. Photo courtesy of Sioux City Public Museum

Asahel Wheeler Hubbard (1819-79) arrived in Sioux City in July 1856 as an established attorney and politician. He became the leader of the young Republican party in this region and served as district court judge from 1858 to 1862. In 1862 he was elected to Congress, where he served three terms during the Civil War and the early years of Reconstruction. Hubbard was the first Sioux Cityan to become a congressman; the second was his son, Elbert H. Hubbard.

While in Congress, Hubbard helped to secure federal funds for the ill-fated Sawyers' Expeditions to Montana. Success in the project would have aided Sioux City; it also would have benefitted Hubbard, who was one of the founders and promoters of Niobrara, Nebraska. As Edward Edwards, one of the members of the first expedition, put it, "One of the great objects of our expedition is to open a highway connecting this town [Niobrara] with Virginia City, for the purpose of putting money in the pockets of the stockholders of this to-be-great city."

Upon his retirement from Congress, Hubbard became one of Sioux City's most influential businessmen. The inscription on a monument in Floyd Cemetery summarizes the early residents' admiration for Hubbard: "Erected by his fellow citizens, in memory of a faithful public servant, a self-sacrificing citizen, a true man." Photo courtesy of Sioux City Public Museum

Edwin R. Kirk (1834-1900) came to Sioux City in 1857 following a foiled attempt to enlist in John Brown's Kansas expedition. He remained in the dry goods business until 1873, much of that time in association with his brother-in-law, Colonel James Sawyers. In his own semi-regular, tongue-in-cheek newspaper designed to promote E. R. Kirk and Company, the self-proclaimed Old Kirk, King Of The Jews expounded on a variety of local issues.

Kirk held several governmental positions, including fire chief, alderman, deputy county treasurer, deputy U. S revenue collector, and, during the Civil War, regimental sutler. He also served as Sioux City postmaster from 1878 through 1894, with a brief interruption during President Cleveland's first term. Photo courtesy of Sioux City Public Museum

Soldier, steamboatman, merchant, and trailblazer, Colonel James A. Sawyers (1824-98) was famous for his flamboyant exploits. Sawyers, a veteran of the Mexican War, migrated to Sioux City from Tennessee in 1857 and formed a mercantile partnership with his brother-in-law, E. R. Kirk. With the outbreak of renewed Indian trouble in 1861, however, Sawyers enlisted as a lieutenant in the Sioux City Cavalry. He resigned soon after, at the request of Iowa Governor Samuel Kirkwood that he accept command of the Iowa Border Brigade, with the responsibility of constructing a series of forts and blockhouses between Correctionville and Chain-of-Lakes, Minnesota.

In 1865 and 1866 Sawyers organized and commanded two overland wagon freighting expeditions from Sioux City in an unsuccessful attempt to popularize a government-funded wagon road to the Montana gold fields. He also owned and operated the river steamers Sioux City and Tiger, and ferryboat Undine, and was responsibile for the construction of Sioux City's first three-story brick building.

The photo shown here was probably taken during the 1860s, at the height of Colonel Sawyers' military and wagon freighting career. Photo courtesy of Sioux City Public Museum

The city's first three-story brick building is shown (in a damaged photograph) nearing completion in 1867 at the northwest corner of Second and Pearl. The Sawyers Block housed the E. R. Kirk and Company dry goods store, Ann Electra Sawyers' millinery shop, the Wise Brothers' New York Store, and other early businesses. Photo courtesy of Sioux City Public Museum

"SAVED AT LAST." The arrival of the first passenger locomotive and train of the Sioux City and Pacific Railroad from Missouri Valley on March 9, 1868, climaxed a decade of hopes and dreams for Sioux City and transformed the river town into a major Midwestern railroad and steamboating center.

The Sawyers Block is visible behind the train at the northwest corner of Second and Pearl streets. Photo courtesy of Sioux City Public Museum

*Second Street between Pearl and Douglas
streets, 1869. This was Sioux City as the
travel-weary steamboat or railroad
passenger first saw it. A cool draught of
genuine Dubuque Lager awaited the thirsty
pilgrim at The Palace.*

*The intersection of Second and Douglas
streets became known as Dead Man's
Corner in the 1870s, after five people were
killed there in a span of just seven years.
Photo courtesy of Sioux City Public Museum*

Chapter 3

Does God Rule, or the Devil, In Sioux City?

1868 - 1886

The arrival of the Sioux City and Pacific Railroad in 1868 transformed Sioux City overnight from a large frontier town on the Missouri River to a small but booming metropolis. It also heralded the community's emergence over St. Louis as the steamboat shipping capital of the West. Eastern manufacturers, who were previously compelled to transfer their Dakota- and Montana-bound goods from railroad to steamboat at St. Louis, were now free to ship by rail direct to Sioux City, thus short-cutting nearly 1,000 miles of hazardous and expensive Missouri River travel. Freight and insurance rates were drastically reduced, and steamboats employed in the lucrative Fort Benton, Montana Territory, gold rush trade could now make more round trips per season.

St. Louis steamboat baron Joab Lawrence was the first to capitalize on Sioux City's new strategic importance. By the spring of 1868, he had moved an entire fleet of five shallow-drafted sternwheelers to Sioux City's levee, erected a rail-to-river transfer depot, and began advertising upriver steamboat schedules to Fort Benton twenty days faster and only two-thirds as expensive as service from St. Louis. A mammoth steamboat drydock and repair yard—the first of its kind to be built north of St. Louis—was added to Lawrence's Sioux City empire soon thereafter. The Kountz, the Coulson, and other lines quickly followed. Over the next five years, these companies built additional warehouses, rail spurs, offices, and repair facilities to cope with the flood of traffic moving across the city's levee.

By the end of 1869, Sioux City's steamboat companies dominated river transportation on the Missouri River, holding monopolies on freight, passenger, and mail service to the nearly two dozen U.S. Army military posts, government Indian agencies, and numerous civilian settlements between Sioux City and the Rocky Mountains. The thousands of tons of river freight moving through its First Street warehouses created a bounty of new businesses and jobs. The city's population exploded. The community, which would claim a mere 1,380 souls in March 1868, boasted of a populace of nearly 4,000 in 1870. Most of these new Siouxlanders linked their livelihood directly or indirectly with the fortunes of the steamboaters. The condition of the river above Fort Berthold, the arrival of a new "mountain boat" from the Pittsburgh boatyards, or the latest exploits of such wheelhouse wizards as Captains Grant Marsh or Joe LaBarge eclipsed even such national news as the Credit Mobilier scandals in the hearts and minds of river-conscious Sioux Cityans.

The city, by 1869, was fast taking on a more exciting, metropolitan look. The downtown business district, which heretofore had hugged the levee, was now expanding at a fevered pace toward the north and east. The new suburbs of Greenville, Coles Addition, and Prospect Hill beckoned to the city's new tide of middle-class homeowners, while Codfish Hill and the near Northside above Sixth Street offered a "country" atmosphere for the more well-to-do.

Culture, too, was coming of age. In 1869 Sioux City voters overwhelmingly approved the formation of the Sioux City Independent School District, thereby vastly improving the quality of public education. The Young Men's Literary Association—the forerunner of today's public library system—was also begun that year, followed by the construction of the Academy of Music in 1870. The *Sioux City Journal*'s change from a weekly to a daily newspaper in 1870, the publication of the first city directory the following year, and the sponsorship of The Woodbury County Agricultural Fair in 1871 highlighted the city's spirit of river progress.

The city's glory as a steamboat capital, however, was as short-lived as it was grand. In 1873 a much-feared and bitterly-fought railroad extension to Yankton, Dakota Territory, caused Sioux City steamboaters to abdicate their dominion over the upper Missouri, for the further western push of the railroad eliminated another ninety miles of costly river travel. More importantly, though, after the completion of the Union Pacific Railroad to Utah in 1869, river shipping simply could not compete financially with the railroads. Even though Sioux City's and Yankton's steamboat companies fought gallantly to survive economically, their slow, plodding, and costly steamers were no match for the Iron Horse's speed and year-round service. While river traffic continued doggedly into the next decade, the glorious age of Western steamboating had all but drawn to a close.

The decline of river traffic in the 1870s, coupled with a national financial panic in 1873, signaled more than the passing of an era for Sioux City. It also marked a new beginning. Sioux City's businessmen, never ones to mourn long over their losses, turned their attentions in the mid-1870s toward developing their city into a transportation and marketing center for the newly emerging agricultural Eden of Siouxland. By 1874 Sioux Cityans could proudly boast three railroads, four grain elevators, two banks, six hotels, a woodworking mill, a lumberyard, and five farm implement dealers, all catering primarily to the burgeoning wholesale and agricultural trade.

One of these local farm suppliers, a young man named Frank H. Peavey, successfully capitalized on the ancient practice of accepting farm produce in payment for his plows and grain drills and laid the groundwork for what was to become an international grain milling and marketing empire. A few years earlier, James E. Booge, a local wholesale grocer and government pork contractor, initiated another industry long important to Sioux City when he constructed the city's first substantial hog slaughtering and processing plant at the corner of Water and Fifth streets. Expansion of Booge's business to the South Bottoms in 1880 and the formation of the Union Stockyards Company in 1884 spurred the city's future emergence as the meat-packing center for the Northern Plains.

Technological advances during this period, though largely in the organizational phase, created somewhat more comfortable surroundings for Sioux Cityans and paved the way for future growth. On March 17, 1873, the Sioux City Gas Light Company lit the town's first gas lights, and the city council sanctioned an electric company a mere ten years later. Creation of the Sioux City Telephone Exchange Company in 1880, and both a municipal waterworks and horse-drawn street railway system in 1884, topped the list of civic improvements begun during this era.

The agricultural boom, the railroad age, and the city's new-found prowess as a packing house center intensified an age-old problem which eventually caused nationwide embarrassment for Sioux City. In 1882 the citizens of this "working man's town" overwhelmingly rejected an amendment to the Iowa constitution banning intoxicating drink, believing that the city's current wave of prosperity and progress required the free flow of liquor. Indeed, the city secured substantial income from saloon licensing and allowed assorted vices to flourish on Lower Pearl and in the infamous dives of the Sudan, located south of Fourth Street and east of Douglas. This debate crested in 1885, when the Iowa legislature enacted a prohibition statute called Clark's Law after the amendment had been overturned.

Tempers soared. In March 1885 local saloon owners and their customers threatened "to pound" Iowa Congressman Isaac Struble, a supporter of the statute, if he dared try to enforce the law in Sioux City. Two weeks later, 136 local business leaders drew up a petition declaring that, while they had no sympathy with the traffic of liquor as a beverage, strict enforcement of Clark's Law would be "extremely detrimental to the business interests of the city."

These men argued for milder regulation of the liquor trade, proclaiming that "at this time we are laboring under a heavy burden brought on by the increased necessities of the city in its change from a thriving village to an important business center, and can ill afford to lose the revenues which may be had if the law is not enforced."

Within a week, however, an opposing petition signed by prominent Sioux City women representing "not less than 460 husbands and fathers and 1,060 children" railed against the city fathers' attempt "to induce our citizens to defy the law and the statute and sully the fair name of Sioux City."

The battle lines had thus been drawn in one of Sioux City's most bizarre conflicts when Reverend George C. Haddock, a vehement prohibitionist, arrived in 1885 to assume the pastorate of Sioux City's First Methodist Episcopal Church. Haddock championed the cause from his pulpit and through his actions, personally seeking out evidence of liquor law violations by saloon keepers and testifying against them in court. Finally, on the night of August 3, 1886, the saloon element retaliated, and the minister was gunned down near the corner of Fourth and Water streets.

Sioux Cityans were outraged, the nation shocked. Haddock became a martyr for prohibitionists nationwide, while Sioux City acquired the unenviable reputation of a town of questionable morality. As one Dakota Territory newspaper asked its readers, "Does God rule, or the devil, in Sioux City?"

Mountain boats Far West *and* Nellie Peck— *large, shallow-draft sternwheelers built to run on the treacherous upper Missouri River above Sioux City—rest at the city levee in the 1870s. The heavy poles suspended over the steamers' bows are "grasshoppers," heavy spars that could be used like giant crutches to "walk" the ships through shallow water. These two powerful steamboats, built in Pittsburgh, were part of Sioux City's Northwest Transportation Company and later Coulson Packet Company fleets. In 1872 these two steamboats paired off in a twenty-nine-day, 3,000-mile, round-trip race on the Missouri from Sioux City to Fort Benton. The victorious* Far West, *(left) gained nationwide fame four years later as the army's ambulance ship at the Battle of the Little Bighorn. Photo courtesy of North Dakota State Historical Society*

The sidewheel steamer Antelope "at the woodpile" near the foot of Douglas Street, circa 1868. The discovery of gold in Montana, Indian warfare, and the subsequent increase in government troop and supply movement above Sioux City brought scores of such rugged little steamboats to Sioux City's levee during the 1860s. A year earlier, the Antelope was riddled with bullets in an Indian ambush on the upper Missouri. Thereafter, steamboats venturing above Sioux City commonly were equipped with boiler plate armor and light cannon for defense. Photo courtesy of Sioux City Public Museum

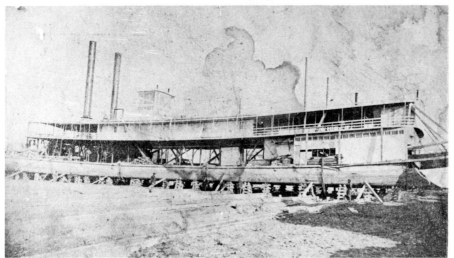

In anticipation of a good shipping season in 1869, Northwest Transportation Company president Joab Lawrence ordered construction of this massive steamboat drydock at the foot of Jones Street in the fall of 1868. The drydock, shown in this damaged view with the Durfee and Peck steamer Key West "on the blocks," was a beehive of activity between 1869 and 1872, employing up to fifty carpenters and mechanics. Photo courtesy of Sioux City Public Museum

By 1871 Sioux City was home port to a triumvirate of steamboat shipping lines: the Northwest Transportation Company, at the foot of Pierce Street; the Yankton Packet Company, also based at the foot of Pierce; and the Kountz Line of steamers, whose warehouse is shown here on the levee west of Perry Creek. In addition to civilian shipping, Sioux City was the supply center to nearly two dozen U.S. Army posts and government Indian agencies on the upper Missouri River. Photo courtesy of Sioux City Public Museum

John H. Charles (1826-1904) survived his first winter's night lodging in Sioux City beneath a buffalo robe on the Hagy House's porch and became a prime mover in Sioux City's nineteenth century financial and cultural affairs. Charles rose from the position of clerk for the pioneer mercantile firm of Milton Tootle and Company to become an independent military contractor, steamboat owner, railroad promoter, real estate developer, and politician, as well as co-founder and president of the prestigious Sioux City Scientific Association. Charles, as a manager for the T. C. Power Transportation Company steamboat line, once advised his firm not to bid too low on a government river freighting contract, reasoning that while they might land the business, they might also lose money in the bargain. "Actually," the Sioux Cityan was heard to comment wryly, "we can make more money staying at home and hauling manure." Photo courtesy of Sioux City Public Museum

Pearl Street was the focal point of Sioux City's downtown district when this photo was taken in late spring, 1869. From the photographer's vantage point atop the Sawyers Block, at the northwest corner of Second and Pearl, the bulk of the city's downtown is visible, as are the growing number of substantial brick buildings—evidence of the railroad's presence.

Next to the Arcade Clothing Company, at the "sign of the elephant," is the firm of W. H. Livingston, the nephew of Milton

Tootle. Across the alley is the hardware store of August Groninger, as well as the office of the Sioux City Register, the town's second newspaper. The three adjacent one-story structures house B. F. Smith's City Drug Store, Schmidt's clothing store, and James M. Bacon's Hardware. Gertz and Doss' Billiard Hall, with workmen on the

roof, doubled as the town's performance center prior to completion of the Academy of Music building. Both Groninger's and Gertz and Doss' upstairs halls served as early city council chambers.

The smaller buildings between Third and Fourth streets include two boot and shoe stores, a confectionery, and a billiard hall. The St. Elmo Hotel is under construction in the background, on Douglas Street between Fifth and Sixth streets. Photo courtesy of Sioux City Public Museum

Throughout the community's history, local photographers have climbed Prospect Hill to document the city's changes and growth. The steamboat capital was in the midst of rapid progress in 1870, when this view was taken. Many substantial business buildings were put up that year. In the center background, Codfish Hill is already emerging as a prestigious neighborhood.

Someone unwittingly marred this beautiful photograph by numbering some structures in ink. That person also failed to list a Number 17.

1. *Residence of lumber dealer A. D. Rice, Douglas between Twelfth and Thirteenth streets*
2. *Residence of dentist A. J. Rederich, east side of Jackson between Tenth and Eleventh streets*
3. *Residence of attorney James H. Bolton, Eighth and Jennings*
4. *Residence of former Congressman A. W. Hubbard, 608 Jones Street*
5. *Hubbard House, northeast corner of Fourth and Pierce*
6. *Millinery shop of Mrs. Catherine Fullen, north side of Third Street between Pearl and Douglas*
7. *St. Thomas Episcopal Church, northwest corner of Seventh and Nebraska*
8. *St. Elmo Hotel, west side of Douglas between Fifth and Sixth streets*
9. *Methodist Episcopal Church, northeast corner of Sixth and Pierce*
10. *Congregational Church, east side of Douglas between Fifth and Sixth streets*
11. *Residence of porkpacker James E. Booge, southwest corner of Seventh and Douglas*
12. *Passenger depot of the Sioux City and Pacific Railroad, at Second and Nebraska, with the roundhouse behind it*
13. *Northwest Transportation Company, at the foot of Pierce Street*
14. *Academy of Music building, south side of Fourth Street between Pierce and Douglas*
15. *McElhaney's Hall, northwest corner of Fourth and Pearl*
16. *Sawyers Block, northwest corner of Second and Pearl*
18. *Sanborn and Follett Saw Mill, Second and Water*

Photo courtesy of Sioux City Public Museum

The Lawrence McCarty home at 215 Sixth Street served as a gathering spot for the large McCarty family and guests, including former Senator George W. Jones. McCarty's grocery store was just to the right of this view, at 601 Pearl Street.

Family members seen, left to right, are: Mrs. McCarty, Emma, Mr. McCarty, Grace, son Thomas (later the Right Reverend Monsignor McCarty), Kate, Alice, Mary, Lizzie, and Loretta. Eva and Laurence are seated in the surrey. Photo courtesy of Sioux City Public Museum

In 1875 the northern reaches of the city were entirely residential. Looking south-easterly from Ninth and Douglas streets, the square brick residence of grocer George Felt stands at the northwest corner of Eighth and Pierce streets. It was torn down in December 1939. The magnificent home of D. T. Hedges, at the southeast corner of Sixth and Jackson streets, rises above John P. Allison's windmill in the foreground. To the left is Codfish Hill, an expanding neighborhood of exclusive homes. The recently-completed First Presbyterian Church (right) stands at the northeast corner of Sixth and Nebraska. Photo courtesy of Sioux City Public Museum

Samuel Tait Davis (1828-1900) was an active leader in Sioux City from his arrival in February 1856. Educated as an attorney, Davis devoted most of his time to real estate, controlling a significant portion of Sioux City's downtown and early residential areas. When Dr. Cook was both postmaster and county judge, Davis often handled the normal duties of the offices. He helped found the Sioux City Journal in 1864 in order to provide a local voice for the Union (Republican) party. He served as editor during the re-election campaign of Congressman Hubbard and President Lincoln.

Davis' most vital roles, however, were in securing rail transportation for Sioux City. He worked tirelessly in the construction of the Sioux City and Pacific, the Sioux City and Pembina, the Sioux City and St. Paul, and the Covington, Columbus and Black Hills railroads. Sioux City voters responded by electing him mayor in 1871.

S. T. Davis remained active well into the 1890s, never fearing to voice his opinions on financial or governmental issues. Ironically, the man who played such a pivotal role in rail transportation died after being struck by a trolley car near his home. He had grown too deaf to hear the car's warning bell. Photo courtesy of Sioux City Public Museum

The S. T. Davis family moved into William H. Bigelow's frame residence at Ninth and Nebraska in 1866. It was the Davis home for the remainder of the century. Davis' first wife, Jane A. Putnam, died in the house in 1877. In 1881, when Davis remarried, he remodeled the structure and added the brick veneer. Seen in this view from the mid-1880s are S. T. Davis, his second wife, Rebecca Smith Davis, and three of his seven children: Mary, Ross, and George Davis. Photo courtesy of Ruth Bailey Iseminger, Spokane, Washington

Early residents considered Dr. Andrew M. Hunt to be Sioux City's first practicing physician. Dr. Cook lived here earlier, but his main interests were in townsite promotion and government service.

As his medical and dental practice did not require all his time, Dr. Hunt also ran a drug and stationery store. Bitten by the Midas bug in 1859, he even panned for gold near Pike's Peak.

A. M. Hunt served five terms on the city council, one year as city assessor, and was a Union army surgeon during the Civil War. The voters elected Dr. Hunt as the first president of the Sioux City School Board on July 26, 1869. After his death in 1873, Central School was renamed Hunt School. Photo courtesy of Sioux City Public Museum

The Sawyers' home, shown here in an 1875 lithograph of Sawyers' Buff, was considered to be one of Sioux City's most lavish estates of the early 1870s. The nineteen-room mansion was built by Colonel Sawyers in 1871 and boasted mahogany paneling from cellar to garret, as well as a breathtaking view of the Floyd and Missouri rivers. It later housed the family of a trotting-horse breeder, a temporary office for Missouri River Railroad Bridge construction engineers, and a city quarantine hospital. It was demolished in 1969.

The ferryboat Undine (lower right) was one of a series of ferryboats and freight steamers owned by Colonel Sawyers. From Andreas' Illustrated Historical Atlas of Iowa; photo courtesy of Sioux City Public Museum

Central School, on the east side of Jackson Street between Fourth and Fifth streets, was the school system's first substantial facility. It began operation in 1870 as both an elementary and secondary school, but later was used solely by younger students. The school board renamed it Hunt School in 1873, in honor of its first president, Dr. A. M. Hunt. They closed the school and sold the entire block in 1887, when the business district began to engulf the area. Photo courtesy of Sioux City Public Museum

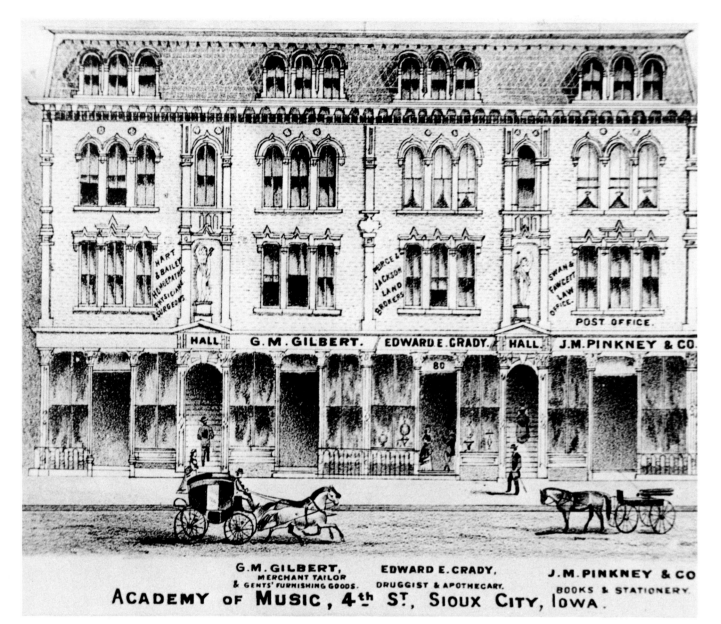

HART & BAILEY HOMEPATHIC PHYSICIAN & SURGEONS

PIERCE & JACKSON LAND BROKERS

SWAN & FAWCETT LAW OFFICE.

POST OFFICE.

HALL G.M. GILBERT. EDWARD E. GRADY. HALL J.M. PINKNEY & CO.

80

G.M. GILBERT,
MERCHANT TAILOR
& GENTS' FURNISHING GOODS.

EDWARD E. GRADY,
DRUGGIST & APOTHECARY.

J.M. PINKNEY & CO.
BOOKS & STATIONERY.

ACADEMY of MUSIC, 4th ST, SIOUX CITY, IOWA.

The Academy of Music, constructed during the heady days of 1870, stood on the south side of Fourth Street between Pierce and Douglas streets. It was erected by the firm of Sharp and Beck, according to the plans of local architect H. O. Ball, with financing provided by A. W. Hubbard, T. J. Stone, and J. C. C. Hoskins. In April 1870 the Sioux City Weekly Journal *described the then-proposed building: "It will be of brick, decorated with terra cotta windowcaps and brackets. Cast iron columns will be put in, and throughout the building will be in the latest style of architecture." The performing hall was located on the second floor, with the remainder of the structure occupied by commercial and governmental offices, including the post office, for several years.*

The academy opened for business in January 1871 under the management of

veteran actor and promoter Seldon Irwin. Irwin's own troupe performed frequently before large audiences in the 800-seat auditorium. Irwin also imported other traveling companies from throughout the United States. In addition, the city's only large hall was used for concerts, high school graduation exercises, political speeches, and prohibition talks. On at least two occasions during the 1870s, Susan B. Anthony occupied the stage and delivered woman's suffrage messages to large audiences.

The opening of the Peavey Grand Opera House in 1888 relegated the Academy to secondary social importance. It served for a time as a "dime museum" and later became a part of Davidson Brothers' Department Store. Lithograph from Andreas' Illustrated Historical Atlas of Iowa; *photo courtesy of Sioux City Public Museum*

George D. Perkins (1840-1914) purchased the Sioux City Journal in 1869, just as the river town was becoming a city. Joined by his brother Henry, he established the city's first daily newspaper in 1870.

George Perkins soon became one of the state's leading publishers, his thoughts carrying great weight throughout northwest Iowa. Politically a staunch Republican, he served one year in the Iowa Senate, was state commissioner of immigration, U. S. marshal for the district, and four-term member of Congress from 1891 to 1899. He later lost a highly-contested bid for Iowa's governorship in 1906.

According to long-time Journal employee A. F. Allen, Perkins performed his greatest editorial work after his return to Sioux City in 1899 and until his death in 1914. Sometimes Perkins described himself as a "plodder," but Siouxlanders generally agreed with his thoughts and ideas during his forty-five years at the helm of the Journal. Photo courtesy of Sioux City Public Museum

George D. Perkins built this house in 1884 on Codfish Hill, at the southeast corner of Ninth and Jackson, following a fire which destroyed the family's earlier residence at the same site. Perkins was an influential publisher and politician, and consequently his house was the scene of innumerable social gatherings. President William McKinley dined at Perkins' home on October 15, 1899. Photo courtesy of Shirley Perkins Ellison

The directors of the First National Bank, 1875. First row (from left): Thomas J. Stone, Judge A. W. Hubbard, and unidentified. Top row (from left): Ed Henn, Robert Buchanan, and Daniel T. Gilman.

T. J. Stone epitomized Sioux City's pioneer financier; in poor health as a young man, he swapped his law studies and family home in Niagara County, New York, to take up a government surveying job in the fresh air of frontier Iowa. Within fifty years he had amassed a fortune in real estate and financial holdings and had become president of northwest Iowa's largest bank. Photo courtesy of Sioux City Public Museum

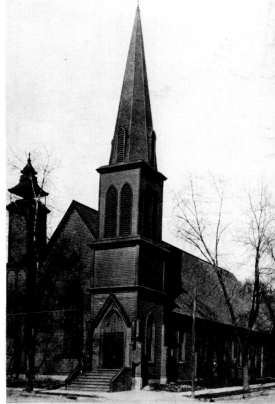

This building, at the northeast corner of Sixth and Nebraska streets, served as the First Presbyterian Church from 1875 to 1906. When the members erected a new church on the same site, they moved the rear portion of this building to Thirty-second and Jackson streets and named it the McClintock Chapel in honor of their late pastor, Dr. John C. McClintock.

Reverend Charles D. Martin held the first Presbyterian service in Sioux City on July 2, 1856. In September 1856 Reverend Thomas Chestnut assumed the pastorate, and the members officially organized on August 2, 1857. After making do with temporary quarters for two years, they erected Sioux City's first church building in 1859, at 814 Fourth Street. By the mid-1870s, membership had outstripped the building's capacities, causing the move to the structure shown here. Reverend Chestnut purchased the church's bell from the owners of the steamboat Kate Kearney, which had sunk near Sioux City a few years earlier. Photo courtesy of Sioux City Public Museum

"Of all the quaint characters who have roved our streets," wrote Sioux City Journal reporter Neil Miller, "probably none wielded a further reaching influence than Charlie Collins, the charmingly eccentric editor of the Sioux City Times."

Erratic, inflammatory, but always entertaining, Collins' contributions to Sioux City journalism as editor and publisher of the Times from 1868 to 1876 included, among other ventures, promotion of an ill-fated Irish-American nation in South Dakota's badlands, a declaration of war on Canada, and a proposal to mine gold from Prospect Hill. The Irish-born publisher left Sioux City in 1876 to establish a series of newspapers in Dakota Territory. He returned to Sioux City, however, and revived the Times from 1881 to 1885. Photo courtesy of Sioux City Public Museum

The Gordon-Russell-Collins Expedition of 1874-1875 was Times editor Charlie Collins' most legendary venture. In 1874, after rumors of gold in South Dakota's Black Hills had been verified by a government expedition, Collins, with the backing of Sioux City businessmen, mobilized a nationwide campaign to colonize the Indian holy lands. A call was issued for volunteers, and, in spite of repeated warnings by the U.S. Army, a secret expedition headed by Collins' associates T. H. Russell and John Gordon departed Sioux City for the hills.

The party of twenty-six men and one woman arrived near what is now Custer State Park, South Dakota, on December 26, 1874, where they constructed the log stockade shown here. Four months later—having found no gold—the entire community was taken prisoner by the U.S. Army and escorted from the territory. Photo from the Stanley J. Morrow Collection; courtesy of W. H. Over Museum, Vermillion, South Dakota.

For nearly twenty years after Sioux City became the seat of Woodbury County's government, there was no permanent county building. Instead, the board of supervisors rented space in existing buildings. In October 1875, however, county voters provided funds for a $75,000 courthouse. A special committee recommended that Des Moines architect William L. Foster's plan be used and that the structure be built of Kasota stone. Sioux Cityans C. E. and D. T. Hedges received the contract and commenced construction in 1876. The Woodbury County Courthouse opened in 1878 and served the county well for forty years. Photo courtesy of Sioux City Public Museum

The Merchants Hotel was constructed in 1876 at the northwest corner of Third and Douglas streets. This establishment stood for nearly forty years and catered primarily to travelers and transportation employees. Photo courtesy of Sioux City Public Museum

James E. Booge (1833-1911) is regarded as the father of Sioux City's meatpacking industry. A Vermont native, Booge staked his California gold prospecting earnings in 1858 on a steamboatload of apples, flour, and whiskey at St. Louis, with intention of peddling these goods among the upper Missouri River settlements. Fate, however, resulted in his arrival in Sioux City with his cargo virtually intact. Soon thereafter he entered into partnership with his brother, the firm being named H. D. Booge and Company Wholesale Grocers.

Booge's baptism into meatpacking stemmed from his purchase in about 1870 of a steamboat's water-soaked cargo of wheat, which he salvaged by feeding to a herd of hogs. The hogs later were butchered and most of the output was shipped upriver to U.S. Army posts. Photo courtesy of Sioux City Public Museum

Booge's profit from his meatpacking experiments led to construction of this three-story brick slaughterhouse—Sioux City's first significant packing plant—at the corner of Fifth and Water streets, in 1873. This building later served as the first home of Chesterman and Barrow Bottling Works. The Chesterman Company, Sioux City's oldest bottlers, continues in business today. Photo courtesy of the Chesterman Company, Sioux City

Demand for increased production capacity and increasing complaints from downtown business owners forced Booge to relocate and expand to a ten-acre site in Sioux City's swampy South Bottoms. By 1884 the James E. Booge and Sons Packing Company, shown in this 1890 lithograph, was advertising a daily slaughter of 2,500 hogs, 100 cattle, and 100 sheep, with an output of $2.5 million in meat products annually. Fully half of this production was marketed in London and Liverpool.

Booge was an organizer and investor in the Union Stock Yards Company, the Sioux City and Northern Railroad, and a number of Sioux City banks. The packing plant shown here stood just north of the Sioux City Stock Yards Company's present covered cattle division facility at Leech Avenue and Cunningham Drive. Lithograph courtesy of Sioux City Public Museum

James P. Wall, contractor, builder, alderman, and fire chief, was one of the most respected citizens of Sioux City from his arrival in 1866 until his death in 1898. On December 2, 1874, he helped organize the colorful Excelsior Hook and Ladder Company No. 1, becoming the group's first foreman. He served as city fire chief from 1880 until 1883, during which period this photo was taken.

Wall was the leading spokesman of the City's Westside during the late nineteenth century. His popularity could be measured by the fact that voters in the staunchly-Democratic district elected Wall, a Republican, to the city council a total of nine times in three different decades.

The contracting and building profession was Wall's primary vocation. Among the numerous structures he worked on were the Academy of Music, the First National Bank, the Hotel Garretson, the Silberhorn and Fowler packing plants, and many fine residences. It is said that during the early days of the "boom years," in the ten months beginning June 1887, his company laid 14 million bricks. Photo courtesy of Sioux City Public Museum

The Academy of Music served a multitude of purposes in the 1870s and 1880s. On June 7, 1884, for example, local residents gave their final performance of Gilbert and Sullivan's musical Iolantha, described in the program as "a clever satire on the 'red tape' formality which pervades English affairs of state." The Women's Christian Association organized this production as a fund-raiser for the Cottage Home, the city's first hospital. Program courtesy of Sioux City Public Museum

Sioux City's horse-drawn streetcar line extended up Pierce Street to Seventeenth Street by the late 1880s, when this view was taken. The sign on the streetcar advertises Pixley and Company clothiers, which was located at 515 Fourth Street. The building on the left is a family dwelling. To the right, at the northwest corner of Seventeenth and Pierce, stands the Samaritan Home, dedicated by the Women's Christian Association on December 11, 1884. Photo courtesy of Sioux City Public Museum

Men and women, blacks and whites, youngsters and old-timers, along with horse-drawn vehicles, all were seen aboard the steamboat Andrew S. Bennett *as it prepared for a trip from Covington, Nebraska, to Sioux City circa 1880. Boats began ferrying freight and passengers across the Missouri River in 1857 and remained popular until the construction of bridges—first the Pontoon Bridge and later the Combination Bridge. Photo courtesy of Sioux City Public Museum*

The marriage of Rosabella "Belle" Smith and Arthur Samuel Garretson, on September 3, 1879, united one of the more established Sioux City families with a young banker on the rise. Garretson came to Sioux City in 1874, at the age of twenty-three. He and William L. Joy opened the Sioux National Bank in 1881. Garretson became Sioux City's foremost developer and promoter of the nineteenth century. Photo courtesy of Sioux City Public Museum

Forepaugh's circus, which billed itself as "The Greatest Show on Earth," drew this large crowd on the grounds of Hunt School circa 1885. Hat manufacturers and merchants obviously were doing a brisk trade during this period. In the background is Deal and Turnbull's grocery, situated along the south side of Fourth Street between Jackson and Jones streets. Photo courtesy of Julie Goodson

These views of Fourth Street were taken on August 8, 1885, when Sioux Cityans paid homage to Ulysses S. Grant, former Civil War general and U.S. president. The impressive Grant memorial arch stood at Fourth and Pierce streets. Sioux City's downtown was in a state of transition, with substantial buildings lining Fourth Street while the sidewalks, sewage system, and street itself lagged behind.

This view looks east from about Pearl Street. McElhaney's Hall is on the far left, with the S. T. Davis Block located across Pearl Street. Construction of both buildings began in 1870, when Fourth and Pearl was the commercial center of the city. Bunting decorated the entire south side of Fourth Street, from the dry goods store of Andrew Larson and Ole Rye, at Fourth and Pearl, to the three-storied First National Bank building, at Fourth and Douglas. Photo courtesy of Sioux City Public Museum

In this photo, looking west towards Pierce Street, members of the B. F. Smith G.A.R. Post No. 22 congregate at the arch. The Hubbard House is on the far right. On March 12, 1870, Sioux City's leading businessmen subscribed more than $40,000 to erect this magnificent hotel. Schulein's Dry Goods store is beyond it. The Sioux National Bank is at the southeast corner of Fourth and Pierce, and Harry Hall's sign is on the Academy of Music. The large, dominating home on Prospect Hill (center) was one of the city's finest when built in the late 1870s for Judge Joseph R. Zuver. It was torn down in the spring of 1979. Photo courtesy of Sioux City Public Museum

The steep terrain of the city's Northside posed a major obstacle to northward expansion. In this 1886 photo, large numbers of horses, mules, and men are lessening the steepness of Pearl Street's 1300 block. The wooden sidewalks have been temporarily taken up and rest along the fence.

From left to right, the homes belonged to the following: district court stenographer William E. Cody; justice of the peace William D. Brown; First National Bank employee Alonzo L. D'Orsay; upholsterer Charles E. Ruggles; attorney Joseph W. Hallam; and (north of Fourteenth Street) railroad agent Edward W. Jordan.

Residents of this area later successfully petitioned the city council to rename the portion of Pearl above Ninth Street to "Grandview Boulevard," in an attempt to disassociate their homes from the sordid reputation of Lower Pearl Street. Photo courtesy of Sioux City Public Museum

These sixteen members of the all-volunteer Hose Company No. 3 proudly display the latest in Sioux City fire-fighting equipment in a photo taken in the latter months of 1886. The firefighters are, from left: Herman Provost, Fred Wyre, Billy Moy, Charles Wright, Pete Kane, John McBride, Pat McBride, Pat Sullivan, August Meyer, Mike Tierney, Gus Hagadorn, Dan Spencer, Louis Warnholtz, Jack Hafie, foreman Frank Draper, and captain Tom Sullivan. Photo courtesy of Sioux City Public Museum

Sioux City's river shipping prosperity had its seamier side as well. This is Hell's Half-Acre, a notorious "red light" district on the banks of Perry Creek. The Durfee and Peck line steamer C. K. Peck can be seen loading near the U.S. government warehouse in the background. Photo courtesy of Sioux City Public Museum

Reverend George C. Haddock moved from Wisconsin to Sioux City in 1885 to assume the ministerial duties at the First Methodist Episcopal Church. He was an ardent opponent of liquor and a staunch believer in prohibition. Haddock did not limit his push for local law enforcement to speaking from the pulpit. Along with a few other clergymen and citizens, Haddock gathered evidence of saloons operating in violation of Clark's Law and presented his findings in court. The minister spent much of Monday, August 2, 1886, serving as a witness against Sioux City's saloon element.

That evening, according to prosecutors in later trials, an organization of tavern owners and brewers met to determine its response to Haddock and his followers. As one brewer had admitted openly several months earlier that the saloon element was prepared to assault northwest Iowa's congressman, a violent course of action against Haddock was a real possibility. The prosecution further related that the brewers and their friends resolved to have two German immigrants, Albert "Bismarck" Koschnitski and Sylvester Ganda, "whip Walker, Wood, and Haddock."

The following evening, Reverends C. C. Turner and Haddock hired a rig at Merrill's livery stable on Water Street, and journeyed to Greenville to uncover evidence against a saloon. Their job completed, Haddock dropped off Turner at his home and returned the horse and buggy. Meanwhile a large number of the liquor sellers congregated nearby at the southeast corner of Fourth and Water. At a little past 10 p.m., as Haddock began to walk home past the Columbia House and into the intersection of Fourth and Water, a member of the crowd fired point blank and mortally wounded the crusading minister. He died a few hours later. Haddock became a nationwide martyr to the cause of prohibition, spoken of in the same breath as other assassinated leaders—Lincoln, James A. Garfield, and abolitionist Elijah P. Lovejoy. Sioux City, on the other hand, received a reputation as a town full of unsavory characters.

The Woodbury County grand jury indicted several men, including "respected citizens" Fred Munchrath, Jr. and John Arensdorf and Standard Theatre manager Harry Leavitt. The murder trial of Arensdorf, which attracted national newspaper coverage, began in April 1887, lasted twenty-two days, and ended in a hung jury standing eleven for acquittal and one for conviction. In the fall of 1887, a jury convicted Munchrath of manslaughter. The prosecution did not attempt to prove that Munchrath himself had killed Haddock but that he was part of a conspiracy to assassinate the pastor. The third and last trial ended in December 1887 with Arensdorf being acquitted in his retrial for murder.

Sioux Cityans may never know for sure who killed Haddock, but the atrocity awakened the community to the moral depths to which the town had plunged. While saloons remained a part of the landscape even after the Haddock affair, the city became less tolerant of such open defiance of the law. (Will Clark, *History of the Counties of Woodbury and Plymouth, Iowa*).

Reverend George C. Haddock (1832-1886). Photo courtesy of First United Methodist Church, Sioux City; rephotographed by B. Paul Chicoine

The First Methodist Episcopal Church, located at the southwest corner of Seventh and Nebraska, was built in 1883-84 and used until 1916. It was the Methodist's third church building in Sioux City, earlier ones being at the northwest corner of Eighth and Douglas and the northeast corner of Sixth and Pierce. It was from this church that Reverend Haddock denounced the lack of enforcement of Iowa's liquor law. Photo by C. N. Taylor; courtesy of R. Scott Key, Murdo, South Dakota

William C. Davenport was deputy sheriff at the time of Haddock's assassination. He learned of the shooting upon leaving a performance of Fielding's Comedy Ideals at the Academy of Music, and after running the two-and-a-half blocks, became one of the first persons at the scene. He was the state's initial witness in the resulting trials, at one point graphically depicting the assault by donning the victim's blood-stained raincoat. He went on to become sheriff, chief of police, and the founder of Davenport Cleaners. Photo courtesy of Sioux City Public Museum

The Haddock murder trials were held in the Woodbury County Courthouse and attracted newspapermen from throughout the nation. This view shows one of the courtrooms where the trials were held. Photo courtesy of Sioux City Public Museum

George W. Wakefield (1839-1905) came to Sioux City in 1868 and studied law under Judge Isaac Pendleton. He married Isaac's sister Kate in 1873. Wakefield served two terms as county auditor and two years as circuit judge. Elected judge of the district court in 1886, he presided over the last two Haddock murder trials. Photo courtesy of Sioux City Public Museum

On December 10, 1887, the day after the jury found John Arensdorf not guilty in his retrial for the murder of Reverend Haddock, Arensdorf wined and dined the jury members, then took them to Florence's photographic studio, less than half a block from the scene of the assassination, for this sitting.

John Arensdorf is seated in the center, with jurors A. J. Thompson (foreman) and J. B. Jones seated on the left and John Tripp and Patrick Collins on the right. Those jurors standing are: P. H. Rush, Peter Hayes, John Harrington, Joseph Stanley, John M. Yockey, George L. Shaw, John Bach, and John Hiatt.

When a Sioux City Journal reporter showed up, Arensdorf said, "You don't like it, I know, but you'll have to stand it," to which juror Tripp shouted, "You bet he will have to stand it." The scribe wrote that "the group was as fraternal as the Fireside Companion club." Photo by Florence Photographic Studio; courtesy of Sioux City Journal

Owner James Finnegan and patrons of the Northern Exchange Saloon at 211 Douglas Street smugly defy public opinion as well as Iowa's liquor statute in this photo from 1891. The city council licensed saloons at that time, requiring tavern owners to pay for the privilege of violating the law. Photo by Charles Bornschein; courtesy of Sioux City Public Museum

Chapter 4

Sowing the Wind – Reaping the Whirlwind

1886 – 1893

The cold-blooded murder of Reverend Haddock in 1886 left Sioux City in a state of embarrassment, its reputation tainted locally and nationally. The storm of public outcry and the intensified law enforcement which stemmed from the tragedy forced some saloon keepers to close their doors. Many others fled across the Missouri River to nearby Covington, Nebraska, transforming that hamlet into one of the most notorious towns in the American West.

Local compliance with Iowa's liquor law remained difficult to enforce. As the *Sioux City Weekly Tribune* acknowledged in early 1887, "The hole-in-the-wall raids have grown monotonous. The joints are generally in full blast again within minutes after the constable makes a seizure and closes the hole that don't close after all."

Fortunately for Sioux City, a significant wave of developmental spirit was engulfing the West in the late 1880s. Community leaders seized this opportunity both to turn attention away from the Haddock affair and to improve local business. Mounting the wave's crest, a clique of leading local businessmen and promoters— A.S. Garretson, John Peirce, D. T. Hedges, William Gordon, and others—launched a campaign to transform Sioux City into one of the most spectacular and trend-setting cities in the nation. Their philosophy, the Sioux City Way—the belief that anything Sioux City wanted, it could obtain—came to represent the progressive spirit that dominated this era.

The need, the individuals, and the prevailing economic climate combined to make the philosophy a reality. As the population swelled from 19,060 in 1885 to a purported 50,000 in 1893, land speculation once again became a major preoccupation. The number of real estate firms jumped from about thirty-five in 1886 to seventy-nine in 1887. Prices for residential and business lots skyrocketed. For the second time in less than forty years, Sioux City became gripped in land-rush fever.

Earlier in the community's history, city fathers had

made few improvements in a neighborhood until the number of people there justified the expenditure. These methods of development changed during the boom years. Sioux City's real estate promoters in the late 1880s began buying up vast tracts of open prairie land and grading the hills into streets and home lots at their own expense. These tracts became the new residential suburbs of Leeds, Riverside, Highland Park, Northside, and Morningside. These districts' boosters vied with each other in devising new and unique transportation systems to link their developments with the city's downtown business center. Electric and steam-powered street railway extensions to Leeds, Highland Park, and Riverside, a cable car railway to the town's hilly Northside, and an elevated railroad to Morningside—one of America's first—reached out to bind the city together. The local government followed suit and increased Sioux City's corporate limits by 1890 to an area large enough to accommodate a population of 250,000. These boundaries remained virtually unaltered for the next sixty years.

Many of Sioux City's major industries emerged or expanded during this period. The Union Stock Yards Company, organized in 1884, enlarged its already massive stock handling facilities and erected new packing houses, adding the firms of Silberhorn and Fowler to that of James E. Booge and Sons. These large meatpacking companies became the new foundation of the city's economy, as well as a major attraction for immigrant laborers. To the north, developers of the new suburb of Leeds touted their district as "Sioux City's new manufacturing suburb," boasting brickyards, a stove manufacturer, and an engine factory. To the west, Riverside came into its own, with a pickling works, a sprawling brick and tile plant, and Riverside Park, which quickly became the city's most popular summertime recreation spot.

The city also achieved improvements in terms of railroads and bridges during the boom years. In 1886, only four railroads entered the city. Within five years, a total of eleven separate rail lines were either in operation or on the drawing boards. The long-awaited Missouri River Railroad Bridge, a goal of Sioux City's boosters since the early 1870s, opened on December 5, 1888. The bridge was owned by the Chicago, St. Paul, Minneapolis and Omaha Railroad. High tolls and other restrictions imposed on competing lines, however, led promoters Donald McLean, John Peirce, and others to organize a company to construct a second Missouri River bridge two miles further upstream. This new bridge, which was intended primarily to carry their proposed Pacific Short Line Railroad, was also designed to serve pedestrian, and wagon traffic—hence it would be a "combination" bridge. The backers selected a site near Prospect Hill and commenced work on the bridge in December 1889.

As Sioux City vied with other Western cities for prosperity and prestige, her residents exerted all effort to advertise and promote the community and region. The construction of Sioux City's corn palaces was a prime example. Businessmen wanted a sensational method to celebrate the 1887 harvest season and advertise the town, and a suggestion to build a palace of corn met with universal enthusiasm.

Within two months, Sioux City's first corn palace opened to the delight of local residents and to the envy of tourists who had taken advantage of reduced railroad rates to attend. An estimated 140,000 people thronged to the palace during the six-day-long celebration. Workmen tore down this first "fairy palace" shortly thereafter, and within a few months a jubilant Sioux City Corn Palace Exposition Company began laying plans for an even more magnificent structure in 1888. In all, Sioux Cityans built five distinct corn palaces from 1887 to 1891.

Sioux City's world-famous corn palaces performed admirably their function of promoting the city and the region. National journals lauded the Corn Palace City, and those who journeyed here were seldom disappointed.

The crowning cultural achievement of the period was the building of the Peavey Grand Opera House, located in the Chamber of Commerce Block. This elegant facility replaced the Academy of Music as the city's cultural center and offered Sioux Cityans the finest in professional entertainment as the managers brought to the Peavey the stars of the American theater.

By the end of 1891, Sioux City was being looked upon—by her citizens as well as her neighbors—as the next great metropolis of the West. The nickname, Little Chicago, never seemed more appropriate. The year of 1892 was less fruitful, however, as an international restriction of capital made further expansion more difficult. After years of unprecedented growth, the sudden slowdown caused many to question the city's boosters.

In April 1892 John Peirce characteristically attempted to shore-up the community's sagging morale by reminding his fellow citizens that, "Eastern people have plenty of confidence in Sioux City. This year is bound to be a year of progress. . . . The town is all right if you just think so."

The new Library/City Hall Building at Sixth and Douglas was completed in 1892, and construction of a new high school began on the former Follett mansion site at Twelfth and Jackson, but for the first time since the boom years began the city found itself faced with grave economic problems. Early in 1892 the McLean-Peirce faction found itself financially unable to continue construction of their Combination Bridge, for which caissons had already been sunk. They surrendered the project to a group headed by A. S. Garretson. Uncertainty struck the corn palaces as well. During a Corn Palace Association meeting on May 6, 1892, some businessmen urged that plans for an 1892 palace be modified or abandoned, fearing that the venture had grown too costly. Backer James F. Peavey rallied to its defense, declaring that what was needed was, "in the language of the illustrious Hedges, to resolve that you want it, then go after it."

A disastrous Floyd River flood, which devastated the city's stockyards and industrial districts on May 18, 1892, however, doomed the festival. On June 15, 1892, banker James F. Toy announced that there would be no 1892 Corn Palace, but that the festival would be resumed in 1893. Mitchell, South Dakota, seized on Sioux City's postponement to erect its own corn palace in 1892.

The Leeds Improvement and Land Company encountered financial troubles later in 1892, and a district court judge appointed a receiver to supervise the company's finances and repay the firm's creditors. The company's failure provoked a general feeling of alarm. These fears deepened when Booge Packing Company, Sioux City's oldest meatpacker, also closed its doors, crippling the area's most important industry. The impact of the Booge failure was moderated somewhat by the announcement in November 1892 that Cudahy and Company would enter the Sioux City market by purchasing the Fowler/Haakinson plant. Meatpacking magnate Edward Cudahy declared his confidence in Sioux City and its developers by predicting, "If I am not mistaken, we will see all the [packing] houses running at full capacity before another year, and a new [packing] house either finished or building. Why do I say that? Because D. T. Hedges has taken hold of the stock yards interests with the intentions of making things hum. And he'll do it!"

Sioux City businessmen thus entered 1893 with guarded optimism, predicting a solid year. They made plans for an 1893 Corn Palace, a move which not only indicated the zeal of the palaces' supporters, but the fear of some of appearing to be in defiance of the Sioux City Way. In a poll concerning whether or not to have an 1893 Corn Palace, jeweler Will H. Beck remarked, "I am in favor of anything, always am." To the same question, grocer Charles Breun responded, "No sir. I am not in favor of a Corn Palace. But here now, if you're going to put me down in the paper, say that I'm in favor of it. I don't want to be put down as against anything!"

An international depression in 1893 drew the final curtain of Sioux City's corn palaces and on the boom years as well. On Black Tuesday, April 25, 1893, one of the lowest points in Sioux City's economic history took place when officers of the Union Loan and Trust Company and the Hedges Trust Company requested the appointment of receivers and announced that they were incapable of paying their local and Eastern creditors. D. T. Hedges also declared that he was personally bankrupt. The panic of 1893 had come to Sioux City. It hit severely because of the Union Loan and Trust Company's role as a source of capital for many of the city's largest local businesses and promotions. More than a dozen of Sioux City's most important companies collapsed within weeks.

The community reacted quickly to the panic of 1893. A. S. Garretson made assurances that, while he and other promoters would be affected by the events, the populace as a whole was secure. Those businessmen who had not been members of the clique generally agreed that the depression had been foreseen, that real estate prices would soon revert to actual values, and that the city's economy was sound overall.

D. T. Gilman, president of the Iowa State National Bank, advised, "Our bank has never had anything to do with the parties involved in the present flurry. They have belonged to a charmed circle into which no one else has been fortunate enough to penetrate."

Marc W. Darling, pastor of the First Congregational Church, after eulogizing the era and its architects, added that, while the promoters had helped to make Sioux City prosperous, they had also "for years been sowing to the wind, and they are now reaping the whirlwind."

In 1887, when the city's economic growth was in its early stages, the Chicago News listed A. S. Garretson (1851-1917) as one of Sioux City's three leading "boomers," describing him as "a young banker, who would be a noticeable figure in any financial circle, lean of person, indifferent of dress, whose hat is an antique whimsey, and whose string necktie is a study of arabesque, an amiable fox, a westernized Yankee."

Garretson played a major role in virtually every large undertaking, either holding an office, securing capital, or advising the principals. A list of his efforts includes expansion of the stockyard industry and downtown improvements, participation in construction of the railroad bridge and early stages of the Combination Bridge, implementation of the corn palaces and Peavey Grand Opera House, development of Leeds and Morningside, and the financing of the Elevated Railroad and numerous other area railroads. He, more than anyone else, had the ability to deal effectively with powerful Eastern and Midwestern financiers and railroad barons.

Garretson's fortune was wiped out by the panic of 1893, yet he worked strenuously to counteract the city's plight. While he never again reached the pinnacle of personal wealth he had known in 1892, Garretson continued to hold an elevated position in the hearts of Siouxlanders. Photo courtesy of Sioux City Public Museum

The Hotel Garretson was the city's finest hotel during the boom years. Built in two stages, in 1884 and 1886, it stood at the northeast corner of Fifth and Pierce streets. The Woodbury County Courthouse sat adjacent at Sixth and Pierce. Visible also in the background is the 1888 Corn Palace during construction. From J. M. Pinckney's Souvenir Album of the 1888 Corn Palace; courtesy of Sioux City Public Museum

Manager D. A. Williams and others peer down from the Hotel Garretson at the City Bus Line about 1890. This transit system shuttled patrons between the hotels and the railroad depots. On the right, a lad has abandoned his high-wheeled bicycle in favor of Moore Pharmacy's five-cent whipped cream soda. Photo by C. N. Taylor; courtesy of R. Scott Key, Murdo, South Dakota

These men sought shelter in the Hotel Garretson from an oncoming April 1887 cold wave. The hotel, at the northeast corner of Fifth and Pierce, had opened just three months earlier, after a massive addition had more than doubled the size of the two-year-old A. S. Garretson office building. A reception, attended by 500 of Sioux City's most influential residents on December 29, 1886, signaled the hotel's birth, but the electric lights shown here were not installed until early February 1887. Photo by C. N. Taylor; courtesy of R. Scott Key, Murdo, South Dakota

Edwin C. Peters (1836-1917), a successful insurance agent, was the original promoter of Morningside. He purchased the acreage, which was then southeast of the city limits, within two years after his arrival in 1870 and devoted most of his remaining energy to Morningside's development. Peters served as president of the Sioux City Rapid Transit Company, the firm that constructed the Elevated Railroad. He also was involved in the founding of the University of the Northwest.

Peters remained in Sioux City despite suffering heavy losses in the panic of 1893. Through diligent efforts he finally repaid all the debts that he had accrued. Photo by Genelli; courtesy of Sioux City Public Museum

A. S. Garretson built this imposing house during the late 1880s in Morningside, overlooking Peters' Park. Three of the family's eight children are seen on the spacious grounds. A cattle grazing area existed beyond the carriage house, on the left, which was built of the same stone as the residence. A gazebo is visible on the right.

The Garretson family lived in this home from 1889 until 1906, when it was purchased by Morningside College. College President W. S. Lewis planned to use the building as a "coordinate college for the education of women." Although this idea was soon abandoned, the building served as

Renaissance Hall, the women's dormitory, for several years. The mansion then became the college president's home and, still later, a fraternity house.

The Sioux City Public Library acquired the Garretson home on December 26, 1931. Following a remodeling project, which included the razing of the carriage house, it opened as the Morningside Branch Library on August 3, 1932. The library board, in a controversial move, tore down the Garretson mansion in 1967 and replaced it with a new branch library on the same site. Photo by C. N. Taylor; courtesy of R. Scott Key, Murdo, South Dakota

This Morningside home and surrounding land belonged to the E. C. Peters family from the 1870s to the early 1890s. The University of the Northwest purchased part of the twenty-acre tract in 1890.

When the Peters family moved in 1892, their old home became a sanitarium for the "tired and ill" until 1894, when this photograph was taken. The wing on the right may have been added during this time. The home later served as a boardinghouse for Morningside College students and as the college's chemistry building. The structure was destroyed by fire on August 22, 1914. Photo by C. N. Taylor; courtesy of R. Scott Key, Murdo, South Dakota

Elmwood was the home of John M. Tredway, the last of three Tredway brothers to live in Sioux City. John came in 1881 and settled on land northeast of the city limits that had been claimed by his brother William in the late 1850s. He sold most of the homestead in 1888 to the Leeds Improvement and Land Company. John

Tredway represented Leeds on the city council from 1895 to 1901.

A large addition to the home, which included the construction of massive columns, was undertaken about 1900. Photo by C. N. Taylor; courtesy of R. Scott Key, Murdo, South Dakota

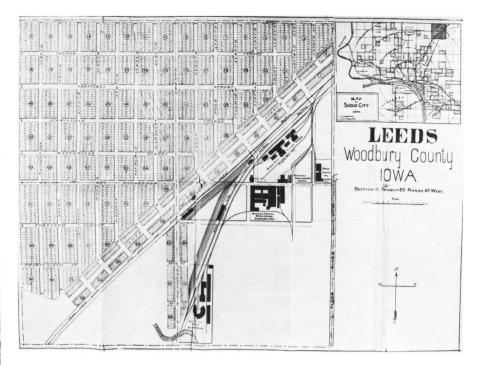

Sioux City's appetite for industrial and residential "elbow room" in the late 1880s manifested itself in the development of Leeds, located just outside Sioux City's 1880 city limits to the north. Touted as an English-style manufacturing suburb-to-be (hence its colorful blend of British and American street names), the district was platted by the Leeds Improvement and Land Company in 1889 as an independent Iowa city and annexed by popular vote of its residents into Sioux City one year later. During the boom years of the late 1880s and early 1890s, Leeds boasted some of Sioux City's largest manufacturers, including the Bonus-Milner Milling Company, the giant Daniel E. Paris Stove Works (once billed as the largest stove works of its kind in the world), the Rathburn Wheelscraper Company, the Sioux City Engine and Iron Works, and a number of smaller businesses. Slightly over 1,000 men, most of them Leeds residents, were employed here by 1892.

While impressively accurate in many details, this map, published in the 1890-91 Sioux City Directory, allowed itself one flight of self-serving fancy: the railroad yard and roundhouse were actually not built until nearly a decade later. From the 1890-91 Sioux City Directory; courtesy of Sioux City Public Museum

The Sioux City Engine and Iron Works, shown here under construction in 1889, was Leeds' second-largest manufacturer from 1889 to 1896. The firm employed 250 men and specialized in the building of stationary steam powerplants, including the patented Sioux City Corliss Engine. The American Pop Corn Company today occupies this site. Photo by C. N. Taylor; courtesy of R. Scott Key, Murdo, South Dakota

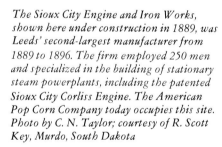

A bounty of private and commercial apple orchards throughout northwest Iowa furnished the raw materials for the Sioux City Vinegar and Pickling Works during the 1890s. The plant, located in Riverside and later known as the Sioux City Cider Company, advertised "Genuine Apple Cider and Apple Vinegar" by the carload lot. Photo courtesy of Sioux City Public Museum

William W. Byam's stately home in Highland Park overlooked many of his investments in the late 1880s and early 1890s. He was instrumental in the development of Riverside Park, the Highland Park streetcar line, and the Westside in general. Byam suffered badly from the panic of 1893 and left town. Photo by C. N. Taylor; courtesy of R. Scott Key, Murdo, South Dakota

Soldiers of the Fourth Regiment, Iowa National Guard, bivouac at Camp Rice in Riverside Park during the summer of 1892. Camp Rice, named in honor of Civil War Brigadier General Elliot W. Rice, who later became a prominent Sioux Cityan, was the site of frequent National Guard encampments and drills throughout the 1880s and 1890s. Many of these men were called out for active duty during the Debs railroad strikes of 1894 and later served in the Spanish-American War. Photo courtesy of Sioux City Public Museum

A view of West Side Park, with Prospect Hill in the backgound. When Dr. John K. Cook laid out Sioux City proper in 1854-55, he called this area Public Square, visualizing the development of government buildings on this site. The business district developed further east, however, and the land remained vacant for years.

In 1871 Sioux City's "fallen angels" suggested that the Public Square be made into the "Social Evil Square," with a ten-foot board fence around it. The suggestion was turned down. Eventually it became a city park, known through the years as West Side, West Third, or Central Park. At the urging of the Woodbury County Pioneer Club, the city council renamed it the Dr. John K. Cook Park on February 21, 1936. The park was relocated in the 1970s during the Hamilton Area Urban Renewal Project. Photo courtesy of Sioux City Public Museum

Dr. William R. Smith subdivided his farm on the city's Westside in the late 1880s and laid out Smith's Villa Addition. In 1892 contractor F. M. Sterling began building this magnificent stone residence for Smith at 1623 Rebecca Street. The doctor died in 1894 and was therefore only able to enjoy the comforts of his new home for a short

while.

The Sioux City school system purchased the Smith mansion in 1899 and turned it into an elementary school. They built additions to Smith School in 1910 and 1916 and extensively remodeled it in 1934. Photo courtesy of Sioux City Public Museum

The frantic, often madcap pace pursued by Sioux City's boom era investors in developing the city's new Northside produced some unusual, if not amusing, results. This photo is believed to have been taken in the vicinity of Sixteenth and Pierce streets. Photo by C. N. Taylor; courtesy of R. Scott Key, Murdo, South Dakota

75

John Peirce and D. T. Hedges purchased a large tract of land north of the city limits in 1886. They began to develop Peirce's Addition the following year. In March 1887, Peirce explained how the method of developing a suburb had changed from earlier times, when improvements had waited until the population merited them. He said, "Street and cable car lines are extended into territories where there are no residents, but residents immediately follow—and this is the modern way of building the western city."

Peirce's plan worked. The large houses, shown here about 1890, were built only after large expenditures in street grading and the creation of the Sioux City Cable Railway on Jackson Street. William Gordon's home, at 2719 Jackson, is in the center, adjacent to Charles Hornick's residence at 2727 Jackson. The Linus Skinner home, at 2813 Nebraska Street, is seen between them. In the background, workmen with horse-drawn graders are cutting down the hilly area near what is now Twenty-Eighth and Pierce streets. The elm trees were planted at nearly the height shown and shaded this neighborhood until the early 1970s. Peirce also was president of the Sioux City Nursery and Seed Company. Photo by C. N. Taylor; courtesy of R. Scott Key, Murdo, South Dakota

Staff and management of the Fletcher and Hutchins Company, 209-223 West Fourth Street, take a break from their lathes and planing tables for this circa 1890 company photo. Fletcher and Hutchins was Sioux City's first wood finishing mill, specializing in doors, window sashes, blinds, and custom moldings for many of the region's finer homes and businesses during the boom years. Photo by L. B. Winslow; courtesy of Sioux City Public Museum

In D. T. Hedges' mansion at 2803 Jackson Street, patterns leaped at the onlooker from floor to ceiling. Photo by C. N. Taylor; courtesy of R. Scott Key, Murdo, South Dakota

The exuberance of the boom years led in 1890 to the creation of the University of the Northwest in Morningside. The Methodist Episcopal Church worked with Eastern and local capitalists to foster the infant center of learning. The original members of the board of directors were: Reverend Wilmot Whitfield, D.D., president; Reverend Ira N. Pardee, financial agent and secretary; E. C. Peters and Reverend R. C. Glass, vice-presidents; and A. S. Garretson, treasurer.

This jasper stone structure constituted the entire college for a decade. It was built in 1890 by J. M. Poorbaugh on a portion of E. C. Peters' former estate. The panic of 1893 curtailed construction of a second, larger building, and indeed, caused the University of the Northwest to cease operation. The Methodist Episcopal Church purchased the property in 1894 and renamed the institution Morningside College.

Fire gutted this original structure, then called the Conservatory of Music, on December 6, 1914. The college was able to reuse the walls, however, as it rebuilt. This building stands today as Charles City Hall. *Photo courtesy of Woodworth Commercial Photos*

Few ventures better exemplified the gambling spirit of Sioux City's boom years than did the construction during 1889-1891 of the Sioux City Rapid Transit Company's celebrated elevated railroad between downtown and Morningside. This elaborate rapid transit system included three miles of surface track from Morningside to Leech Avenue and another two miles of double-tracked iron trestlework. More than $500,000 was expended on the construction and equipment. Local "boomers," including A. S. Garretson, James A. Jackson, E. C. Peters, and James E. Booge, launched the project, but most of the capital came from Eastern investors.

In this view of September 1890, employees of the King Bridge and Iron Company of Cleveland, Ohio, contractors for the project, display the techniques of steam and muscle power used to erect the "el's" extensive trestlework, as they approach the intersection of Third and Virginia streets. The Peavey Grand Opera House and the 1890 Corn Palace are in the background. Photo courtesy of Sioux City Public Museum

On April 16, 1891, the Sioux City Rapid Transit Company—the third elevated railroad in the world—opened for business with the departure of this two-car excursion train from the "el" station above the corner of Third and Jones streets. Two trains, each powered by a double-ended steam locomotive, left this station every thirty minutes thereafter for the distant suburb of Morningside and points between. Fare was only a nickel. Photo courtesy of Sioux City Public Museum

Completion of the Elevated Railroad to Morningside in 1891 fueled speculators' hopes and kindled a boom in affluent home building in the new suburb. This view, taken from an upper-floor window of the A. S. Garretson home, shows a west-bound "el" train on the line's surface grade on Morningside Avenue. The James A. Jackson home stands at upper left. Photo courtesy of Sioux City Public Museum

The Sioux City Cable Railway was the largest inducement engineered by land developers John Peirce and D. T. Hedges to lure prospective home buyers up the slope to Peirce's Addition, the city's newly-opened northern suburb. The line, which began operation on May 30, 1889, traveled up Jackson Street from Third to Twenty-ninth Street. It soon was extended north on Jackson to Fortieth Street and west on Third to Water Street.

The cable system powerhouse and car shops, shown here with the shop crew and three of the company's thirty-four single- and double-decked cable cars, was located on Twenty-ninth Street near Jones Street. A similar view today would overlook Hubbard Park. The building's generators propelled an endless cable which ran in a sunken slot between the rails. A hand-operated clutch, or "grip," controlled by the car's conductor, extended into the slot to engage the constantly-moving cable. In addition to powering the cable cars, the facility also provided electricity for arc lights on Jackson Street and steam heat for several nearby mansions.

Sioux City's cable line was electrified in 1894 and eventually incorporated into the city's streetcar system. A cinder pile in the park below is all that remains of Iowa's first cable railway. Photo by C. N. Taylor; courtesy of R. Scott Key, Murdo, South Dakota

Sioux City Cable Railway Company president and developer John Peirce (in bowler hat far left) halted two of his company's streetcars and their crews for this circa 1894 photo at the intersection of Twenty-ninth and Jackson streets. Peirce's newly-completed mansion, later home to the Sioux City Public Museum, is prominent in the background.

Despite evidence of the line's recent conversion to electric trolley power, the old cable grip slots remain between the rails. From a damaged Charles Bornschein glass plate negative; courtesy of Sioux City Public Museum

Jennings and Pierce Street motormen pose with their streetcars adjacent to the Hotel Booge (earlier the Hubbard House) at Fourth and Pierce in 1890. The exquisite carriage on the right is parked in front of Will H. Beck's jewelry store. Photo by C. N. Taylor; courtesy of R. Scott Key, Murdo, South Dakota

The opening of the Missouri River Railroad Bridge on December 5, 1888, climaxed sixteen years of efforts by Sioux City manufacturers, businessmen, and railroad developers to tap the markets of nearby northeast Nebraska. The bridge, built for the Chicago, St. Paul, Minneapolis and Omaha (later Chicago and Northwestern) Railroad, boasted four, 300-foot iron spans supported by stone piers sunk ninety feet below the Missouri's surface. While the bridge was regaled as an engineering marvel of the time, its glory was tarnished by the Omaha line's refusal to allow other railroads to use the bridge at a reasonable fee, a violation of the original charter. The ensuing litigation resulted in the promotion of a new multipurpose bridge two miles further upstream, the Combination Bridge.

The passenger train seen here descending the bridge's Iowa approach is passing the massive Silberhorn Packing Company complex, later the home of Armour and Company. A section crew of the Sioux City Rapid Transit Company is working on the surface portion of the Elevated Railroad, near what is now Pulaski Park. Highway 75 passes through this site today. Photo courtesy of Sioux City Public Museum

Long hours, low pay, and primitive if not outright hazardous working conditions awaited the flood of immigrant packing house workers seeking employment in Sioux City during the 1880s. This scene is thought to be the boning room of the Silberhorn Packing Company (later Armour and Company). Photo by C. N. Taylor; courtesy of R. Scott Key, Murdo, South Dakota

By the end of the nineteenth century, Sioux City had blossomed into a major rail center, boasting eight trunk lines and five branch lines linking its industries to the world's markets. These railroads included the Chicago and Northwestern; Chicago, Milwaukee and St. Paul; Fremont, Elkhorn and Missouri Valley; Illinois Central; Sioux City and Pacific (Chicago, St. Paul, Minneapolis and Omaha); Sioux City and Northern (later Great Northern); and a northeast Nebraska branch of the Union Pacific (later owned by Chicago, Burlington and Quincy).

Thirty passenger trains arrived and departed daily, with local industries contributing a yearly average of 80,000 carloads of freight by 1892.

The Union Passenger Station, shown here nearing completion at Third and Douglas streets in 1893, was one of three downtown stations. It was built by A. S.

Garretson's Sioux City Terminal and Warehouse Company and served as the depot and business quarters for the Great Northern, Illinois Central, and Burlington roads until its demolition in 1952. The Siouxland Senior Center today occupies this site. Photo by C. N. Taylor; courtesy of R. Scott Key, Murdo, South Dakota

"This is the first really new thing that has been shown me," remarked President Grover Cleveland after his grand tour of Sioux City's first corn palace on October 12, 1887. Indeed, the five Sioux City corn palaces, constructed between 1887 and 1891, were the embodiment of Sioux City's boom years and the age of the Sioux City Way.

The idea of building a corn palace, the first of its kind in the world, was conceived during an August 20, 1887 meeting of local businessmen planning a harvest celebration worthy of the town's growing fame. After hearing several proposals, including decorating the courthouse and piling corn at the city's major intersections, they decided to erect a palace of corn. The organization selected the northwest corner of Fifth and Jackson as the site and contracted with architect E. W. Loft to prepare the building plans.

In large measure, the promoters' thinking was to use the area's agricultural bounty to advance the city's interests. As jeweler Will H. Beck proclaimed after the meeting, "It [the corn palace] is the greatest thing that could be done to advertise and show the world in black and white that we have reasons for claiming a city of 100,000 in a few years."

As a rough, wooden-frame building emerged, boosters decided that Sioux City needed an even larger edifice. The adjoining Goldie Roller Rink, on the left, became an addition to the original building and was used as a hall for band contests and public speaking. The entire region backed this grandiose project, with farmers donating produce, businessmen advancing funds, workmen supplying labor, and the women of Sioux City furnishing the interior's artistic details.

Inside the main entrance was a large copy of the municipal seal—a buffalo being driven from a railroad track by a locomotive—while on the floor stood two large, stuffed hogs with ears of corn in their mouths. As journalist E. P. Heizer later described it, "The interior of the palace was a realm of enchantment. Under the white glare of twenty-seven electric lights, it was a vision of fairyland."

Formal dedication of the 1887 Corn Palace took place on the evening of October 2. The building was thrown open to the public the following day, and approximately 140,000 persons toured its wonders before the palace closed on October 8. President Cleveland and railroad magnates Chauncey DePew and Cornelius Vanderbilt later examined the palace and applauded Sioux City and Siouxland for its progressiveness. "No visitor," Heizer stated, "could fail to receive enlarged impressions of the northwest, and of Sioux City as the capital of the northwest."

The 1887 Corn Palace. Photo by Genelli; courtesy of Sioux City Public Museum

With more time to plan, Sioux City's Corn Palace Association devised an even larger and more elaborate palace in 1888. Located at the northeast corner of Sixth and Pierce, this palace opened on September 24 and closed October 6, 1888. Photo by John E. Johnson; courtesy of Sioux City Public Museum

A huge throng of people assembled at the Chicago and Northwestern Railroad depot on February 28, 1889, to provide a rousing send-off for Sioux City's Special Corn Palace Train, carrying a delegation of local businessmen and political supporters to the presidential inauguration of Benjamin Harrison.

Large crowds gathered at every station between Sioux City and Washington, D.C., hoping to catch a glimpse of this rolling "panorama of corn." Returning by way of New York City and Philadelphia, the Corn Palace Train served as "a moving pageant that spread abroad the fame of Sioux City and vicinity," attracting many Eastern visitors to the 1889 Corn Palace. (Will Leach, History of the Counties of Woodbury and Plymouth, Iowa). Photo courtesy of Division of the State Historical Society, Iowa City, Iowa

Each of Sioux City's corn palaces was unique. The 1889 palace, also erected on the "corn palace lot" at Sixth and Pierce, featured an archway over Pierce Street and a 200-foot tower. Also visible in this view, beyond the corn palace, is Armstrong School, at Eighth and Pierce. In the foreground, John Peirce's land office faces the Woodbury County Courthouse.

Reduced railroad fares brought many people to this year's festivities, which were held from September 23 to October 5, 1889. Photo courtesy of Sioux City Public Museum

Several local photographers ascended the tower of the 1889 Corn Palace to capture the city in a time capsule during an era of unprecedented growth.

Pierce Street provides the focus of this residential view, with the street cut through the hills at the city's north end. Armstrong School, built in 1882 at the southeast corner of Eighth and Pierce streets, is in the foreground, while the First Congregational Church is under construction at the southwest corner of Eighth and Nebraska streets. The white-frame J. L. Follett residence on the spacious grounds to the right occupies the future site of the city's new high school. Photo courtesy of Sioux City Public Museum

The business district southeast of the corn palace includes the First Baptist Church in the foreground, with the six-story Metropolitan Block behind it, at the northeast corner of Fourth and Jackson streets. The Metropolitan Block, constructed by Narcisse Desparois and opened in 1889, was Sioux City's first skyscraper and boasted the town's first passenger elevator. Old Hunt School sits adjacent to the Metropolitan Block in front of the Peavey Grand Opera House. A considerable building boom is just beginning, with many more substantial structures about to become a reality within the next year. The railroad district and railroad bridge are visible in the background. Photo courtesy of Sioux City Public Museum

The just-completed Iowa Building, at the southwest corner of Fifth and Pierce streets, dominates this view looking south and west. C. Shenkberg and Company's building is at the northwest corner of Third and Pierce, with the Chicago, Milwaukee and St. Paul Railroad depot just behind it. Lower Douglas and Pearl streets formed much of the city's wholesale district at this time. The Pontoon Bridge is in the background. Photo courtesy of Sioux City Public Museum

In this view looking southwest, with Fifth and Douglas streets intersecting in the foreground, the older business district is visible. Prospect Hill is on the right, sporting a large number of fine and commodious homes. Photo courtesy of Sioux City Public Museum

A Turkish theme highlighted the 150-foot
square 1890 Corn Palace, located on the
"corn palace lot." The celebration that year
was held from September 25 to October 11.
Attendance figures dwindled, however, due
to inclement weather and competition from
other festivals, the most notable being
Ottumwa's Coal Palace Festival, which
opened in 1889. Photo courtesy of Sioux
City Public Museum

This rare interior view of the 1891
Corn Palace testifies to the artistry
and workmanship that went into these
temporary structures. Decorations abound
from floor to dome, while the goddess Ceres
looks down upon a stage enhanced by
numerous incandescent lights placed to
resemble stars. Local business displays are
prominent around the dome's gilded
perimeter. Photo by Genelli; courtesy of
Sioux City Public Museum

The 1891 Corn Palace, by far the largest
of these unique palaces, stretched a full
block in length along the north side of
Sixth Street and spanned Pierce Street.
Organizers of the October 1-17 extrav-
aganza spent heavily and predicted great
success for the 1891 palace, but drizzly days
and disappointing attendance figures
jeopardized the festival's future. In an
attempt to recoup financially, the
association extended the closing date to
October 24. Photo by Philip C. Waltermire;
courtesy of Sioux City Public Museum

The Peavey Grand Opera House, March 1891. As early as 1881, a movement had been under way to refurbish or replace the Academy of Music, which had opened in 1871. By the mid-1880s, the business community also sought a chamber of commerce building. The result, in 1887, was the creation of a joint chamber/opera house building at the northwest corner of Fourth and Jones streets.

While the theater was conceived initially as a minor part of the overall project, it grew in size as planning progressed. Local architect J. W. Martin designed the near portion of the building, with widely acclaimed theatrical architect Oscar Cobb of Chicago taking charge of the theater's interior. The Romanesque-style structure featured a French mansard roof. Upon completion, the Iowa State National Bank occupied the first floor corner, while Bosshard's Drug Store flanked the main entranceway to the west. The chamber of commerce and the weather bureau, as well as transit, real estate, and "boom era" offices filled its upper floors. Photo courtesy of Sioux City Public Museum

Promoters of Sioux City's Peavey Grand spent lavishly in making their opera house one of the finest facilities in the West. Brass railings and Oscar Cobb's innovative "NaCelle" boxes, to the upper left and right, highlight this scene from the late 1880s. The first floor, or "parquet circle," seated 523 people. The balcony, directly above the parquet circle, held an additional 246 persons. Another 400 or more could cram into the cheap seats in the gallery, at the extreme top, for a total seating capacity, counting the boxes, of over 1,300 spectators.

Frank H. Peavey, a Minneapolis-based grain tycoon and former Sioux Cityan, was the largest non-local contributor in this undertaking. The opera house was named the Peavey Grand in his honor. Photo by C. N. Taylor; Courtesy of R. Scott Key, Murdo, South Dakota

This view from the late 1880s shows the Peavey's stage, which hosted some of the world's greatest talents during the late nineteenth century. The dedication of the Peavey Grand and the first performance, on September 24, 1888, coincided with the opening of the 1888 Corn Palace celebration.

W. I. Buchanan became manager of the Peavey Grand following a lengthy stint with the Academy of Music. He worked diligently to secure the stars of the theater for Sioux City. Through his efforts and those of his successors, such notables as Edwin Booth, Lawrence Barrett, Maude Adams, Sarah Bernhardt, Joe Jefferson, and many others were honored to "play the Peavey." Photo by C. N. Taylor; courtesy of R. Scott Key, Murdo, South Dakota

This Fourth Street parade was likely held during the Corn Palace celebration of 1890. The float in front of the Peavey Grand Opera House proclaims the "Morningside Way of Doing Things." Equipment for the weather bureau is seen on the roof of the Peavey.

A. S. Garretson brought nearly 100 Eastern investors to the 1889 Corn Palace to show off the city. They were very impressed with the city's progressive spirit and invested heavily, especially in the Lower Fourth Street area. In this view, the Toy Building is under construction at the southeast corner of Fourth and Jackson, and the Wales Block, at the northwest corner of Fourth and Jennings streets, is emerging beyond the Chicago House. By the end of 1890, the Boston Investment Company owned the following buildings: Plymouth Block, Bay State Block, Massachusetts Block, Lexington Block, Bolton Block, and the Merchants' Club House. Photo by C. N. Taylor; courtesy of R. Scott Key, Murdo, South Dakota

The Sioux City Cornhuskers baseball team, in 1891. Sioux City promoters of the 1880s and 1890s viewed the Huskers as an extension of the Sioux City Way and invested lavishly in their backing. Joy reigned supreme, thus, when the Huskers, the Western Association's pennant winner, edged out "Cap" Anson's Chicago Colts for the 1891 World Championship at Sioux City. The glitter of Sioux City's "Corn Palace series" was dulled, however, when the National League awarded its pennant to Boston rather than Chicago. Photo by Philip C. Waltermire; courtesy of Sioux City Public Museum

Successful real estate agent Daniel Hector Talbot (1850-1911) purchased a secluded domain northwest of the city limits in the 1880s. At Talbot's Farm, he pursued his interests in plants and animals and experimented extensively in crossbreeding. His farm became a sanctuary for unusual animals. Talbot was an organizer of the Sioux City Scientific Association, the ancestor of the Sioux City Public Museum

Talbot was one of Sioux City's most unique personalities, but apparently he was well accepted. The Sioux City Journal ran the following advertisement in 1889 without comment: "For Sale—3 buffalo, 10 head of elk, and 3 bear—D. H. Talbot." Photo by Genelli; courtesy of Sioux City Public Museum

Students of teacher Kate Davis at Jennings Street School (now Irving) primped their curls, greased down their cowlicks, and succeeded (almost) in holding still long enough to have their class picture taken in 1888.

Shown here (but not identified by position) are Nellie Leander, Anna Stuart, Pearl Hughes, Louise Knott, Winifred Smith, Lulu Krammer, Jennie Ford, Carrie Hughes, Bessie Hood, LaVon Philbrook, Lida Richardson, Maude Galbraith, Cilla Richardson, Blanch Price, Julia Murphy, Kate Reynolds, Sam Price, Fay Bissell, Mat Gray, Bert Van Keuren, George Smith, Robert Calder, Sam Perkins, Humphrey Statler, Christian Peterson, Judson Follett, Jr., Walter Ingersoll, Bob Ridruch, and Hakin Halseth.

The Jennings Street School served a mixture of white working class students as well as the children of a few of Sioux City's more affluent families of the late 1880s. Photo courtesy of Sioux City Public Museum

Everett School boys and girls, however, managed to hold their heavy dumbbells ever-so-still for this demonstration of a pre-1900 calisthenics class. Everett School, originally known as the Davis Addition School, was built at West Third and Rebecca streets in 1888 and was added to in 1891 and 1917. Photo by C. N. Taylor; courtesy of R. Scott Key, Murdo, South Dakota

The relocation of the James E. Booge and Sons pork packing plant to the Floyd City Addition of Sioux City, coupled with the organization of the Union Stock Yards Company, brought a flood of new residents to the South Bottoms. In 1885 the school board established the Fifth Ward School at the northeast corner of Dace and Wall streets, soon changing its name to Worcester School (photo dated circa 1890). The rapid influx of people to the area necessitated additions in 1888, 1890, and 1907.

The school was renamed Hobson School in 1926, in honor of the late J. G. Hobson, former principal of Worcester School for thirty-six years. In 1938, through the assistance of the Public Works Administration, a new Hobson School was built on the same site. Photo by C. N. Taylor; courtesy of R. Scott Key, Murdo, South Dakota

This 1890-vintage Webster School class photo portrays the wide mix of ethnic backgrounds then flourishing in the West Fifth and Market streets district, including many of the city's Bohemian, Irish, Jewish, and Scandinavian immigrants, as well as a large number of early black families.

Webster School, first called Westside Brick School, was built in 1872, with additions placed on the original structure in 1883, 1891, and 1912. By the 1930s the old school had become a fire hazard, and WPA workers demolished it in 1938. The current Webster School was dedicated on February 10, 1939. Photo by Charles Bornschein; courtesy of Sioux City Public Museum

A damp day on September 13, 1889 failed to dull excitement of Grand Opening Day at The Fair, located at 320 Fourth Street. Eugene H. Gilmore was proprietor of this store, which specialized in Queensware, crockery, glassware, household goods, and notions. On this day, however, a coaster sled could satisfy a young lad's Christmas dreams for only fifty-eight cents! Photo by Lovell; courtesy of Sioux City Public Museum

Fire struck the old Sawyers Block at Second and Pearl streets—with its newer fourth floor addition—on February 8, 1891. The wholesale hardware firm of Baker and Bissell occupied the structure at the time of the blaze. The Tolerton and Stetson wholesale grocery company, which wrapped around the old Sawyers building, suffered the worst damage.

City fire records list another casualty of the conflagration—the enterprise of Mollie Van Sickels, described as a "sporting house." Mollie endured an unexplained $150 loss on "stock." Photo by C. N. Taylor; courtesy of R. Scott Key, Murdo, South Dakota

94

Ben Davidson, a youthful Russian immigrant, came to Sioux City in 1882. He spent the next two years as a peddler, carrying his supply of thread, needles, thimbles, tinware, and more on his back from house to house throughout Siouxland. Brother Dave arrived in 1883 and younger brother Abe a few years later.

In 1884 Ben and Dave Davidson opened B. Davidson's Bankrupt Store in a ten-by twenty-foot storeroom at 822½ Fourth Street and let the customers come to them. The company prospered and soon moved to the building shown here, at the northwest corner of Fourth and Nebraska. By the late 1880s, when this image was made, Davidsons' store was growing both in popularity and in the size of the staff. The company needed even more space and relocated in 1891 to a two-story structure at the southwest corner of Fourth and Pierce. The store was expanded on many occasions during the ensuing decades and became one of the best-known in the Midwest. Younkers Department Store purchased Davidsons' operation in 1947, first calling the business Younker-Davidsons then, since 1969, Younkers.

The Davidson brothers launched other ventures in the early 1900s. Several large downtown office buildings and stores were constructed by the Davidson Building Company and the Sunset residential area was a project of the Davidson Realty Company. They also were leaders of Sioux City's Jewish community. The Sioux City Journal aptly summarized the three Davidson brothers and their success story in the following headline: "Peddlers to Merchant Princes: Story of Opportunity and Ambition." Photo courtesy of Woodworth Commercial Photos

Grand Rapids, Michigan, natives Martin and John Bekins had already amassed ten years' moving and wagon freighting experience in 1891, when they moved to Sioux City. They opened their first hauling and storage company barn in the wide-open spaces of Twenty-first and Pierce streets.

By the time of this photo, believed to be taken in the early 1890s, the two Bekins brothers had been joined by younger brothers Taeke and Daniel and operated a fleet of seven wagons. In addition to hauling and storage services, the Bekins Van and Storage Company specialized in moving and hoisting such items as bank safes, boilers, and heavy factory machinery. Today's nationally-known warehousing, moving, and furniture divisions are the direct descendants of this early Sioux City firm. Photo courtesy of Sioux City Public Museum

The stark glare of a "new-fangled" electric light bulb fails to cut the gloom of this unidentified Sioux City meat market. In the days before electrical refrigeration (and health inspectors!) the discriminating grocery shopper might choose her family's Sunday dinner from a selection of beef, pork, lamb, and goose, or possibly a locally-cured ham from the ceiling-height wall racks. The huge meat cooler visible in the rear was likely supplied with ice from any one of a number of local Floyd River ice cutters. Photo by C. N. Taylor; courtesy of R. Scott Key, Murdo, South Dakota

Activity abounds at the southeast corner of Fourth and Nebraska streets in this view from the early 1890s. The Bolton/Commercial Block housed doctors, lawyers, realtors, and grain brokers in its upper floors; the Iowa State National Bank, after moving from the Peavey Grand Opera House, occupied the main floor. Bekins Van Line had its offices in the basement of the Commercial Block and its warehousing facilities in the Plymouth Block. On the left, along Fourth Street, two adjacent boot and shoe stores, probably C. A. Howe's and Snyder and Reid's, had succumbed to economic pressure and were conducting half-price sales prior to closing their doors. Photo courtesy of Julie Goodson

The third floor of the Bolton and Commercial blocks exemplified the ornate building styles of the boom years. While called separate names, the buildings were actually interconnected, with the Bolton Block in the foreground. In this view, taken about 1890, the Close Brothers and Company real estate office is on the right, and the law firm of Lothrop and Dott is in the background. Photo by C. N. Taylor; courtesy of R. Scott Key, Murdo, South Dakota

"Rooms to Suit Tenant, apply to A. E. Truesdell, Iowa Savings Bank" reads the sign in the recently-completed Plymouth Block, located at the southeast corner of Fourth and Court streets. Finished by 1891, it was the largest structure to be built along Lower Fourth Street during the boom years. Major occupants through the years have included the Sioux City College of Medicine, the Sioux City Iron Company, Aalfs Wall Paper Company, and many more. It became the Call Terminal Building in 1930. Photo by C. N. Taylor; courtesy of R. Scott Key, Murdo, South Dakota

Photographer Philip C. Waltermire provided this in-depth study of Sioux City in the fall of 1890. Panning his camera east from Prospect Hill, he captured a city on the move, with many of its buildings decorated as part of that year's corn palace festivities.

To the right, with the Missouri River Railroad Bridge in the background, a temporary railroad pile trestle serves as an extension of Water Street to connect Sioux City with the nefarious Nebraska towns of Stanton and Covington. Promoters of the Pacific Short Line (Combination Bridge Company) erected the temporary trestle to transport people and materials for construction of the new Combination Bridge (far right). Photo by Philip C. Waltermire; courtesy of Sioux City Public Museum

The Massachusetts Block (opposite), constructed in 1890 at the southwest corner of Fourth and Jackson streets, housed the Pelletier Department Store prior to the great fire of December 1904. The slotted streetcar track on Jackson Street (lower left) is the end-of-the-line for the Sioux City Cable Railway. Photo by C. N. Taylor; courtesy of R. Scott Key, Murdo, South Dakota

The Major Block, located at 1012 Fourth Street, housed the University of the Northwest's College of Commerce and Law Department when this view was taken in 1891. Women students were entering the previously male-dominated secretarial field, and Sioux City had a few women attorneys. Photographs of District Court Judge George W. Wakefield and former judge C. H. Lewis hang above the students. Photo by C. N. Taylor; courtesy of R. Scott Key, Murdo, South Dakota

Nationwide observance of Labor Day was just two years of age on September 7, 1891, when Sioux City's thirty-five union plumbers joined an estimated 1,000 fellow tradesmen, city officials, soldiers, and musicians in a gala seven-block-long Labor Day parade through Sioux City's Westside and downtown.

Their appearance pleasantly shocked one Sioux City Journal reporter, who commented, "In the whole array there was not one anarchist—not one. The red flag was not in sight—but everywhere the stars and stripes!" Photo by Philip C. Walter-mire; courtesy of Sioux City Public Museum

Sioux City firefighters proudly display their hook and ladder wagon in front of the main fire station at 408 Water Street about 1890. The building housed both Hose Company No. 1 and Hook and Ladder Company No. 1. William Burns' Sioux City Cornice Works was at the near left, at 412 Water Street, Photo by C. N. Taylor, courtesy of R. Scott Key, Murdo, South Dakota

After utilizing the old, relocated Tremont Hotel for fifteen years, members of the First Baptist Church dedicated this building in August 1882. It was located at the northeast corner of Fifth and Nebraska streets and boasted the city's first pipe organ. Larger buildings were beginning to surround the church by 1890, when this photo was taken. The United Bank Building, on the right, was at the northwest corner of Fifth and Jackson streets. The Goldie Roller Rink sat between the bank and the church.

The First Baptist Church sold this property in 1916, during the midst of another building boom that shifted the downtown area to the east. The members dedicated their new quarters at the northeast corner of Ninth and Douglas on April 6, 1919. Photo by C. N. Taylor; courtesy of R. Scott Key, Murdo, South Dakota

Under Reverend George H. Cornell's guidance, W. E. Phelps, "The Most Worshipful, the Grand Master of Masons of the Grand Lodge of Iowa, assisted by the Grand Officers," lays the cornerstone for St. Thomas Episcopal Church on August 12, 1891. The Knights of Pythias were holding their state convention in Sioux City that week and therefore took part in the ceremony.

J. M. Poorbaugh built this magnificent edifice at the northeast corner of Twelfth and Douglas. It replaced an earlier St. Thomas at the northwest corner of Seventh and Nebraska. Photo by C. N. Taylor; Courtesy of R. Scott Key, Murdo, South Dakota

This image portrays the beautiful cherrywood interior of the St. Thomas Episcopal Church. The congregation dedicated the structure on September 25, 1892. Photo by C. N. Taylor; Courtesy of R. Scott Key, Murdo, South Dakota

Maris Peirce, like his more famous brother John, was a real estate dealer who branched into other ventures in the 1880s. Unlike his brother, however, Maris entered the political arena in 1892, announcing his candidacy for mayor as head of an Independent ticket just four days prior to the election. He campaigned in opposition to the existing saloon licensing system. Amazingly, he garnered a majority of the votes in a three-man race.

John Peirce proclaimed his brother's victory to be a defeat for vice in Sioux City and a triumph for the capitalists, artisans, and laboring men. Less than two months later, however, eighteen of Sioux City's most prominent businessmen convinced Mayor Peirce that his election was not due to the liquor enforcement issue, and that the licensing system should be reinstated. Photo by J. H. Hamilton; courtesy of Sioux City Public Museum

On May 18, 1892, a wall of muddy water six feet high and nearly a mile across swept without warning down the Floyd River Valley to wreak havoc over Sioux City's "bottoms" district. Between 400 and 500 homes were carried into the Missouri River, or as shown in this photo of the 1700 block of Fourth Street, left in jumbled piles.

The 1892 Floyd River flood—considered one of the worst disasters in Sioux City's history—left ten persons dead, thousands more homeless, and the city teetering on the brink of financial ruin. Photo courtesy of Sioux City Public Museum

The muddy waters had barely begun to subside, on May 19, 1892, when throngs of Sioux Cityans filed out upon the el line past Iowa Street for their first close-up look at the Floyd's devastation. This elevated station and others along Third Street had been a God-send to hundreds of East Bottoms residents the previous day. Many of them, rousted from their beds by the roar of the sudden wall of water, scrambled to safety on the el's girders and stairways. The less fortunate took refuge on the roofs of their homes.

The hero of the day was thirty-eight-year-old Swedish immigrant Andrew Anderson, who was credited with saving twenty-seven lives before he lost his own. Photo by Brown and Wait Studio; courtesy of Sioux City Public Museum

The Iron Horse imprisoned. Officials and employees of the Sioux City and Northern Railroad survey the damage wrought by the 1892 flood to the railroad's roundhouse and shops at 2121 Fourth Street. This photo was taken from atop the adjacent Elevated Railroad trestle. Photo courtesy of Sioux City Public Museum

Sioux City High School in 1893—a Richardsonian Romanesque "Castle on the Hill."

The school board, attempting to deal with rapidly rising school enrollments which had overcrowded Armstrong School, purchased the entire block bordered by Twelfth and Thirteenth streets between Jackson and Nebraska streets in 1890 as the

site of a new high school. The Judson L. Follett home, formerly at that location, was moved to the east side of Nebraska Street's 1300 block and served as the interim high school.

Board members selected the plan of Joliet, Illinois, architect F. S. Allen in 1891 and awarded the construction contract on March 10, 1892, to Eric Lund of Minneap-

olis. Most subcontracts went to Sioux City businesses. The 100- by 160-foot Norman castle-like school was built of Prentice brown sandstone from the Lake Superior area. Its massiveness reflected Sioux City's ebullient spirit at the time.

The community's mood changed drastically, however, before the building's opening. The panic of 1893 struck just four weeks prior to the May 23, 1893, dedication of the Sioux City High School, and tight budgets restricted its programs for several years. Despite these problems, the city possessed a marvelous structure capable of supplying admirable service to the community for many decades. Photo courtesy of Sioux City Public Museum

Daniel T. Hedges moved into this impressive home at the northwest corner of Twenty-eighth and Jackson in 1889. The structure signified the exuberance of his hopes and plans.

Hedges characterized the city's history from the 1850s to the 1890s. He and his brother Charles were among the town's pioneers. They were partners in many ventures—real estate, fur trading, general merchandising, freighting, and construction. Their brother Nat was a casualty of the Sawyers Expedition of 1865, and Charles died in Dakota Territory in 1877.

D. T. Hedges was one of the leaders of the boom years, playing important roles in the Elevated Railroad, the development of Leeds and Morningside, and the expansion of the meatpacking industry. In one of his biggest undertakings, he and John Peirce began developing the city's far Northside in 1887 and constructed the cable railway.

Hedges's speculative ventures ended on April 25, 1893, when the panic of 1893 struck with a vengeance. He was totally ruined financially. He first denied he would leave Sioux City, but after nearly forty years of good and bad times, Hedges was unable to start over again amid his former associates. The 1892-93 city directory reads, "Hedges, Daniel T., Capitalist, residence 2803 Jackson." The 1893-94 volume notes, "Hedges, Daniel T., moved to Los Angeles, Cal." Photo by C. N. Taylor; Courtesy of R. Scott Key, Murdo, South Dakota

Chapter 5

Reorganization and Rebirth

1893-1910

The panic of 1893 and the financial collapse of the Corn Palace City's boosters shocked the community's residents, causing some of them to deny that the boom had ended. Indeed, just four days after Black Tuesday, the *Sioux City Journal* stubbornly brushed aside the events of recent days, insisting, "It is settled, that we are to have a Corn Palace this year, that Sioux City is still the only Corn Palace city of the world; that the old union is unbroken—that we still hold the key to 'The Sioux City Way'."

The "Way," however, had become a temporary victim of the panic. Sioux City had been engulfed in speculation during the late 1880s and early 1890s as the town's promoters had striven to increase the local business activity, population, and prominence. Consequently, the investors' losses caused Sioux Cityans to suffer acutely from the panic of 1893, and the resulting depression lingered longer here. The stockyards industry was in a state of confusion. Work on the Combination Bridge had ground to a halt. Numerous other businesses and promotions suddenly existed only as memories. The city, faced with a plunging economy and a drop in census figures of over 10,000 people from 1890 to 1895, demanded herculean efforts from its residents in order to regroup.

The reactions of the promoters varied widely. D. T. Hedges, whose personal financial troubles had precipitated many of the city's failures, left town soon after the panic. John Peirce made several attempts in the 1890s to regain his status as the city's most boisterous booster, but finally he migrated to Seattle in 1901. Other promoters, however, including E. C. Peters, William Gordon, and A. S. Garretson, remained in Sioux City despite their losses, repaid their debts over the course of years, and continued to be respected leaders of their city.

Eastern bankers and speculators who had lost heavily when the panic hit Sioux City organized the Credits Commutation Company in 1894. This company's purpose was to recoup as much of the shareholders' investments in Sioux City as possible. F. L. Eaton, a financier from Montpelier, Vermont, came to Sioux City as the Eastern creditor's chief representative. Although many of these shareholders were leery of investing further in Sioux City, Eaton, together with Captain John Ellis, convinced a majority of the investors that an economically healthy Sioux City would ultimately increase the financial return to the Credits Commutation Company. The key to this turnaround, Eaton and Ellis reasoned, would be the completion of the stalemated Combination Bridge project. Local citizens, also sensing the importance of the Nebraska trade to the city's recovery, dug into their own pockets and self-imposed a 2 percent tax to aid construction of the bridge. The Credits Commutation Company voted to support the project, construction resumed, and on January 21, 1896, the Combination Bridge opened to traffic.

The Credits Commutation Company organized the Sioux City Stock Yards Company to manage the city's badly-ailing main industry. They also created the Live Stock National Bank to provide financing in the immediate area. The May 1901 announcement that Armour and Company would purchase the former Silberhorn/Anglo-American/International packing plant highlighted the Credit Commutation Company's rescue of the meatpacking industry. The presence of Armour and Cudahy gave Sioux City two national packing companies and spurred greater activity at the local level. F. L. Eaton (and his Eastern employers) was a major influence in leading Sioux City out of the depression and to economic recovery. The recovery brought on a wave of civic pride.

Sioux City was financially solid, its businesses were productive, and its credit was secure by 1902. In a retrospective view of the past decade, the *Sioux City Tribune* ventured this opinion: "There have been years, since 1893, when the city was viewed, both at home and abroad, in the light of those calamitous events of '93. It required time for things to adjust themselves anew, for affairs to get on their proper foundation, for men to take their bearings and discover that the foundations were as solid as ever, though the superstructure had suffered."

Sioux City flourished during the first decade of the 1900s. Even a major catastrophe such as the Pelletier fire, on December 23, 1904, caused only temporary difficulties. Community leaders quickly rebuilt the fire-ravaged downtown district. The city's population rebounded from 33,111 in 1900 to 47,828 in 1910, and Sioux City rose from fourth place to become the second-largest city in Iowa. With the stockyards, meatpacking, railroad, and wholesale industries once again firmly entrenched, the citizens looked ahead to a prosperous future.

A faction began a movement to change the shape of local government during this period of reorganization. The ward system, which consisted of part-time aldermen and a mayor, had existed since 1857 with but minor alterations. Advocates of the relatively new commission plan argued that, with the increases in the city's population and business activity, a part-time government could not provide the services or efficiency needed for the bustling community. In addition, they believed that the abandonment of the old wards would alleviate petty jealousies between neighborhoods. The proposed commission plan contained five full-time department heads elected at large: commissioner of public affairs (mayor), commissioner of accounts and finance, commissioner of public safety, commissioner of parks and public property, and commissioner of streets and public improvements. Candidates would run without political party designations, and those elected would serve two-year terms. Sioux City voters sustained the ward system in a 1908 special election. After the passing of the required interval of two years, though, the citizens adopted the commission plan by a 747-vote margin, and the ward system became a thing of the past.

Sioux City residents had demonstrated great resilience in their ability to rebound from the panic of 1893. The prevailing economic conditions of the new century had taught them the value of slower, more deliberate advancement. The citizens adapted well to this new growth style. A new development cycle was sweeping the city by 1910, more far-reaching and more lasting than that of the late 1880s and early 1890s. As early as 1902, the *Sioux City Tribune* summarized this period of regrouping: "Sioux City. It was built with a rush; it fell with a crash, to be more slowly resuscitated, put upon a firm foundation and set ahead with a vim which none but a truly western metropolis could expect to have. It is now going ahead with speed beyond expectations."

John Peirce (1840-1910), a real estate agent for the first fifteen years after his arrival in 1869, became the epitomy of the boom-time promoter during the 1880s and 1890s. He struggled to develop new rail lines for the community, and working with D. T. Hedges, popularized Peirce's Addition, the city's far northern reaches, as a residential area. Early in 1889, despite being over-extended with numerous railroad ventures, including the Sioux City and Northern (derisively call the Sioux City and Nothin), Peirce became a staunch backer of Donald McLean's Pacific Short Line Railroad and Combination Bridge, breathing life into the project, and personally seeking out the $500,000 needed from local sources.

The panic of 1893 devastated Peirce and the other large-scale promoters. Yet, his spirit remained intact. As late as 1898, he remarked enthusiastically before departing for Black Hills mining talks in England:

O, the turn is coming, and we're going to see such a boost in times as will make us wonder how this old nightmare of depression could ever have galloped over us as she has been doing. All the capital which we'll bring over for development of those mines out there will breed fortunes for all of us, and the hard times will become only a reminiscence.

Photo courtesy of Sioux City Public Museum

With the failure of the Black Hills mining project and other ventures, John Peirce finally gave up on Sioux City. Needing funds to relocate, he devised a scheme to sell his beloved home by instituting a nationwide lottery. Raffle tickets sold for one dollar a chance. Department stores, such as Pelletier's, Davidsons', and T. S. Martin's, also gave out one chance free with purchases of five dollars (lowered at the end to $1.98). Approximately 40,000 tickets were distributed.

The lucky number initially was to be drawn on November 6, 1900, at the Peavey Grand Opera House, as shown in this ticket. The event was rescheduled for December 24, 1900, and moved to the Union passenger depot. It was first announced that Bert M. Bills, a jeweler from Vinton, Iowa, held winning ticket number 35,365, but, on January 5, 1901, it was revealed that William Barbour, a millionaire New York threadmaker, was the lucky man. It was reported that Barbour and two other friends of Peirce's had bought all unsold tickets on the day of the drawing.

On February 12, 1901, Peirce and his family left for Seattle, Washington. Upon departure, Peirce uttered his oft-quoted "Farewell to Sioux City":

Goodbye, Sioux City, perhaps for aye. You are at once the birthplace of all my ambitions and the graveyard of all my hopes.

After dedicating thirty years of my best strength to your development you are not a city but a town, with an interesting past, an uneventful present, and a peaceful and conservative future.

No devotion of mine could prevent the calamity which spread your broken idols all around, and unrelenting fate still holds the ruins in her embrace. No period of prosperity can lend new animation to your fettered limbs, for commerce has her lines not laid within your favored zone.

Yet, old girl, there burns within my bosom that youthful first love that knows no death, and my hope is that, while you lie bound Prometheus-like, no vultures will further pluck your vitals.

Goodbye, goodbye.

The above, while interesting, tells only half the story. The abstract for Peirce's mansion reveals that a warranty deed transferring title to William Barbour was actually drawn up on December 17, 1900, one week before the drawing and fully nineteen days before Barbour was known to hold the "winning" ticket. The vultures were still plucking at Sioux City's vitals. Peirce had fixed the lottery. Raffle ticket courtesy of Sioux City Public Museum

The career of William Gordon (1857-1933) spanned many eras of Sioux City's history. Gordon emigrated from Ireland in 1882, came to Sioux City the following year, and married Stella Davis, the daughter of pioneer Sioux Cityan S. T. Davis, in 1884. The business and real estate aptitudes of both William and Stella soon propelled Gordon into the community's economic stratosphere. During the boom years he was the chief developer of Leeds, helped create the Elevated Railroad, and promoted many new industries and businesses.

Gordon withstood the panic of 1893 far better than many of his fellow boomers, remaining an economic force in Sioux City for virtually the remainder of his life. One of his greatest ambitions was the development of Sioux City's riverfront, a cause he advocated for decades. The "river road," dedicated in 1949, was named Gordon Drive in his honor. Photo by Genelli; courtesy of Sioux City Public Museum

Fred L. Eaton (1859-1925) arrived in Sioux City in 1894 as secretary and general manager of the Credits Commutation Company. It was his job to try to rebuild a local economy shaken to its foundations. The stockyards, the mainstay of the city's development during the preceding decade, was in total disarray. The Combination Bridge, the key to Sioux City's claim to the northern Nebraska trade area, remained far from complete.

Through the work of Eaton and others, the Combination Bridge Company, a division of the Credits Commutation Company, finished the bridge nearly seven years after Donald McLean had initiated the project. Eaton also assumed the heroic task of reorganizing the stockyards, first as secretary-treasurer and later as general manager of the Sioux City Stock Yards Company. In 1903 he became company president, a position he retained until his death.

In the spring of 1903, F. L. Eaton became president of the newly-formed Inter-State Live Stock Fair Association. Through his dedication, the Interstate Fair grew to be the largest private fair in the nation, attracting thousands of spectators and rivaling nearby state fairs. From 1903 until 1924, Eaton and the Interstate Fair were synonymous.

To Fred L. Eaton, more than to anyone else, goes the credit for revitalizing Sioux City's economy after the panic of 1893 and resurrecting the spirit of the community. Photo courtesy of the William Eaton Palmer Family

Together with F. L. Eaton, these three men represented Sioux City's Eastern creditors and played important roles in the city's economic regrouping during the late 1890s. Unlike Eaton, however, they did not take up permanent residence here, and faded from the scene about 1900.

D. L. Plumer, of Wausau, Wisconsin (opposite, top), was president of the Credits Commutation Company from 1894 to 1900.

Isaac C. Elston, of Crawfordsville, Indiana (opposite center), served as president of the Live Stock National Bank and the Sioux City Stock Yards Company.

Captain John Ellis, of Kewanee, Illinois (opposite, bottom), was vice-president of the Sioux City, O'Neill and Western (formerly the Pacific Short Line) Railroad and president of the Combination Bridge Company. He was a chief spokesman in convincing shareholders of the Credits Commutation Company to undertake the completion of the Combination Bridge. Photos courtesy of the William Eaton Palmer Family

When plans for the Missouri River Railroad Bridge were altered to exclude a wagon and pedestrian thoroughfare, a long-sought avenue between Nebraska and Iowa was temporarily delayed. In 1889, however, E. C. Palmer, John M. Moan, A. L. Stetson, and William Luther opened Sioux City's Pontoon Bridge, anchoring it at the foot of Pearl Street in Sioux City and at the minute town of Stanton, Nebraska.

Just as the name implies, the Pontoon Bridge was a series of floating platforms. It cost five cents to traverse the bridge on foot. During the aftermath of the Haddock assassination, when greater diligence was exercised in the local enforcement of Iowa's liquor and vice laws, the bridge was described as "a row of boats with a thirst at one end and a beer saloon at the other end."

The completed Combination Bridge, shown here on the left, served as the death knell for Sioux City's Pontoon Bridge in 1896. Photo courtesy of Sioux City Public Museum

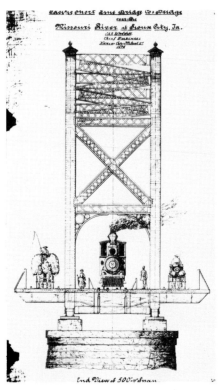

Caisson for Pier No. 7 July 23 95. Shortly after Launching.

Promoters Donald McLean, John Peirce, and others formed the Pacific Short Line Railroad Company in 1889. As a result of exorbitant tolls charged by the Omaha line to use the recently-completed Missouri River Railroad Bridge, McLean determined to build a second bridge for his proposed line.

Phoenix Bridge Company engineer James A. L. Waddell submitted this plan for the Pacific Short Line bridge. It graphically illustrates how the bridge received its name of the Combination Bridge. Although it was engineered to carry railroad, pedestrian, and wagon traffic. Waddell's design from 1889 proved so adaptable and the bridge so durable that motorized vehicles from the twentieth century were easily accommodated. Drawing courtesy of Iowa Department of Transportation, Ames, Iowa

The interest of Sioux City's neighbors in the progress of the Combination Bridge is demonstrated by the crowd which gathered on the Nebraska side of the Missouri River on July 23, 1895, for the launching of pier caisson no. 7. The hollow iron cylinder, like the six which preceded it, was constructed on land and towed by rowboat to the pier site, where it functioned as a water-tight chamber for underwater pier excavation,

and later, when filled with concrete, as the foundation for the stone pier itself. Laboring from inside these pressurized cylinders, workmen, known as "sandhogs," removed gravel, sand, and mud from beneath the caissons, enabling them to settle to bedrock footings seventy-four feet beneath the river's surface. Photo courtesy of Sioux City Journal

After an initial burst of energy, difficult economic conditions, culminating in the panic of 1893, brought bridge construction to a standstill. Ownership of the "bridge" passed from the McLean-Peirce faction, to a group headed by A. S. Garretson, to the Credits Commutation Company.

In an effort to spur construction, Sioux Cityans passed a 2 percent tax referendum and the Credits Commutation Company assessed its shareholders. These two acts provided the funds to complete the project.

This September 20, 1895 photo, taken from atop a pile of steel girders near the bridge's Iowa approach, demonstrates the massive logistical and muscle requirements needed to assemble the bridge. The men in the foreground are loading steel tie rods

onto a horse-drawn rail carriage for delivery to the nearly-completed north swing span. Beyond the span, two wooden, temporary trestles provide access for a train of miniature "stone cars" for pier construction, as well as support for the yet-to-be-built north fixed span.

The opening of the Combination Bridge on January 21, 1896, was a triumph of engineering skill and a significant economic boost for financially-scarred Sioux City. The entire bridge superstructure of two swing spans and two fixed spans had been completed in just under eight months. It served Siouxland, with only minor interruptions, for eighty-five years. Photo courtesy of Sioux City Public Museum

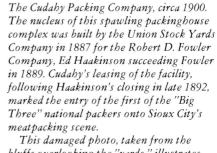

The Cudahy Packing Company, circa 1900. The nucleus of this spawling packinghouse complex was built by the Union Stock Yards Company in 1887 for the Robert D. Fowler Company, Ed Haakinson succeeding Fowler in 1889. Cudahy's leasing of the facility, following Haakinson's closing in late 1892, marked the entry of the first of the "Big Three" national packers onto Sioux City's meatpacking scene.

This damaged photo, taken from the bluffs overlooking the "yards," illustrates the sprawling nature of nineteenth century meatpacking technology. The two railroad tracks in the foreground belong to the surface line of the Elevated Railroad (near) and the bridge approach for the Chicago and Northwestern Railroad's Missouri River Railroad Bridge to Nebraska (far). Cudahy and Company was an important economic force in Sioux City for over sixty years, employing nearly 1,700 workers at the time of its close in 1954. Photo courtesy of Sioux City Public Museum

Pioneer banker John P. Allison's home, at the northeast corner of Eighth and Douglas, was perhaps the city's finest residence when it was built in the late 1870s. By the late 1890s, when this view was taken, it served as the Hawkeye Club's headquarters. Photo courtesy of Sioux City Public Museum

This 1895 photo reveals that the membership of the Hawkeye Club spanned many years. Allison is seated in the middle of the front row.

The Hawkeye, Euclid, and Mondamin clubs played important roles in Sioux City's economic and social history. According to the Sioux City Tribune, during the boom years the Mondamin Club rooms "were made the headquarters of the men who controlled the city's destiny. It was here that visiting capitalists where entertained, and in its rooms many of the great financial transactions of the time were conducted." Photo courtesy of Sioux City Public Museum

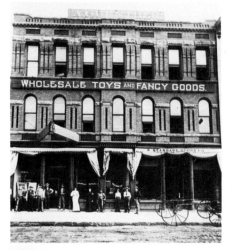

The entire staff of Anton A. Guenther's Toy and Fancy Goods Store, 315 Fourth Street, stepped outdoors for this 1894 company photo.

Fourth Street still boasted cedar block paving in 1894, a popular surface composed of six-inch-thick blocks of untreated cedar set in sand and sealed with a thin coat of tar. Quiet, durable, and easy on horses' hooves, cedar block paving drew only one criticism from city engineers: in floods the street tended to float away. Photo by Charles Bornschein; courtesy of Sioux City Public Museum

According to an 1893 directory of "Protestant, English-speaking Churches," Reverend John W. Malone, of Des Moines, organized Sioux City's African Methodist Episcopal Church in August 1884. (The church, however, dates its existence from 1883.) Services were held first at a building at Third and Court streets, but the congregation moved to the west side of Main Street's 500 block within a few years.

The structure shown here was built at the turn of the century on the site of the previous Main Street Church. Malone A.M.E. Church continues today to meet the needs of its members. Photo courtesy of Sioux City Journal

This turn-of-the-century Westside view brings together three Sioux City businesses in their effort to serve the consumer. Dineen Brothers' Company, at 208 Fourth Street, manufactured the delivery wagon for its neighbor, John Schwinn's grocery. The wagon, in turn, is hauling Splendid flour from Martens Brothers' mill, located at Eleventh and Howard streets. Photo by Charles Bornschein; courtesy of Sioux City Public Museum

The Palmer Candy Company, 209-211 Douglas Street, in 1906. This candy plant was an outgrowth of the family's original fruit warehouse at 301 Pearl Street, which had been founded by brothers Charles and William Palmer in 1893.

At the time of this photo, the Palmer Candy Company was billed as one of Iowa's largest candy manufacturers, employing nearly 100 workers in the production of fudge, caramels, nougat bars, marshmallows, and countless other sweet delights. The company added a fifth floor to this building within three years after this photograph was taken.

Palmer Candy remains an important Siouxland business. The plant is now located at 311 Bluff Street, in the old Chesterman Bottling Company building. Photo courtesy of Palmer Candy Company

Chocolate Dipping Room No. 2, Palmer Candy Company, circa 1898. Photo courtesy of Palmer Candy Company

The Sioux City Brewing Company, nearing completion in this 1899 view, bottled "Specialties, Bavarian Export, and Extra Pale Select" in its Park Street building, between Second and Third streets. Joseph Baumgartner and Abel Anderson began the business, which was later purchased by George Kingsbury and F. L. Eaton. The Sioux City Brewing Company remained in operation until Iowa went "dry" on January 1, 1916. Photo courtesy of Sioux City Journal

Sioux City's police station was located at 211 Third Street from 1893 to 1916. The heavy, indigenous-stone structure was typical of many local buildings of the time. In this view, taken shortly after 1893, a horse-drawn ambulance is on the right, and a horse-drawn "paddy wagon" is in the center. When the police department relocated, this building was used for commercial purposes until destroyed by fire on July 21, 1946. Photo courtesy of Sioux City Public Museum

Flags, bunting, and signs welcome Iowa's Civil War veterans to Sioux City in June 1898, with GAR members congregating in front of the Mondamin Hotel. The hotel's central location, at the northeast corner of Fourth and Pierce, made it the ideal encampment headquarters.

Built as the Hubbard House in 1870, the hotel was remodeled as the Hotel Booge in 1887. Still later, in 1895, it acquired the name of the Mondamin Hotel. It was destroyed by fire on January 30, 1912. Photo courtesy of Sioux City Public Museum

The Grand Army of the Republic, a national organization of Union army veterans, was a major social and political force in the late 1800s, carrying great weight in local, state, and national elections. Sioux City had two GAR posts from 1885 to 1892, before they united to form the General Hancock Post No. 22. Sioux City hosted the state encampment on three occasions.

This 1914 view, taken nearly fifty years after the end of the Civil War, shows the GAR thinning in membership and slowing in step. The local post continued until November 17, 1940, however, when death claimed Sioux City's last surviving Civil War veteran, Michael Hawk. Photo courtesy of Sioux City Public Museum

The Big Sioux River along Riverside Park was a favorite weekend and holiday retreat for Sioux Cityans of all persuasions. The river, then over 200 yards wide in places, was navigable by steam and motor launches, rowboats, racing shells, and canoes; ample public and private facilities ashore accommodated picnickers, campers, and Sunday strollers.

The Commercial Men's Boat Club, later the home of Sioux City's Community Theatre, graces the riverbank in the distance. Photo courtesy of Sioux City Public Museum

114

Sioux City's five Big Sioux River boat clubs played an important role in summertime social activities at the turn of the century. In this view from 1903, offices of the Farmers' Loan and Trust Company and their families, headed by Sioux City financier James F. Toy (seated immediate front right), enjoy an afternoon of picnicking and posing at the Riverside Boat Club. Toy's bank was later reorganized as the National Bank of Commerce, the forerunner of today's Toy National Bank. Photo courtesy of Sioux City Public Museum

Local nabobs in surreys, carriages, buckboards, and on foot flank the right-of-way of the Riverside Park Railway, circa 1892, for festivities at Riverside Park. The roller coaster standing in the background is the Switchback Pleasure Railway—part of Sioux City's first amusement park. Photo by Philip C. Waltermire; courtesy of Sioux City Public Museum

Riverside Park was the scene of many events—church socials, Prohibition party rallies, and Woodbury County Anti-Saloon League gatherings. This photo, however, was taken on another occasion. Photo by Charles Bornschein; courtesy of Sioux City Public Museum

Spectators lounging in right field undoubtedly are enjoying the Sioux City Packers' double-header sweep of Omaha on September 13, 1908. Playing before a crowd of 8,000 at Riverside Ballpark, the home team shut out Omaha 5-0 and 9-0 behind the iron-man pitching of Al Furchner. The Packers won sixteen of their last seventeen games that season to capture the Western League crown. Photo by Philip C. Waltermire; courtesy of Sioux City Public Museum

Marenus Sorensen, a laborer at the Sioux City Brick and Tile Works, proudly displays his catch of a 102-pound catfish snagged in the Big Sioux River near Riverside Park in 1909.

Shown here at Carl Nelson's Boat Livery are, from left: (in motor launch) Mrs. Gus Danielson, Mrs. C. D. Barboe, Mrs. Marenus Sorensen, an unidentified woman, Mrs. Carl Nelson, and Mrs. Hugh Retag; (on shore) Marenus Sorensen, Gus Danielson, Carl Nelson, Milo Thompson, an unidentified man, and local rag picker Sandy Anderson.

The sternwheel towboat Mandan, seen across the river at the top of this photo, is moored at the U.S. Army Corps of Engineers' winter ice harbor, a facility maintained by the corps at North Riverside from the 1890s until the mid-1920s. Photo courtesy of Sioux City Public Museum

This lawn party took place at the home of Mr. and Mrs. William B. Lower in North Riverside, circa 1910. Lower was an officer and major shareholder in the Lower Brick Company, the Sioux Paving Brick Company, and later the Great Western Land Company. His home, near the Big Sioux River Bridge, marked Sioux City's western-most corporate limits. Courtesy of Sioux City Public Museum

The Terrible Railroad Collision drew thousands of spectators to Sioux City Day at the 1896 fair. In a staged event popular with the catastrophe-conscious public of the times, two twenty-five-ton steam locomotives and their trains were paired off smokebox-to-smokebox at opposite ends of a mile-long track, with a midpoint centered directly in front of the grandstands. Their throttles were then lashed down, and their crews "joined the birds" to create this spectacular finale. An unknown Sioux City photographer, risking his life for this rare example of pioneer stop-action photography, captured the two charging monsters at the instant of their embrace. Photo courtesy of Sioux City Public Museum

For twenty-four years (1903-1926), the Interstate Fair, held at Woodland Park (later called Interstate Park and Riverview Park) was Sioux City's premier autumn attraction. Farmers and ranchers and their families from throughout South Dakota, Nebraska, and Iowa vied for honors in animal, crop, and home management during the week-long competition.

Along with the attractions of the ever-present midway, farm and city fairgoers thrilled to such daily exhibitions as sulky, draft horse team, and fire horse racing, bicycle and foot contests, and auto racing on the fairground's one- and two-mile tracks. Photo courtesy of Sioux City Public Museum

This four-man crew prepares to clean one of the Sioux City Traction Company's open-air cars in this late-1890s view of Water Street between Second and Third streets. This type of streetcar, used solely in the summer, became obsolete in 1903, when the company changed from narrow gauge to standard width tracks.

On the left is the powerhouse for the old Sioux City Street Railway Company, the predecessor to the Sioux City Traction Company. On the right is the warehouse for the Sioux City Implement Company. Photo courtesy of Sioux City Public Museum

These twelve men constituted the fire fighting force of Hose Company No. 3, located at 1211 Fifth Street, about 1900. The horse-drawn pieces of equipment are (left to right) a hook and ladder truck, a "Pumping Billy," a hose cart, and the chief's buggy.

This building, replete with brass beds for the fire fighters, served as a station house for the Sioux City Fire Department from 1891 to 1929, when a new station, designed by prominent local architect William L. Steele, replaced it. The Pumping Billy came out of storage in September 1942 and was sold for its metal content as part of the war effort. Photo courtesy of Sioux City Public Museum

The Security Bank Building, one of a number of bank and office complexes built of quartzite from the Sioux Falls and southern Minnesota area, stood at the northwest corner of Fourth and Nebraska from 1893 to 1945, when it was replaced by another building.

The Security Bank, founded in 1884, opened for business in this building on March 27, 1893, less than one month before the panic of 1893 struck. The bank, however, withstood the tide, survived, and prospered. It eventually sought newer quarters in the mid-1940s.

In this early circa 1910 view, the building also houses the Woodbury County Savings Bank, the freight and ticket offices of the Chicago and Northwestern Railroad, Moore's drugstore, Edwards and Bradford lumber office, and a host of doctors and lawyers. Photo courtesy of Sioux City Public Museum

With their shining horse-drawn equipment in the background, Sioux City fire fighters pose ready for action in the headquarters of Chemical Company No. 2, located at 1414 Nebraska Street, circa 1900. This building housed Chemical No. 2 from 1891 to 1913. Photo courtesy of Sioux City Public Museum

Sioux City became a powerful jobbing center during the early 1900s. In this view of the wholesale district, looking north from Second Street on Nebraska Street, Tolerton and Warfield Grocery Company (later the I-Go Building) is on the left, and Knapp and Spencer Hardware Company is on the right. Both structures were built in 1901 for established Sioux City firms and were described by the Sioux City Tribune as "two new, mammoth, six-story warehouses, near the terminal systems, each costing $100,000." The old Tolerton and Warfield building was being torn down in 1982 when a spectacular flash fire leveled the remainder of the structure. Photo courtesy of Sioux City Public Museum

Tolerton and Warfield's wholesale grocery warehouse crew congregate at one of the company's loading bays for this 1905 photograph. Photo courtesy of Sioux City Public Museum

Workmen and spectators gather around the foundation of the Federal Building and Post Office on August 1, 1894. On the right is the Library/City Hall Building, finished in 1892 at a cost of $122,000. In the background is the rambling Hotel Oxford, at the southwest corner of Sixth and Douglas.

Federal officials in the 1890s faced what seems to be an unbelievable situation—how to get ride of a surplus in the federal treasury. The main source of revenue was the tariff, which many representatives wanted to keep high enough to favor "home manufactories." Their solution: increase expenditures! Many federal buildings were put up during the 1890s, including Sioux City's at the corner of Sixth and Douglas. Photo courtesy of Sioux City Public Museum

The post office occupied the basement and first floor of the Federal Building. Mail sorting was completely done by hand in 1910, as shown in this view. The mail sorters are, from left: William Lewis, Virgil

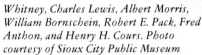

Whitney, Charles Lewis, Albert Morris, William Bornschein, Robert E. Pack, Fred Anthon, and Henry H. Cours. Photo courtesy of Sioux City Public Museum

By January 2, 1896, when this photo was taken, the Federal Building's exterior was nearly complete, with the clock tower yet to be added. It opened on February 14, 1897 and housed the post office, federal court system and federal offices until the end of 1933. It remained empty during the remainer of the 1930s, maintaining only a handful of New Deal recovery projects.

The city of Sioux City purchased the old structure in 1940 with the intention of tearing it down and erecting a new city hall on the same site. World War II interrupted those plans, and a fire which gutted the old city hall on October 14, 1944, ended the proposal for good. Four years later, after extensive remodeling, the old Federal Building reopened as City Hall. Photo courtesy of Sioux City Public Museum

Sioux City policeman Christian Steinbeck and his son about 1900. Retired school-teacher Marian Steinbeck described her father-in-law in a 1978 interview:

> Chris Steinbeck was very tough, a great big man with a big walrus moustache, very commanding, and with a voice that could be heard all over. He could send kids flying, and anybody else that didn't want the cop after him! His beat [during the 1890s] was down on the East Fourth Street in the area around Steuben Street. Because of his manner he was known as "The Kaiser of Steuben Street."

Photo courtesy of Sioux City Public Museum

Rapid expansion of the local meatpacking industry during the late 1890s and early 1900s created economic opportunities for thousands of European immigrants. Frank Tocko, his wife Frances, and their children Helen and Joseph arrived in Sioux City from Suwalki, Poland, in 1901 and became the first Polish family to settle in the South Bottoms (photo dated 1905). The Tockos later operated a small neighborhood grocery store and boardinghouse for packing house workers and were one of the original families of St. Francis Catholic Church. Photo courtesy of Mrs. Helen Kuchis

Women of the Anton and Rosina Hacker family, of Greenville, circa 1900. Left to right: daughters Margaret Ellen, Rose Marie, Christina, mother Rosina Hurth Hacker, and daughters Sophia, Agnes, and Mayme.

The Hackers were one of Greenville's pioneer families, arriving in Sioux City from Hurth, Germany, in 1875. The original one-acre homesite purchased by Anton Hacker along Bacon Creek is now the northeast corner of Fairmount and Correctionville Road. It constitutes a major portion of Greenville's neighborhood business area. The family residence, shown here in the background at 2715 Correctionville Road, still serves as the home of Hacker family descendants. Photo courtesy of Kenneth C. Johnson

On this spring day of 1898, Sioux City volunteers from Company L of Iowa's Fifty-second Infantry Regiment muster on Douglas Street prior to debarking for the Spanish-American War. The crowd is gathered in front of the old Hotel Oxford. On the left, the Washburn and Crosby Gold Medal flour sign identifies the Masonic Block (later the Continental Building) at the northeast corner of Fifth and Douglas.

These Sioux City troops never reached Cuba, but they did encounter deadly enemies. While stationed for training at Camp Chickamauga, Georgia, the heat and lack of sanitation inflicted heavy casualties. So many young men were suffering from typhoid fever and other ailments by August 1898 that a special hospital train was required to deliver them back to Iowa. Photo courtesy of Sioux City Public Museum

The Floyd Monument cornerstone-laying ceremony, on August 20, 1900, marked the ninety-sixth anniversary of Sergeant Charles Floyd's death.

The rediscovery of Floyd's journal in 1894 kindled local and national interest in the lone casualty of the 1804-1806 Lewis and Clark Expedition. On August 20, 1895, after an intensive search had revealed the location of the sergeant's grave, citizens held a reinterment service and placed a marble slab over the site.

That same day, many of Sioux City's leaders organized the Floyd Memorial Association. The organization's purpose was to raise funds to erect a more suitable Floyd Monument. They secured over $12,000 from individuals, businesses, and the federal, state, and local governments. U.S. Army Corps of Engineers Captain (later Colonel) H. M. Chittenden supervised the planning and construction of the monument, and many workmen took part in laying the monument's foundation on May 29, 1900. The cornerstone laying followed on August 20, 1900. Photo by Philip C. Waltermire; courtesy of Sioux City Public Museum

The completed Floyd Monument was a solid
masonry obelisk patterned after ancient
Egyptian models and built of Kettle River
sandstone. It measured a trifle over 100 feet
high. The May 30, 1901 dedication ceremony, attended by an estimated crowd of
2,000 persons, climaxed nearly six years of
concentrated effort by the Floyd Memorial
Association. It also provided a vivid
reminder of the importance of the Lewis
and Clark Expedition. In 1960 the Floyd
Monument became the first historic
landmark registered by the United States
government. Photo by Philip C. Waltermire; courtesy of Division of the State
Historical Society, Iowa City, Iowa

J. Herbert Quick (1861-1925), lawyer,
mayor, businessman, and author, is shown
presumably working in his beautiful
Morningside home on his manuscript
Virginia of the Air Lanes in January 1907.
    John Herbert Quick was born on a farm
in Grundy County, Iowa. After a teaching
stint, he studied law, secured his degree, and
moved to Sioux City in 1890. Famous car-
toonist Jay N. "Ding" Darling, the son of
Congregational minister Marc Darling,
recalled that Quick's reading and thoughts
"were in a path along which few people
found it convenient to travel, reaching out
mentally, occupying a firing-line far in
advance of the army."
    In addition to his legal career, J. Herbert
Quick became involved in the Citizens'
Committee during the mid-1890s, in an
attempt to clean-up alleged abuses in county
government. Quick ran unsuccessfully for
mayor as head of the Democratic ticket in
1896 but emerged victorious two years later
with the strong backing of the Citizens'
Committee. Once in office, though, Quick
seemed as stymied as his predecessors in
dealing with liquor and gambling abuses.
He lost his bid for re-election in 1900.
    After leaving public office, Quick devoted
most of his energy to writing. Alladin and
Company, published in 1904, was his first
major success. Although he left Sioux City
in 1908, the community continued to cheer
its most noted author's later hits, including
Vandemark's Folly and The Hawkeye.
Photo courtesy of Division Historical
Museum and Archives, Des Moines, Iowa

Mary A. Safford, Marie H. Jenney, and
Eleanor E. Gordon (left to right) in about
1896. These were the first three ministers
of the Unitarian church in Sioux City.
    The liberally-oriented Unitarian church
began in Sioux City in 1885, with services
being held in the reconverted Goss' Roller
Skating Rink at the southwest corner of
Sixth and Douglas. Mary Safford was the
first minister and her life-long friend,
Eleanor Gordon, became her assistant.

Through their leadership and teaching,
the church grew steadily. On April 28, 1889,
the congregation dedicated a new building
at the southeast corner of Tenth and
Douglas. Following her ordination, Gordon
became associate minister in May 1889. She
left Sioux City to accept the pastorate of the
Iowa City church in 1896 and was succeeded
by Miss Jenney. In 1899 Safford and Jenney
moved to Des Moines. Photo by Genelli;
courtesy of Sioux City Public Museum

Sioux City High School's Herperian Club, assembled at the corner of Seventh and Douglas, helped to usher in the new century during this 1900 parade. Photo by Genelli; courtesy of Sioux City Public Museum

Looking east on Fourth Street from Douglas in 1901. The old Academy of Music building, on the right, long since replaced by the Peavey Grand Opera House as the city's cultural center, continues to function as part of Davidson Brothers Department Store. Davidson's business grew tremendously during the first two decades of the twentieth century, leading to the construction of a new main building and several additions. The old Academy gave way to a new wing of the store about 1910. Photo courtesy of Sioux City Public Museum

The YMCA building anchored the northwest corner of Seventh and Pierce from 1893 to 1956. Thousands of men and boys participated in the YMCA's recreational, educational, social, and religious exercises. In this view from about 1910, the Iowa (Bell) Telephone Company is on Seventh Street at the left, and the Gladstone Medicine Manufacturing Company, on the right, is at 707 Pierce Street. Photo courtesy of Sioux City Public Museum

Students of the Sioux City College of Medicine look on intently as the technique of skin grafting is demonstrated at the YMCA auditorium in 1903.

When the panic of 1893 forced the University of the Northwest at Morningside to close its doors, Doctors William Jepson, George W. Beggs, Hiram A. Wheeler, and Frank J. Murphy decided to continue the university's medical department. They added other local physicians to the faculty and renamed the institution the Sioux City College of Medicine.

The college rented office space throughout the city, including the Plymouth Block, until 1898, when it built its own structure at the corner of Fourteenth and Jones streets. In 1902, seeking larger quarters, it moved to the YMCA building, but returned in 1905 to the Fourteenth Street location. The Sioux City College of Medicine closed in 1909. Photo courtesy of Sioux City Public Museum

A chill drizzle fails to dampen the solemnity of a Knights of Columbus initiation portrait, taken in front of Sioux City's Cathedral of the Epiphany at Tenth and Douglas streets, circa 1906.

The Roman Catholic Diocese of Sioux City was created from the Archdiocese of Dubuque by Pope Leo XIII on January 15, 1902, with the Right Reverend Bishop Philip J. Garrigan, former vice-rector of the Catholic University of America, (seen first row center) named as the diocese's first bishop. At the time of its creation, the Sioux City diocese represented over 50,000 Catholics in twenty-four northwest Iowa counties, and included eighty-four parishes and forty-three parochial schools.

The cathedral was less than two years old when this photo was taken. The magnificent edifice, begun in 1891 and finished in 1904, was originally known as the New St. Mary's. It succeeded two earlier Catholic churches in the city by the same name: the first St. Mary's was a wooden frame structure erected at West Seventh and Perry streets in 1862; the second, a substantial brick structure, was located at the corner of Sixth and Pierce in 1876.

Careful shooting by the photographer mercifully deleted the two as-yet-uncompleted church spires from this photo. They would not be added until forty-two years later, in 1948. Photo courtesy of Sioux City Public Museum

The massive destruction of the Pelletier fire is depicted in these views from the roof of the Knapp and Spencer Building, located at the southeast corner of Third and Nebraska streets. This was the city's worst fire, in terms of property damage. It began the evening of December 23, 1904, in the Pelletier Department Store, at the southwest corner of Fourth and Jackson streets. Before it was extinguished, nearly two-and-a-half blocks of downtown had been gutted, reaching from Third and Pierce streets to the alley east of Fourth and Jackson streets.

Eight pages of meticulously-kept Sioux City Fire Department records provide in-depth information on losses resulting from the fire. Fire fighters laid over 10,000 feet of hose and battled the blaze for thirty hours, using horse-drawn equipment and a limited quantity of water. The estimated monetary loss on buildings and stock amounted to $1,703,928. Prominent buildings destroyed by the fire included the Massachusetts Block (home of the Pelletier store), the Toy Building and annex, the Brown Block, the Bolton and Commercial Block, the North-western National Bank, and others. The fire claimed one life, when Genoa B. Brockway attempted unsuccessfully to jump to safety from his room on the fourth floor of the Massachusetts Block. The fire department listed the cause of the fire as, "Boy threw match in decorations."

In an oral history interview conducted by the Sioux City Public Museum seventy-four years later, the boy, E. Porter Hunt, related the circumstances leading to the fire:

The Pelletier Company instructed Mr. A. P. McKown to have the store decorated up in a holiday style, and

McKown devised a method of using these colored napkins. That thing was one solid bunch of paper napkins.

The Santa Claus cave downstairs was constructed out of light material—muslin—and over this muslin was batten after batten of just genuine pure cotton. From the roof of the cave we had strung and formed icicles out of cotton. There was a Christmas tree over here, and a Christmas tree over there, and the walls were just one mass of cotton. We used bale after bale after bale of cotton.

In the middle of the Santa Claus cave was a table covered with asbestos. On this table we had mechanical toys, and in this group of toys was one hot-air engine. This engine propelled a lot of different mechanical toys, like derricks and piledrivers, and maybe a washing machine. Up above it was a gas jet, an open gas flame.

Ned Brown was Santa Claus and I was his assistant. I'd always go ahead of him and get my toys and stuff lined up. Ned came down and he said, "Are you about through fixing your toys? You

had better go and start it. I just turned the gas on upstairs."

So I opened the drawer, pulled out a searchlight match, and pulled it across the top of the asbestos to light it. The head flew off and flew into the standard of this tree. Well, if you ever saw cotton when it's all frayed out on flame.....I grabbed the tree and pulled it away, but I wasn't fast enough. It went up the wall, went up in the trapdoor in the window, and that was it.
Photos courtesy of Sioux City Public Museum

The Davidson Realty Company (opposite page) built these houses in 1905 on the east side of Pierce Street between Fifteenth and Sixteenth streets. Davidson's Court, as the complex was called until 1926, remained a fixture of the region for several decades. The area presently is occupied by the Siouxland Community Blood Bank. Photo courtesy of Woodworth Commercial Photos

A large crew of men in 1906 stand ready to transform the Hotel Garretson into an office building. The Crowe Brothers Construction Company of Chicago lowered the massive structure several feet, removed the balconies, and added several outside doors. The remodeled Hotel Garretson, then called the Grain Exchange Building, burned on May 24, 1914. Photo courtesy of Sioux City Public Museum

The Simmons Hardware Company of St. Louis built this unique branch at the southwest corner of Fourth and Water streets in 1905-06. The Columbia House and Merrill's livery stable had earlier located on this site. Rather than demolishing the Columbia House, however, it was relocated to the northeast corner of Third and Water.

In this view from about 1920, early trucks are visible in front of the building. The clock is unusual. Rather than the normal numerals, it contains letters, clockwise from the bottom, "TROQRLATPIF." This stood for the company's slogan: The Remembrance of Quality Remains Long After the Price is Forgotten.

The building remained a wholesale hardware store until 1933. It was vacant until 1939, when Kollman-Warner Company, which dealt in wholesale seeds, occupied the structure for three years. From 1944 until 1956, the Sioux City Battery Company was located there, hence its nickname of "the Battery Building." It stands today as a warehouse for the Bomgaars Company. Photo courtesy of Sioux City Public Museum

A rampaging Perry Creek, on July 10, 1909, badly damaged these pile trestle railroad bridges, hurtling several cars off the track. The view also shows the old City Mill structure, flanked on the right by Strange Brothers' Hide Company and on the left by the newly-completed Simmons Hardware Company.

Long-time Westside residents will recall numerous Perry Creek floods, including a severe one in almost every decade. Photo courtesy of Sioux City Public Museum

This circus was held near West Ninth and Cook streets in the early 1900s. Most of these spectators are enjoying the antics of the high-wire artist. A few on the right, however, prefer looking at a camel and eating Whittemore's ice cream.

The road on the left is Fourteenth Street. The three visible towers point out (left to right) St. Thomas Episcopal Church, Bancroft School at Eleventh and Pearl streets, and St. Mary's School at Tenth and Pearl. Photo courtesy of Sioux City Public Museum

David A. and Adelia Magee are looking serene and happy at their 309 Thirteenth Street home. Adelia was the daughter of Gottfried Hattenbach, the first Jewish resident of Sioux City. Adelia's nephew, Monroe Hattenbach, related the story of Dave Magee's struggle to marry Adelia:

> Dave Magee was a miller, and he fell in love with the only Hattenbach girl, Adelia. Of course, the old folks didn't want her to marry a gentile. So they made her stay in her room; they wouldn't let her out. So she would drop messages down [from] the window to Dave Magee. Well, he finally decided he would become a Jew if they would let her marry him. So he did, he became a Jew. In fact, I think he was a better Jew than any of the Hattenbachs.

After the marriage in 1876, Magee entered the grocery business with Ludwig Hattenbach and became influential in Sioux City's economic and political circles. He served as four-term alderman, sheriff, and mayor. Photo courtesy of Sioux City Public Museum

The Republicans were hot on the campaign trail in 1907, with visits to Sioux City from two high-ranking party leaders.

Secretary of War William Howard Taft, probably testing the presidential waters at the time, fills the Chicago and North-western depot with his presence on June 16, 1907. He defeated William Jennings Bryan in the 1908 election. George D. Perkins, editor and former congressman, is standing at left of Taft, while attorney and local historian Constant R. Marks, in the white hat, looks on. Photo courtesy of Shirley Perkins Ellison

Morningside College lettermen, the Men of the M, escort college President Wilson Seeley Lewis and U.S. Vice President Charles W. Fairbanks past Main Hall (later Lewis Hall) on October 8, 1907. Photo courtesy of Sioux City Public Museum

Grandview Park, north of Twenty-fourth Street and west of Douglas Street, became a city park on August 1, 1908. The 3,500 people attending the ceremony enjoyed music by Mose E. Reed's band and listened to several speeches.

The thirty-acre tract had been purchased in 1906 by the park commission, which then operated outside the city government's framework. Park commissioner E. C. Peters stated that 2,200 trees had been planted from 1906 to 1908, some of which are seen in this view. The Sioux City Journal described the park commission's work as "the transformation of several acres of pasture from a practically useless piece of ground to a beauty spot."

In this circa 1908 view, looking northwest, only a handful of homes grace the rolling hills. In time these hills would be filled with a college, a major shopping center, a medical complex, and a multitude of residences. Photo by Hoyt Sterling; courtesy of Sioux City Public Museum

City voters opted to change the form of city government in February 1910 from the ward system to the commission plan. The first election was held less than two months later, at which time a mayor and four commissioners were selected. The winners determined among themselves who would supervise each commission. This was amended during the 1920s, so that candidates ran for a specific position.

This relatively new form of government is being ushered in by the five Sioux City officials aboard another innovation of the times, a "horseless carriage." At the wheel is Mayor (Commissioner of Public Affairs) A. A. Smith. Also in the front seat is Commissioner of Public Safety Roy S. Whitley.

In the back (from left to right) are Commissioner of Streets and Public Improvements E. O. Wesley, Commissioner of Parks and Public Property G. B. Healy, and Commissioner of Accounts and Finance Jonathan W. Brown. Photo courtesy of Sioux City Public Museum

Chapter 6

War Clouds and Storm Warnings

1910 - 1930

Sioux City, mirroring the nation, rolled into 1910 on a crest of optimism, with a sound economy and a seemingly bright future. Packinghouses, railroads, and wholesale firms buzzed with activity, and the city's population swelled from 47,828 in 1910 to 71,227 in 1920. Sioux City's public school system, flooded with enrollments, more than doubled the size of the Sioux City High School in 1913-1914. Although the rate of population increase slackened during the 1920s, Sioux City maintained its ranking as Iowa's second-largest city.

The population explosion and the destructive effects of a series of major downtown fires in the early 1910s spawned private and public construction projects unequalled since the city's boom years of the 1880s and 1890s. The public library, having outgrown its portion of the old Library/City Hall Building at Sixth and Douglas streets, erected a new main branch at Sixth and Jackson in 1912-1913. The county board of supervisors, seeking to move from its old quarters at Sixth and Pierce, adopted local architect William L. Steele's bold and innovative plans for a new county building in 1915. The new Woodbury County Courthouse, completed in 1918, blended the twentieth century functionalism and beauty of "prairie school" architecture. It remains today as both the centerpiece of Sioux City's skyline and the nation's finest example of a government building in the prairie school style.

Sioux City's stockyards area bustled with energy, as hogs, cattle, and sheep from Iowa, Nebraska, South Dakota, Montana, and Minnesota were prodded to nearby packinghouses. By the mid-1920s, over 300 carloads of livestock were being unloaded daily by the chute crews. The giant firms of Cudahy and Armour anchored Sioux City's meatpacking industry in 1910. Cudahy, the city's largest employer, provided jobs for 2,000 workers in the conversion of livestock into trainloads of refrigerated fresh meat. Swift and Company, which had had a small Sioux City plant for several years, greatly expanded its local operations when its purchased the scandal-plagued Midland plant.

The Big Three dominated the local economy for several decades, while other, smaller packing plants also played significant roles.

Industries in the stockyards district were the major employers of the multitudes of southern and eastern Europeans who flocked to Sioux City each year. Most of these new arrivals—Greeks, Syrians, Lithuanians, Poles, and others—resided in the "bottoms" south and east of downtown. Little was done to help these immigrant groups during the 1910s, and an unfair stigma was attached to these new Siouxlanders. In 1921, however, concerned citizens organized the Community House at 1604 Fourth Street. In this meager headquarters, immigrants received assistance in learning the English language, studying for citizenship exams, and adapting to their new social and economic lives. Churches also played a major role in protecting and advancing the interests of their new members, and the number of ethnic churches increased significantly. The eastern and southern Europeans joined with Sioux City's Scandinavians, Germans, Russians, Italians, blacks, Jews, and countless others in creating a homogeneous and dynamic community.

The progressive era of the 1910s heightened political interest locally, and the issues of women's suffrage and prohibition were debated hotly. Sioux City males went to the polls on June 5, 1916, to decide if adult Iowa women should be granted the franchise. The local results were very close, but the measure failed by 10,000 votes at the state level. Women achieved this inherent right four years later, with the enactment of the Nineteenth Amendment.

Iowa reinstated state prohibition on January 1, 1916, and three years later the ratification of the Eighteenth Amendment instituted a ban on liquor sales nationally. Sioux City had never supported curtailments of intoxicating beverages, and local enforcement of prohibition was spotty at best. The city's nickname of Little Chicago took on a new meaning during the 1920s. Instead of connoting the next great city of the West, it then implied that Sioux City's abuse of prohibition rivaled that of Capone-ruled Chicago. The parallel was vastly overdrawn.

Local attorney William Lloyd Harding emerged as a state political leader in the 1910s. After three terms in the state House of Representatives, Harding was elected Iowa's lieutenant governor in 1912. Four years later, Iowa Republicans nominated him as their gubernatorial candidate, and Harding easily defeated his Democratic opponent. Harding was an enigmatic figure, combining a "stand-pat Republicanism" philosophy with a "wet" stance on prohibition. Sioux City's only governor served two stormy terms (1917-1921) as Iowa's chief executive.

Military events were the biggest news items from 1916 to 1918. President Woodrow Wilson issued a call for state troops in June 1916 in response to Mexican bandit-general Pancho Villa's bloody raid on American civilians in Columbus, New Mexico. More than 200 Sioux Cityans in Companies H and L of the Iowa National Guard's Second Infantry mobilized for action and served along the Rio Grande River for nearly seven months. Townsmen toasted the soldiers' return to Sioux City in March 1917. The welcome included flag waving, tears, and a massive parade up Pierce Street.

It was a short-lived furlough, for less than six weeks later—on April 6, 1917—America entered World War I by declaring war on Germany. Sioux City's soldiers went back into service. This "war to end all wars" touched the lives of many Sioux Cityans. Nearly 5,000 local men and women entered the service, and more than 100 of them gave their lives at such places as Verdun and Belleau Wood.

Siouxland's homefront was also active. The *Sioux City Tribune,* on June 16, 1917, published page after page of names of local males registered for military service as of June 5. The newspaper urged the citizens to read the list carefully and "report any slackers to city authorities at once." Morningside College and the Sioux City High School added military training courses to their curriculums. While area farmers went all out for production and reached record harvest levels, consumers rationed foodstuff. This provided great quantities of grain and meat to feed the doughboys and the starving masses of our European allies.

Raising money for the war effort was another important task. Sioux City's Four-Minute Men, a quasi-governmental organization of super-patriots, interrupted theater performances, picnics, and other public gatherings to exhort onlookers to the need for more troops and to push the sale of war bonds. When a theater owner seemed uncooperative, yellow paint was always handy. Sioux City was the first city in the nation to subscribe its quota in the Third Liberty Loan drive.

Sioux City's considerable German population frequently was held in suspicion during World War I. Nebraska and Iowa officials placed sufficient credence on the rumors that German infiltrators or sympathizers planned to disrupt the nation's railroads that troops were stationed for a time on the Missouri River Railroad Bridge. Governor Harding's Language Proclamation banned the speaking of the German language—and indeed any foreign language—in schools, churches, public gatherings, and over the telephone.

All Sioux Cityans rejoiced on Armistice Day, November 11, 1918, and the strains of "Keep the Home Fires Burning" and "The Rose of No Man's Land" still cause a catch in the throats of those who worried through Sioux City's eighteen months of participation in the war.

A period of volatile politics swept through Sioux City in the late 1910s and early 1920s. Former Congregational minister Wallace M. Short ran for mayor in 1918 at the head of a labor-supported ticket. The business community strongly opposed his candidacy, doubting his ability to manage the city and admonishing his ties to organized labor, especially his tolerance of the widely-feared Industrial Workers of the World (the I.W.W. or Wobblies).

Controversy surrounded Mayor Short's tenure. In his first term, the Ruff Disaster, a terrible influenza epidemic, malfeasance by another labor-supported councilmember, and the I.W.W. issue culminated in the only recall election of a local official in Sioux City's history. The voters, however, reaffirmed their faith in Short in the special election. They also returned him to office in 1920 and 1922. A strike at Sioux City's Swift and Company plant occurred during Short's second term and led to a violent confrontation between law enforcers and strike sympathizers. Shots were exchanged, and a striker and a special deputy, the son of Sheriff W. H. Jones, were fatally wounded.

Short's administration achieved numerous successes despite this pronounced lack of tranquility. The completion of a new Big Sioux River Bridge in 1923 provided a vastly improved highway transportation link with Sioux City's South Dakota neighbors. The city council made significant additions to the municipal parks system. It also centralized the city's police and fire departments and court system in 1924 with the opening of the new Municipal Building at Sixth and Water streets. Short's tenure proved to be a boon to local labor unions, as his support helped worker advocates spread their message to the wary populace.

While the 1920s generally are remembered for flappers, hip flasks, and lavish spending, the Roaring Twenties were anything but a party for the agricultural sector of Siouxland's economy. When Europe recovered agriculturally after World War I, continued high levels of production by American agrarians glutted the domestic market and drove down prices. The decline in farm purchasing power was felt acutely in Sioux City.

The nationwide speculation fever and "the business of America is business" atmosphere of the 1920s came to a screeching halt with the stock market crash of 1929. Few Sioux Cityans truly understood what lay ahead, but most felt sure that an era had ended.

This view of Pierce Street, looking north from near Third Street, shows that motorized traffic is outnumbering horse-drawn wagons in 1913. Beautiful street lamps are in evidence at very close intervals.

Davidson Brothers' department store is on the left, at the southwest corner of Fourth and Pierce. Beyond W. H. Beck's jewelry store, at the northwest corner of the intersection, are the Pelletier department store and, in the old Iowa Building, the Seney shoe store.

On the right, a number of well-known businesses are south of Fourth Street, including John C. Kelly's Sioux City Tribune, the Empress Theatre, August Williges' furrier establishment, Charles Selzer's wholesale liquor store, and the Northwestern National Bank. The Martin Hotel, completed only months before, anchors the northeast corner of Fourth and Pierce, and the Grain Exchange Building and the Davidson Office Building are in the background. Photo courtesy of Division of the State Historical Society, Iowa City, Iowa

Sioux City's stockyards by the 1910s had become a city unto itself with numerous barns, shops, commission offices, packing-houses, and even its own railroad line surrounded by a sea of busy livestock pens and unloading chutes. This view was taken from the northwest corner of the Livestock Exchange Building, looking toward Sioux City's downtown. Photo courtesy of Sioux City Stock Yards Company

Armour and Company purchased the old Silberhorn plant in May 1901, and joined Cudahy as the second national packing company to locate in Sioux City. This early 1920s photograph shows Armour's side-tracks, railroad cars, and the maze of inclined ramps through which livestock were herded to slaughter.

Armour and Company closed this Sioux City plant in 1963. Photo courtesy of Woodworth Commercial Photos

This sprawling meatpacking plant was built during the late 1910s for the Midland Packing Company. It was dedicated on January 23, 1920. Massive and flagrant stock manipulations by management and sales-men, which resulted in a shortage of working capital, caused the company to declare bankruptcy and cease operations on May 1, 1920. Receiverships and court cases followed.

The plant remained closed until 1924, when Swift and Company purchased the buildings. This created an envious position for Sioux City, for with Cudahy, Armour, and Swift the city had three established, national packers.

This 1927 photograph shows the Swift plant at its peak of operation, with the company's own railroad cars advertising Swift's Premium Hams, Premium Oleo-margarine, and Silverleaf Brand Pure Lard.

Swift remained in the building complex until the mid-1970s. Sioux City busi-nessman Kermit Lohry then purchased the structures and developed KD Stockyards Station, a collection of retail shops, eating establishments, a bowling alley, and other businesses. Photo courtesy of Woodworth Commercial Photos

The management of the Sioux City Stock Yards Company gather in F. L. Eaton's new office on the third floor of the Livestock Exchange Building for this photograph, circa 1920. They are (from left to right): superintendent Harry H. Burdick, purchasing agent Edward L. Evans, Sioux City Terminal Railway general manager Charles F. Morrison, president F. L. Eaton, secretary George F. Silknitter, and traffic manager William H. Benn. Photo courtesy of William Eaton Palmer family

The Northwestern passenger depot at 124 Nebraska Street (shown here in a 1923 photo) was the largest and most pretentious of Sioux City's three downtown railroad stations. Dozens of trains and hundreds of passengers on both the Chicago and Northwestern and Illinois Central railroads arrived and departed the facility daily. The C&NW discontinued passenger service to Sioux City in 1959, and the Illinois Central followed suit in 1971. During World War II, however, passengers departing here aboard the C&NW Corn King could expect to arrive in Chicago in just ten hours and twenty-five minutes! Photo courtesy of Woodworth Commercial Photos

The Chicago and Northwestern Railroad (formerly the Chicago, St. Paul, Minneapolis and Omaha) roundhouse at Eighteenth and Howard streets, circa 1920.

John I. Blair's Chicago and Northwestern Railroad empire (the parent road to the Sioux City and Pacific) assumed formal control of the Omaha Road in 1882 along with another locally-based railroad, the Sioux City and St. Paul, to create northwest Iowa's largest railroad transportation network. This unusual thirty-six-stall, full-circle roundhouse was the hub of operations for the C&NW/Omaha road in Sioux City. The extensive fueling, repair, and storage requirements of a first-class railroad at the turn of the century are evident in this photo, which was taken during steam railroading's finest hour.

The smaller roundhouse (upper right) belonged to the Illinois Central Railroad, another major Sioux City rail line, which shared trackage with the C&NW as far as LeMars, Iowa. Both roundhouses were demolished in the late 1940s as diesel locomotives made steam engines—and their massive service facilities—obsolete. Much of the area in the foreground is today buried under Floyd Boulevard. Photo courtesy of Woodworth Commercial Photos

Hostlers, boilermakers, machinists, and their assistants line the transfer table pit of the Chicago, St. Paul, Minneapolis and Omaha Railroad (later Chicago and North-western) roundhouse backshop at Eigh-teenth and Howard streets, circa 1910. Photo courtesy of Sioux City Public Museum

The Chicago, Milwaukee, St. Paul and Pacific Railroad shops at North Riverside, circa 1922.

The Sioux City and Dakota Division of the Milwaukee Road had its origins in Sioux City in 1873 with the completion of the Dakota and Southern Railroad to Yankton, Dakota Territory, a line which was later absorbed by the Milwaukee Road in 1879. This division, for which Sioux City was headquarters, consisted of over 550 miles of track, much of which reached into South Dakota.

The giant facility shown here was constructed by the railroad in 1918 to replace its flood-prone, smaller roundhouse at Second and Division streets. The entire engine terminal occupied over fifty acres and employed approximately 400 men in repairing and fueling the more than twenty-five locomotives dispatched daily on trains from Sioux City on the Milwaukee's tracks. The Big Sioux River and the line's West Yard at Stevens (now North Sioux City, South Dakota) are visible in the back-ground. Photo courtesy of Woodworth Commercial Photos

LeRoy Minear, driving truck no. 1, and his
cohorts show off the Walker electric trucks
used by the Moore-Shenkberg Grocer Company in the late-1910s. The trucks are
loaded with merchandise for retail grocers
in the area. Moore-Shenkberg occupied both
buildings in the background, on the north
side of Third Street between Douglas and
Pierce streets.

Conrad Shenkberg came to Sioux City in
1882 and established a wholesale grocery
business with twenty-two railroad carloads
of goods. As the company grew, the four-
story (later six-story) structure in the
foreground was built in 1892, and the eight-
story building in the background followed in
1910. The company was renamed Moore-
Shenkberg in 1916 and O. J. Moore Grocer
Company in 1920.

The nearer building became a ramp-
garage in 1933. After sitting virtually vacant
for several years, it was torn down in 1982.
The other structure presently functions as a
warehouse for Younkers department store.
Photo courtesy of Sioux City Public Museum

Bountiful deposits of rich glacial clays,
combined with ready markets for the
finished products, made brick and tile
manufacturing a major industry for Sioux
City for many years. The largest and
longest-lived of the city's many brick
companies was the Sioux City Brick and Tile
Company, located in North Riverside. This
firm manufactured common brick, hollow
tile block, facing brick, and builder's sand,
with a peak capacity of 100 million bricks
and tiles yearly.

This photo, taken in 1922, shows Plant
No. 2, which specialized in the Nu-Soo
brand of hollow tile block. Sioux City Brick
and Tile was Riverside's second-largest
employer for many years. The company
closed its Riverside plant and moved its
base of operation to Sergeant Bluff in 1964.
Photo courtesy of Sioux City Public
Museum

Completion of the Sioux City Traction Company's Westside car barns at West Third and Ross streets in 1906 occasioned this gathering of conductors and their "steeds."

Beginning in 1882 public demand for speedy, efficient, scheduled service between Sioux City's downtown and rapidly expanding suburbs resulted in the formation of no less than twenty separate street railway and power companies, most of which came under the control of the Sioux City Service Company by 1909.

Although Sioux City's streetcars and their crews racked up millions of miles of safe, uneventful service to the public between 1884 and the end of operations in 1948, some of the cars shown here were not so fortunate: No. 21, the first car on the left, was reduced to kindling during a one-sided duel with a railroad locomotive at the corner of Third and Wesley Way; No. 127 was destroyed by fire at the Greenville car barns in 1921. Photo courtesy of Sioux City Public Museum

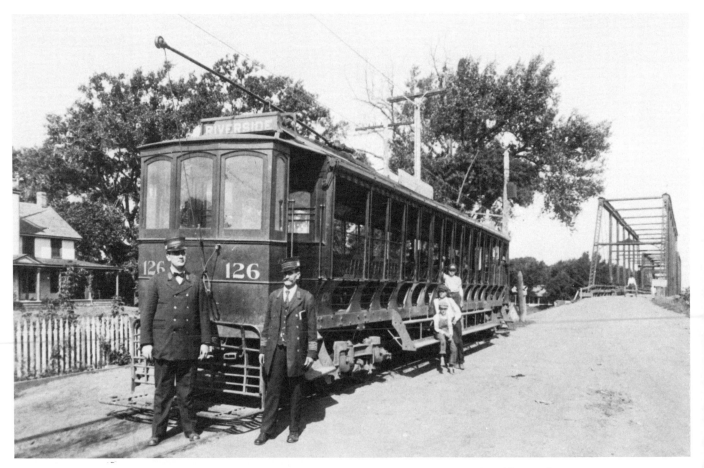

North Riverside and "end of track" for Sioux City's streetcar system looked like this in 1913; conductor A. H. Amundson and trainman Olof Oien pose with Sioux City Service Company Car No. 126 on the Iowa side of the old Big Sioux River Bridge.

A. L. Grabbe, who owned Grabbe's Park across the river in Stevens, South Dakota (now North Sioux City), can be seen coming across the bridge with a pushcart. Photo courtesy of Mrs. A. H. Amundson

A crowd of 25,000 people swarm into Mizzou Park on September 3, 1910, to hear a talk by former President Theodore Roosevelt. Reporters are busy at work as Roosevelt gives a ringing endorsement of President Taft and a recently-passed, stringent tariff. Significantly, the former president's show of support for Taft came in "insurgent territory," as Congressman Elbert H. Hubbard from Sioux City and Iowa Senator Jonathan Prentiss Dolliver, both opponents of the tariff, were also on the platform. They defended their positions in brief messages following Roosevelt's speech.

Mizzou Park was located at the foot of Douglas Street, on grounds now occupied by the Municipal Auditorium. In the background, the Tolerton and Warfield Building is on the left, and the Northwestern passenger depot, where another 25,000 people met Roosevelt, is on the right.

Roosevelt's trip to Sioux City in 1910 was very short. He arrived at 10:48 a.m., spoke at the ball park, and departed for Sioux Falls a few minutes after noon—a schedule that effectively rules out a supposed Roosevelt side-trip to the yet-unbuilt Interstate Speedway in Stevens (North Sioux City), South Dakota. Still, TR pronounced himself "DEE-lighted" with his Sioux City stopover. Photo courtesy of Sioux City Public Museum

With Durphy's orchestra readying a waltz in the background, some of Sioux City's social elite gather for this late 1910s Christmas party in the Martin Hotel ballroom. Photo courtesy of the William Eaton Palmer Family

The Sioux City school system was in a state of almost total disarray in 1910, brought on by disputes between the school board and a series of somewhat weak superintendents, as well as vigorous battles between fellow board members. New superintendent Melvin G. Clark (1867-1931) stepped into the fray in July 1911. Over the course of the next twenty years, the progressiveness of the Clark administration marked Sioux City's educational system as a model to which other communities only could hope to measure up.

The list of accomplishments accrued under M. G. Clark (shown here) seems almost endless. The system's curriculum received Clark's close attention. He introduced the "motivated course of study," which placed particular emphasis on English and history. Undaunted by what he deemed a lack of adequate textbooks expressing these ideals, Clark simply wrote his own. These included: Progress, a history book highlighting chief problems which humanity had sought to solve (1916); Motivated Language and Habituated Arithmetic (1919); Applied English (1924); Progress and Patriotism, embodying his idea of "spiritualized citizenship" (1924); and the three-volume Language in Use (1925-26). He also diversified the school's programming, instituting domestic and manual science departments, upgraded the

divisions of art and music, and replaced the "preliminary grade" with kindergarten.

Although essentially an educator rather than an administrator, M. G. Clark possessed the business acumen needed to bring his ideas to fruition. When teacher training seemed insufficient, he began Sioux

City's Normal School in the old Armstrong School building, where prospective teachers undertook a three-year program preparatory to teaching in the Sioux City schools. A thorough pragmatist, Clark dropped the project in 1927, when enough trained teachers were emerging from colleges and universities.

Clark believed that adolescent youth could better be served through regional junior high schools. The theory was that, by utilizing an enriched curriculum and providing and intermediate step between elementary and high school, more students would progress beyond the eight grade. The school board built the city's first four junior highs during Clark's tenure: East in 1917, West in 1919, North in 1922, and Woodrow Wilson in 1925. The resulting attendance boost was staggering. In 1915 there were 526 students in eighth grade and 205 in tenth; in 1925 these numbers grew to 940 eighth graders and 772 high school sophomores. While undoubtedly other factors played a part, the junior high schools were a major cause for this jump. The greater percentage of students staying a longer number of years, coupled with an increase in population, necessitated the building of several new high schools during and after Clark's administration. Photo by Genelli Studios; courtesy of Sioux City Independent School System

In this enhanced presentation, photographer Philip C. Waltermire captures fire fighters battling the Lindholm Furniture Company fire on March 19-20, 1912. A large crowd gathers near the Continental Building to view the destruction. The Lindholm store had been at the southwest corner of Fifth and Douglas streets since the early 1890s. Photo by Philip C. Waltermire; courtesy of Sioux City Public Museum

Few structural changes, other than new facades, have taken place near the northwest corner of Fifth and Nebraska since 1911, but the changes in the buildings' uses have been considerable. In this 1911 image, Max McGraw's Interstate Electric and Manufacturing Company is in the old Marks-Joy Block on Fifth Street. McGraw later became an executive of the McGraw-Edison Company. The Peavey Furniture Company, Electric Supply Company, and W. P. Jones's "Grow-Sir" occupy the first floor of the Lytle Block.

On the right, the nearer structure at 511 Nebraska holds Harmon Smith's livery stable. It became the Strand Theatre in 1914 and, during the 1930s, was reputed to be one of Sioux City's largest gambling dens. The light-colored building houses the Seymour White Laundry Company and the YMCA in 1911. It had many occupants, including the Moose Lodge, before becoming the Sioux City Art Center in 1966. Photo courtesy of Sioux City Public Museum

The Sioux City Public Library had outgrown its portion of the City Building at Sixth and Douglas by 1911, when the city council received a $75,000 gift from Andrew Carnegie's library fund. After much discussion, the northeast corner of Sixth and Jackson was selected as the site for a new library.

Library board members, city officials, and project staff convened for this photograph after the laying of the new library's cornerstone on March 5, 1912. Shown, left to right are: Commissioner of Parks and Public Property G. B. Healy, supervising architect William L. Steele, board members R. H. Burton-Smith, Mayor A. A. Smith (with trowel), board president Dr. J. P. Savage, board member A. L. Fribourg, and building contractor George J. S. Collins. The building opened on March 8, 1913. Photo courtesy of Sioux City Public Library

A 2 million-gallon water reservoir was built in Grandview Park during the 1880s. The city's growing water needs required expansion by 1912, however, when this photograph was taken. Workmen have already completed the 4 million-gallon north reservoir, in the background, and are preparing to form higher concrete walls for the original reservoir, thereby doubling it to a capacity of 4 million gallons. The Boys' and Girls' Home, at Twenty-Sixth and Douglas streets, is on the right. Photo by W. S. King; courtesy of Sioux City Public Museum

The Municipal Auditorium, seen here in 1923, was built in 1909 at the southwest corner of Seventh and Douglas. The community used the structure for theatrical performances, automobile shows, lectures, and much more, including a meeting place for the Monahan Post, the Sioux City Consistory, and the Rotary Club. For ten years, beginning in 1945, it housed the Tomba Ballroom, and since 1955 it has been the home of KVTV (later KCAU) television station. Photo courtesy of Woodworth Commercial Photos

After building a radio set out of makeshift parts in 1912, George R. Call (1898-1974) received the first radio message ever transmitted in Sioux City. In this 1915 photo, taken at the Call residence at 1529 Grandview Boulevard, high school student Call is plying his avocation intently. Two years later, during World War I, the government closed down all amateur radio operations. Call and several other young men, however, soon found themselves serving as instructors of semaphore and radio theory and operation at Sioux City High School. After the war, these radio pioneers organized Sioux City's first radio station, constructed hook-ups for railroad trains, and maintained an office between the water reservoirs at Grandview Park. Call remained a ham radio enthusiast the rest of his life. He also engaged in business, joining his father in the Call Bond and Mortgage Company, and serving as a diligent advocate of the development of the Missouri and other rivers. Photo courtesy of Sioux City Public Museum

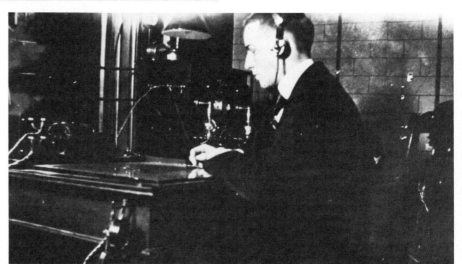

A Keystone Cops short and the 1915 silent film Simple Life starring Fatty Arbuckle drew this crowd to the Olympic Theatre. The movie house was located on the north side of Fourth Street between Douglas and Pierce streets. Photo courtesy of Sioux City Public Museum

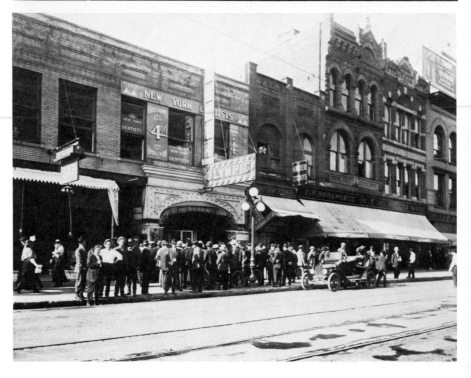

By the 1910s, the Woodbury County Courthouse at the southeast corner of Sixth and Pierce had been outgrown. County voters approved the construction of a new courthouse in June 1914 and selected the building's site, the southeast corner of Seventh and Douglas, in November 1914. On January 5, 1915, the board of supervisors chose local architect William L. Steele to design the building; they accepted his preliminary drawings on March 23, 1915.

Steele, who had worked under Louis H. Sullivan in Chicago, was a leading exponent of prairie school architecture. He came to Sioux City in 1904 and soon became the community's best-known and most daring architect. Upon securing the courthouse job, he brought in fellow prairie schoolers William Gray Purcell and George Grant Elmslie to assist him. While Steele was the architect on record for the project, the building's amended design was chiefly Elmslie's.

The Minneapolis firm of Splady, Albee and Smith received the contracting bid on February 15, 1916, and work began as soon as weather permitted. On June 27, 1916, when this view looking southeast was taken, the foundation is in place and the first floor is being built. The cornerstone would be laid just thirteen days later. Horse-drawn wagons and what seems like primitive machinery are being employed to assist the workmen.

On the left is St. Vincent's Hospital, located in the old Fred T. Evans home at the southwest corner of Seventh and Pierce. The Trimble and Davidson office buildings rise above the Overland and Willys-Knight automobile dealership, and the Federal Building is on the right. Photo from William L. Steele's Courthouse Scrapbook; courtesy of Sioux City Public Museum

The ornate Woodbury County Courthouse rose quickly and was nearly finished on November 26, 1917, the date of this photograph. The county occupied the $850,000 building on March 1, 1918. While the radically-innovative plans of Steele, Purcell, and Elmslie were met with distrust and some hostility in 1915, the beauty of the completed structure stifled such thoughts. The major complaint voiced over the past sixty years has been that a full block of land should have been utilized to allow a better look at the building. It stands today as the foremost example of a public building in the prairie school style. Photo by W. S. King; from William L. Steele's Courthouse Scrapbook; courtesy of Sioux City Public Museum

The Sioux City Police Department operated this substation on the grounds of the 1911 Interstate Fair. These officers scoured the grandstand and midway areas in search of ticket scalpers, pickpockets, and other law violators. Photo courtesy of Sioux City Public Museum

Sioux City car enthusiasts promoted automobile races from 1908 to 1915, first at the Interstate Fair grounds and later at a racetrack in Union County, South Dakota.

Promoters heavily advertised the 300-mile July 4, 1914 race, and a crowd estimated as high as 47,000 people jammed into the Interstate Speedway bleachers. The day was hot and dry, conditions that resulted in only seven of the initial seventeen cars finishing the race. Barney Oldfield was the odds-on favorite to win, but he was one of those who did not complete the race. Instead, unknown Eddie Rickenbacher powered his Deusenberg Special to victory. He averaged 78.8 miles per hour during his 150 sweeps of the two-mile track. The first place finish netted "Rick" $10,000 and projected him into the national limelight. Photo courtesy of Woodworth Commercial Photos

Eddie Rickenbacher returned to the Interstate Speedway in 1915 to defend his title, this time operating a Maxwell automobile. On July 3, 1915, in a race marred by the fatal crash of another driver, Rickenbacher again triumphed. The volume of attendance was sharply reduced from the previous year, however, as was the purse. Rickenbacher's 1915 victory brought him only $6,000.

The 1915 race was the last big automobile event at this track. Rickenbacher became a World War I flying ace (and changed his name to Rickenbacker), an automobile executive, and general manager of Eastern Airlines. The track became the first aviation landing field in the Sioux City area, eventually named Rickenbacker Field. Photo courtesy of Sioux City Public Museum

The Sioux City Journal, *which had occupied a building at 413 Douglas Street since 1876, erected this structure at the southwest corner of Fifth and Douglas after the Lindholm fire. This photograph was taken about 1915, when the building opened. George D. Perkins, who had published the* Journal *for forty-five years, had died just one year before. This building served as the* Journal's *headquarters until November 1972, when the newspaper moved to its present home at Sixth and Pavonia, in the Mary J. Treglia urban renewal district. A parking ramp now occupies the* Journal's *old site. Photo courtesy of Sioux City Public Museum*

A. M. Cleary (left) and employees of his New Exchange Saloon, located in the Livestock Exchange Building, stand amid cuspidors, beautiful wooden furnishings, and advertisements for Sioux City's Western Brew beer in this September 1915 photograph. They appear calm despite the realization that Iowa would be a "dry" state in less than four months.

Iowa had instituted the Mulct Law in 1894, which had combined prohibition, local option, and licensing. The Iowa legislature voted to return to prohibition, however, at the end of 1915. A sign of the wall sums up these employees' thoughts: "Don't Ask Me What I am Going to Do after January 1, 1916—BUT—What the Hell are YOU Going to Do?" Photo courtesy of Sioux City Public Museum

The advent of state prohibition in 1916 and national prohibition in 1920 did not noticeably stem the tide of alcohol, and liquor busts like this one were common in Sioux City and other cities and towns. Bootlegging continued even after prohibition's repeal as criminals competed with state-owned liquor stores and the lack of "liquor by the drink."

The community's long-held nickname of Little Chicago took on a new connotation during prohibition. Rather than signifying the next great city of the West, Little Chicago then meant that wide-open conditions rivaled those of Capone-dominated Chicago. While illegal liquor certainly was available, any comparison with Chicago's plight is highly romanticized. Photo courtesy of Sioux City Public Museum

147

The old Woodbury County Courthouse, at the southeast corner of Sixth and Pierce, serves as a backdrop for this circa 1910 political photograph. In what may have been a staged shot, the horse-drawn, driverless rig sitting idly along Pierce Street is marked "Democratic." In contrast, the Chalmers-Detroit "30" automobile, driven by Harry A. Wetmore and full of Republicans, appears ready to speed ahead.

William Lloyd Harding is seated behind Wetmore. A native of the Sibley, Iowa area, he came to Sioux City in 1897 to attend Morningside College, where he drew local notice for his oratorical abilities. After receiving his law degree in 1905, Harding entered Republican party politics and advanced quickly. Voters elected him to the Iowa House of Representatives in 1906. He was vying successfully for re-election at the time this photograph was taken. After serving three terms in the House, Harding sought and secured the office of Iowa lieutenant governor, serving under Governor George W. Clarke for two terms (1913-1917).

Local attorney Ole T. Naglestad is the tall gentleman wearing the winter coat and standing along the courthouse fence. He was then justice of the peace. Naglestad served as Woodbury County attorney from 1915 to 1931, by far the longest tenure for that position. Photo courtesy of Sioux City Public Museum

148

William L. Harding (1877-1934) became the Republican candidate for governor in 1916 after a spirited and divisive primary race. His Democratic opponent was publisher Edwin T. Meredith. Prohibition, women's suffrage, and "good roads" were key issues in one of Iowa's fiercest gubernatorial campaigns. Because of the liquor question, the president of Morningside College and the minister of Grace Methodist Episcopal Church (of which Harding was a member) opposed Harding, a "wet," and endorsed Meredith, a "dry." In the end, however, Harding swept to victory with nearly 70 percent of the vote. He became Iowa's twenty-second governor at the age of thirty-nine. His overwhelming popularity led to an early "booming" of Harding for the vice-presidency in 1920.

The United States entered World War I soon after Harding's inaugural, making the responsibilities of guiding the state during wartime his primary concerns. Iowa ranked high in securing its wartime quota of men and money. Harding's zeal in managing the homefront, however, led to a major political blunder. In May 1918, he issued his famous Language Proclamation, which outlawed the use of foreign languages in public, in schools, in churches, or on telephones. Most residents approved his ban on the German language, but the disallowance of the use of all foreign languages infuriated citizens of foreign birth.

Harding successfully stood for re-election in 1918, although his margin of victory was reduced substantially from his 1916 landslide. The armistice ending World War I, signed only days after Harding's re-election, should have allowed the governor to shift his efforts to other projects, such as state road improvements, park development, and state tax reforms. The mismanaged pardoning of a convicted rapist on November 16, 1918, though, dashed these plans. It was a major news story for months, with anti-Harding forces condemning the governor's action and questioning his motivation, hinting at bribery.

The Iowa House of Representatives investigated the matter in March 1919. The legislators instigated impeachment proceedings against Harding at one point, the only time an Iowa governor has been subjected to such a move. While the measure was halted the next day, with Harding only censured, the Sioux City governor's political career had ended. He limped through the remainder of his term, did not seek re-election, and did not run for any office again. The Republicans would not have a Harding/Harding slate in 1920.

Still a skillful orator, however, he traveled the Chautauqua circuit, became a chief spokesman for the St. Lawrence Seaway, and campaigned for Republican candidates in other Midwestern states. Photo courtesy of Sioux City Public Museum

With only fifteen minutes left to go until game time—according to Thorpe and Company's clock—Mose E. Reed's band leads a parade on Pierce Street, harkening spectators to Mizzou Park for the May 1 home opener of Sioux City's 1917 baseball season.

The Western League offered a prize of the Governor Capper silver loving cup to the city with the largest opening day attendance, and employees of many Sioux City businesses received this Tuesday afternoon off in order to take in the game between the Sioux City Indians and the Denver Bears. Pre-game festivities included the appearances of two nineteen-year-olds from Anthon, Iowa, as the battery for throwing out the first pitch. Bernard Coyne, at 7'9" regarded as "Iowa's tallest boy," initiated the game, hopefully with a drop ball, to fellow townsman Verby Admire, who at 3'9" was deemed to be Woodbury County's shortest man.

Sioux City took a 5-3 record into the game, after series in St. Joseph and Wichita. They looked forward to another championship in 1917. This was not their day, however. Denver's tough pitching, and Sioux City's lack of timely hitting, resulted in a 7-0 shutout of the home team. They also failed to received the Governor Capper cup. Photo courtesy of Sioux City Public Museum

A detachment of Sioux City World War I enlistees prepare "to make the world safe for democracy," as they muster prior to train-time in front of the Union passenger depot at Third and Pierce in 1917. The Moore-Shenkberg Grocer Company is at the right. Photo courtesy of Sioux City Public Museum

H. M. S. White (back to camera) instructs members of the Signal Corps battalion in semaphore, or flag signaling, on the lawn of Sioux City High School (later Central) in the summer of 1918. The soldiers are demonstrating the alphabet. The two groups on the right are deciphering messages, Morse code in the foreground and semaphore in the background. Photo courtesy of Sioux City Public Museum

Mother Gertrude and the Benedictine Sisters purchased the old Fred T. Evans home at the southwest corner of Seventh and Pierce streets in 1898 and began St. Vincent's Young Ladies' Home. In 1907 it became St. Vincent's Hospital.

In less than ten years the hospital required larger quarters. Local architect William L. Steele designed a new structure, which was built along Jones Street north of Sixth Street. It opened in 1917 (shown here in a 1923 photograph). Major additions were built in 1951-1953 and in 1969-1971. Photo courtesy of Woodworth Commercial Photos

150

A successful library program for recuperating servicemen during World War I led Sioux City librarian Clarence W. Sumner and Rose O'Connor, an assistant librarian, to implement a similar idea with Sioux City's hospitals in November 1919. The Sioux City Library Hospital Service was perhaps the nation's first cooperative venture between private hospitals and a public library.

Each hospital developed a suitable collection, and materials were brought to the patients' beds. Safeguards were installed to minimize the spread of disease through the use of the books and magazines. Rose O'Connor (1874-1939) directed this important program until her death. She is shown here distributing books in the surgical ward of St. Vincent's Hospital in 1920. Photo by W. S. King; courtesy of Sioux City Public Museum

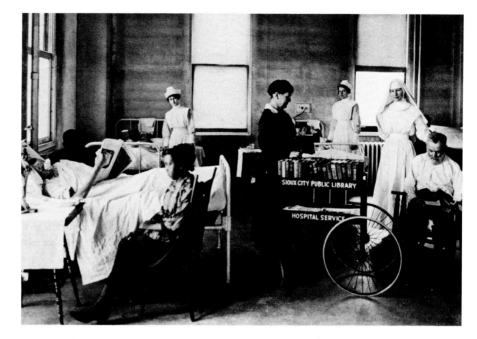

Wallace Mertin Short (1866-1953) is perhaps the most interesting and controversial figure in Sioux City's history. Born near College Springs, Iowa, he attended Amity College, Beloit College, at which he was valedictorian, and the Yale University Seminary, where he graduated Phi Beta Kappa. Short's first two pastorates as a Congregational minister were at Evansville, Wisconsin, and Kansas City, Missouri.

Reverend Short began his four-year tenure at Sioux City's First Congregational Church in May 1910. He emerged as a folk hero within weeks of his arrival, when he thwarted an attempted robbery by breaking his cane over the head of one of the three assailants. His views on prohibition and labor unionism, however, polarized the church members and eventually led to his forced resignation in 1914.

Several months later, Wallace Short organized the Central Independent Church. The new church, which first held services in the (Peavey) Grand Theatre, attracted former members of the First Congregational Church as well as liberal spirits and supporters of organized labor. Short became identified at that time with the Industrial Workers of the World, the Wobblies. The business community feared the left-wing I. W. W. and consequently distrusted Short.

Labor advocates convinced Wallace Short to run for mayor in 1918, and he won handily despite the intense opposition of both major newspapers and the business leaders. A combination of factors—the Ruff Disaster, a massive influenza epidemic, and, primarily, Short's continued tolerance of the I. W. W., fueled by vigorous anti-Short editorials in the Sioux City Tribune—led in 1919 to a recall election of the mayor. Short's opponents attempted to split the labor vote in the lone recall in Sioux City's history by running railroad engineer Hugh

Carney against Short. Carney was no match for Short, however, and the mayor garnered over 60 percent of the vote. He was re-elected in 1920 and 1922.

Critics of Short called Sioux City the Wobbly Capital during his stormy tenure. Intense labor/management relations led to several strikes in the early 1920s, and a revitalized Ku Klux Klan raised its bigoted head in Sioux City and throughout the nation. In combating these and other problems, Wallace Short attempted to put into practice the "social gospel" ideas of his mentor and hero, Reverend Washington Gladden.

After leaving the mayor's chair in 1924, Short served one term in the Iowa House and made unsuccessful bids for the U.S. Congress in 1924, mayor in 1926, and the Republican party nomination for governor in 1934. He was the gubernatorial candidate of Iowa's Farmer-Labor party in 1934, 1936, and 1938.

Short founded a union newspaper in 1927, The Unionist and Public Forum. He served as editor and publisher until prevented by illness late in life. The former mayor was also a major force in northwest Iowa during the Farmers' Holiday movement in 1932 and 1933. Most of the ideas Short proposed and worked to enact eventually came into being. The cliche that "he was ahead of his time" is appropriate. Photo courtesy of Sioux City Public Museum

The four-story, mansard-roofed Hedges Block, built in 1873 at the northeast corner of Fourth and Douglas, houses the Oscar Ruff Drug Company and several smaller tenants in this 1909 image. Photo courtesy of Sioux City Public Museum

On June 29, 1918, the old Hedges Block collapsed, and fire engulfed the ruins. The Sioux City Fire Department fought the blaze for nearly thirty-six hours, while combined forces of the police, fire, and volunteers struggled to free trapped victims. In total, the Ruff Disaster claimed thirty-nine lives and injured scores of people. In terms of loss of life, it was the city's worst disaster.

Commissioner of Public Safety W. R. Hamilton drew heated criticism for supplying whiskey to the rescue workers, a practice stopped by Sheriff W. H. Jones. Hamilton was suspended and removed from office in September 1918, due in part to his actions at the scene of this tragedy. Photo courtesy of Sioux City Public Museum

The Ruff Disaster occurred while the Hedges Block, owned by the Western Iowa Company, was being extensively remodeled, with the first floor being lowered to ground level. In fact, the sign seen between the pillors reads: "REMODELING. OPEN FOR BUSINESS. WALK RIGHT IN." Photo by Ricard Photograph Company; courtesy of Sioux City Public Museum

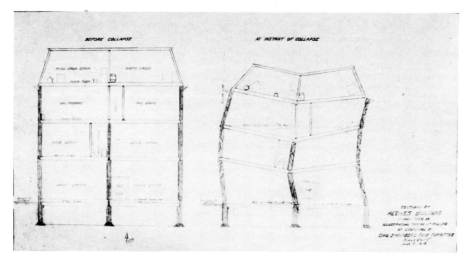

A crowd flocks to this mid-1910s sale at the T. S. Martin store, located on the north side of Fourth Street between Pierce and Nebraska streets.

Thomas S. Martin came to Sioux City in the 1870s, before spending three years in Deadwood, Dakota Territory. He started the T. S. Martin store on April 10, 1880. Later, his brothers James P. and Louis B. Martin joined the firm. The company had several different downtown locations prior to this Fourth Street site. Photo courtesy of Sioux City Public Museum

Ten days after the Ruff Disaster, the members of the Civil Engineers' Club offered their theory on the cause of the catastrophe. They concluded that the remodeling project had been ill-advised because of the age and generally poor condition of the Hedges Block. According to their renditions, the shifting of the floor line placed undue strain on the exterior and load bearing walls, causing them to collapse.

The Ruff Disaster further embarrassed the already-besieged administration of Mayor Wallace M. Short. Upon taking office, Short and the two other victorious labor-supported candidates, Commissioners W. R. Hamilton and Henry Michelstetter, passed a resolution loosening the qualifications of the office of city building inspector in order to appoint their campaign manager, E. J. O'Connor, to the post. The Civil Engineers' Club opposed the measure, stating that letting down these standards was "dangerous and objectionable."

O'Connor, occupying the position of assistant building inspector during the interim, reviewed the remodeling plans for the Hedges Block, but apparently was not competent enough to comprehend the inherent dangers of the project. The coroner's jury, however, placed primary responsibility for the thirty-nine deaths on the owners of the Hedges Block, for not fully appreciating the deteriorated condition of their building, and on the city's building inspection department, for not overseeing the project adequately. Less than two months later, professional architect F. E. Colby replaced O'Connor as city building inspector. Photo courtesy of Sioux City Public Museum

T. S. Martin died in 1915, and the company passed to his three sons—J. Earle, Jules T., and Howard V. Martin. The brothers moved the store to this six-story structure at the northeast corner of Fourth and Nebraska in 1919 (photo dated 1928).

The Martin brothers died in the 1940s, and the family's store was sold in 1948 to the May Company of St. Louis. The Younkers Brothers Company, in turn, purchased the operation in 1957. This elegant structure was torn down in 1970 as part of the city's urban renewal program. Photo courtesy of Woodworth Commercial Photos

The T. S. Martin store opened to the public on March 19, 1919, but a dedication party was held the evening before, when Iowa Governor William L. Harding (center) and South Dakota Governor Peter S. Norbeck (right), together with 200 newspaper editors and writers, held a Press Club frolic there.

The Sioux City Journal reported that, after punching in on special time cards, "the governors were compelled to make the first purchase in the new store, one cent being the coin of the realm, and silk shirts being their prizes."

Standing behind the counter (left to right) are Howard V., Jules T., and J. Earle Martin. The governors' bargain certainly fit the company's motto, "where quality is higher than price." Photo by W. S. King; courtesy of Sioux City Public Museum

Sioux City policemen Earl Morgan (left) and Tom Green show off two of the department's motorcycles at the police station at 315 Sixth Street about 1917. Morgan and Green drove a Harley-Davidson and an Indian motorcycle, respectively. Photo courtesy of Sioux City Public Museum

Trinity College, established in 1913 on this rugged hilltop between Sioux City's Northside and the "suburb" of Leeds, flourished alternately as a Catholic men's college, a high school for boys, a convent, a seminary, and as the temporary home for Western Iowa Technical Community College until it closed in 1974. This building, together with three others, still stands at 3075 Floyd Boulevard. Photo courtesy of the Sioux City Journal

Trinity High School football lettermen donned their brand-new team jerseys for this traditional team portrait, made in 1919. Shown here, left to right, first row, are: Abrose Kirwin, "Tip" O'Neil, Eddie Hickey, Matt O'Keefe, Vincent J. "Tub" Harrington, and Denis Chicoine. Second row: Lawrence Verzani, Jack McBride, and, on the far right, Eddie Meylor. The remaining members are unidentified.

Vincent Harrington starred in football as a guard on Notre Dame University's famous "Four Horsemen" team in the 1920s. He became the Democratic party's nominee for the Iowa Senate in 1932 and swept to victory in the FDR landslide. Harrington was elected to the U.S. Congress in November 1936 and re-elected in 1938 and 1940. He resigned his seat in Congress during World War II, however, to join the Army Air Corps. The immensely-popular Harrington died in the line of duty on November 29, 1943. He was only forty years of age. Photo courtesy of Denis Chicoine, Elk Point, South Dakota

Sioux City's Masonic fraternity purchased lots in 1920 and 1921 at the southeast corner of Ninth and Nebraska, formerly the site of the S. T. Davis residence. The Masonic Temple, which opened in December 1922, housed a membership of 6,500 Masons in the Sioux City district. Nine different bodies originally used the building as their meeting place and business headquarters. The firm of Beuttler and Arnold designed the $500,000 structure in a Moorish and Spanish architectural style. Photo courtesy of Woodworth Commercial Photos

Ralph A. Bennett's Motor Mart Building, at the southeast corner of Sixth and Nebraska, opened in 1912. The first major occupant was the Bennett Auto Supply Company, wholesalers of Moon, White, and Knox automobiles.

Prominent tenants in the 1920s, when this view was taken, include: Frank Buckwalter's real estate agency, ground floor on right; the New York Life Insurance, occupying most of the third floor; the Sioux City Chamber of Commerce and its related organizations (for which the building was renamed), using most of the fourth floor; and Tom Archer's Roof Garden night club, in the peaked portion on the right. The dance hall later was named the Skylon. The same portion housed the Sioux City Art Center from 1954 to 1961.

The Sioux City Gas and Electric Company is occupying the north half of the ground floor in this view. In 1930 Bishop's Cafeteria took over this section. Photo courtesy of Woodworth Commercial Photos

John J. Lessenich started the Chicago House at the northeast corner of Fourth and Jones streets in 1867. That wooden building burned in 1881 and was replaced. In 1905 the structure shown here was erected. In June 1923, when this image was made, the Chicago House was considered one of Sioux City's five finest hotels and convention centers. The 112-year history of the hotel and roominghouse ended with its demolition in 1979. Photo by N. N. Woodworth; courtesy of Sioux City Public Museum

This westerly-looking view reveals a number of small retailers clustered around the intersection of South Fairmount and Correctionville Road in 1927. They all served the long-established neighborhood of Greenville.

On the left is Chain Store No. 9, one of a series of Barney Baron's corner grocery and meat markets; on the north side of Correctionville Road is a competitor, E. A. Welding's market.

To the east of South Fairmount is A. F. Singer's drugstore, adjacent to J. A. Graham's Fairmont Garage. The multi-purpose garage sold Hudson, Essex, and Chevrolet automobiles, repaired vehicles, and pumped gas. At the time of this photograph, gas sold for 16.9 cents per gallon, which included a two-cent tax. Photo courtesy of Woodworth Commercial Photos

This rare and damaged photograph provides a glimpse of what the Peters Park area of Morningside was like in 1923. Looking south on Morningside Avenue towards South St. Aubin Street, E. C. Peters' legacy, Peters Park, is on the left. On the right are the Morningside State Bank, Morningside Pharmacy, and the College Inn. The Morningside Savings Bank building is in the background. Photo courtesy of Woodworth Commercial Photos

The J. C. Rennison Company in 1922, at the east end of Morningside, was then Sioux City's largest and most modern greenhouse, with over 85,000 square feet under glass and over 40,000 geraniums in bloom.

The business was already over forty years old when this photo was taken in 1922. It had earlier been located at the northwest corner of Seventh and Pierce, the southwest corner of Ninth and Pierce, and, for many years, at the northeast corner of Twenty-fifth and Jones streets. The firm had a retail shop on Pierce Street and served over 225 stores in Iowa, South Dakota, Nebraska, and Minnesota. The business required the burning of over 800 tons of coal yearly to keep the greenhouse warm.

In 1922 Miss Fannie L. Rennison headed the company, and Newell F. Guernsey had charge of the landscape and nursery department.

These buildings remained a fixture along the Smithland Road until the early 1980s, when they were torn down. Photo courtesy of Sioux City Public Museum

A Reo Cab Company driver waits on a summer day in 1923 in front of the Iowa State Automobile and Tractor School, at the southwest corner of Eighth and Nebraska streets. Frank D. Hennessy began the school in 1917 on Pearl Street. The next year, he moved into the newly-constructed Davidson Day-Light Block, the north half of the structure shown. As the school grew, the south half was added. By 1922 there were 150 students learning to repair internal combustion engines, cars, tractors, farm lighting plants, and accessories. The faculty also taught general business practices.

This photo also shows the Hennessy-Fennell Tire Company, which sold Goodyear's "Barney Oldfield" tires. J. H. Hansen's Cadillac dealership is on the left, and Brown Van Storage is on the top floor.

The older portion of the building was badly damaged by fire on November 27, 1939, and was remodeled as a one-story structure. General Business Equipment Company presently occupies the portion on the left. Photo courtesy of Sioux City Public Museum

J. R. McGowan's Tire Company, at 901 Pierce Street, sells Firestone and General tires in this 1929 view. The firm also retailed oil, gasoline, and road-service batteries, while providing car washing and vulcanizing services. A branch of the Security National Bank now occupies this site.

In the background, the First Baptist Church is on the left, and the First Unitarian Church is on the right. Photo by N. N. Woodworth; courtesy of Sioux City Public Museum

Mayor Wallace M. Short and others pose during construction of the Big Sioux River Bridge in late 1922. The long-awaited replacement of the old bridge, declared unsafe by city engineer G. Y. Skeels some fifteen years earlier, brought relief to the business community, who feared the loss of its trade area, and to the traveling public, who motored along such majestically-named roads as the Sunshine Highway, the King of Trails, and the George Washington National Highway.

The city of Sioux City and Union County, South Dakota, jointly funded the $63,000 bridge, with Sioux City paying two-thirds of the cost. It was dedicated on March 1, 1923, and formally opened on May 12, 1923. Photo courtesy of Sioux City Public Museum

Mayor Wallace Short's third term (1922-1924) was a building period for the city. The local government approved bonds for a new Municipal Building in January 1923 and selected the plans of local architect E. R. Swanson. Contractor B. E. Short (no relation to the mayor) began construction that same year. In early 1924 the Sioux City Police and Fire departments and the police court system moved into the new structure, located at the southwest corner of Sixth and Water streets.

In 1931, the date of this photograph, the fire department (on the left) fronted on Water Street, while the police department occupied the Sixth Street portion, on the right. The courtrooms and related facilities were located on the third floor.

The situation remains virtually unchanged fifty-one years later. The size and deteriorated physical condition of the building, especially when compared to present police, fire, and jail requirements, have led to repeated efforts to secure new quarters. Photo courtesy of Woodworth Commercial Photos

The Methodist Hospital, as shown in an architectural rendering by the firm of Beuttler and Arnold, opened to the public on December 2, 1925. Contractor B. E. Short built the $410,000 structure at the southwest corner of Twenty-ninth and Douglas streets. It contained five surgical rooms on the top floor and had a capacity of 164 patients.

The Methodists had operated a hospital in Sioux City since about 1920, first in St. John's Hospital at Fourteenth and Jones streets, which had been given to the church by Dr. William Jepson, and later at the somewhat larger Samaritan Hospital at Seventeenth and Pierce.

The new Methodist Hospital, with several additions, continued in operation until 1966, when it joined with the Lutheran Hospital to form St. Luke's Medical Center. As new facilities were constructed in the 1970s, the former Methodist Hospital complex undertook a supporting role, housing services such as treatment centers, family planning, and a day care center for children of hospital employees. Photo courtesy of Sioux City Public Museum

One of Siouxland's earliest farm-to-market truckers delivers a load of milk cans to the Fairmont Dairy in 1925. Fairmont moved into the old Sioux City Brewing Company plant (later numbered 223 Wesley Way) in 1920, operating there until the company relocated to Highway 75 North in 1963. Photo courtesy of Woodworth Commercial Photos

Demonstrating the manner in which supple, young bodies were made strong and healthy, 3,000 Sioux City junior high school sudents take part in this monster, physical education exhibition, held at Gilman Terrace on June 1, 1926. This view includes only the East Junior High School contingent. The spire on the horizon belongs to St. Boniface Catholic Church. Photo courtesy of Sioux City Public Museum

Policemen direct traffic at the corner of Dace and Steuben streets during the Floyd River flood of September 18-19, 1926. The flood began after seven inches of rain fell in the Sheldon, Iowa region, sending the meandering Floyd out of its banks once again. The remodeled Stockyards Ballpark, dedicated just four months earlier, is on the right, and the Swift and Company plant is in the background. Photo courtesy of Sioux City Public Museum

A Sioux City Journal photographer captures 1,000 baseball enthusiasts on Sunday afternoon, October 3, 1926, as they congregate at Fifth and Douglas to watch the play-by-play report of the second game of the World Series via the Journal's electric scoreboard. The St. Louis Cardinals defeated the New York Yankees this day by a 6-2 margin behind the four-hit pitching of veteran hurler Grover Cleveland Alexander. The Cardinals triumphed in the series 4-3, winning the last two games in Yankee Stadium.

Fifth Street is in the background, with the Continental Building on the left and the First National Bank and the Frances Building in the center. Below the Harper Wall Paper and Paint Company sign, a dilapidated old car rests quietly on a lot which had held the old Lerch Block before fire gutted the structure on August 3, 1918. The lot later became the site of the Sioux City Transit System's Central Transfer depot. Photo courtesy of Sioux City Public Museum

The Fairmount Park Library, one of five public library branches financed through a 1926 $100,000 bond issue, opened in June 1927 and succeeded a branch library which had been started fourteen years earlier. William L. Steele and George B. Hilgers were the architects for all the new structures. The Fairmount Library, shown here in 1927, was one of the last local buildings designed in the prairie school style. F. J. Sulzbach was the contractor.

The building housed the branch library until 1970 and served as a social service neighborhood center during the remainder of the 1970s. Photo courtesy of Woodworth Commercial Photos

World War I veterans formed the Edward D. Monahan American Legion Post Band No. 64 and, in 1920, organized the Monahan Post Band. For twenty-eight years, the band was both a local and a national institution. It won first place honors at seven American Legion competitions, soon becoming known as the legion's official band.

The highlight of the band's impressive history, however, came in September 1927.

After scrimping and saving for months, most members were able to attend the American Legion convention in Paris. Their hard work and practice paid off, as the Monahan Post Band (shown here in Paris) was deemed the best band in attendance. Additional honors came in later years, and in 1948 the legion group disbanded and the Municipal Band was organized. Photo courtesy of Sioux City Public Museum

The Hawkeye truck (right) was a Sioux City product. Ralph A. Bennett organized the Hawkeye Truck Company in the mid-1910s as part of his local automotive empire. The first trucks were built at 313-315 Jennings Street. As the business expanded, the company moved in 1918 to two, single-story, day-light structures at 2700 Floyd Boulevard (later Hawkeye Drive).

By the early 1920s, Hawkeye Truck Company employed sixty-five people and assembled a number of models, ranging from a one-ton to a three-and-a-half-ton truck. A large number of the parts also were manufactured in Sioux City. The trucks were extremely well-built and were christened the Rolls Royce of Commercial Vehicles by the British press after a truck show in London. They also were very popular among area farmers and Midwestern business firms.

The 41,000 square-foot Hawkeye plant, shown behind the truck in this photo, was the headquarters for the company until 1934. The firm closed its doors that year, a victim of "hard times" and a nationwide restructuring of the auto and truck manufacturing industry. The plant became the temporary home of Wincharger in 1935 and today is used by the Means Towel Service Company. Photo courtesy of Woodworth Commercial Photos

"Here's another fine mess you've gotten me into, Stanley!"

Comedy film partners Oliver Hardy and Stanley Laurel lend their approval—and Ollie's weight—to a promotion of Sioux City-manufactured Kari-Keen auto trunks in 1930.

Mitchell, South Dakota, inventor Paul Lier designed this expandable, steel luggage and produce carrier in 1925. The Lier (later Kari-Keen) Manufacturing Company assembled its product in a series of locations as the company grew: the Warnock (Benson) Building, 3925 Floyd Avenue in Leeds, 509 Plymouth Street, and the Morley Twine Company's former plant at East Seventh and Division streets. The Kari-Keen Company employed over forty people and produced seventy-six types of attachments to accomodate virtually every make of automobile. The carriers were very popular as 1920s-vintage cars were not equipped with large trunks.

The Kari-Keen Company went out of existence in 1937, the victim of over-production and a change in automobile styles. The plant was the home of the Wincharger Corporation for many years. In 1982 the East Seventh Street structure was torn down. Photo by N. N. Woodworth; courtesy of Sioux City Public Museum

Flight instructors and students prepare for a hard day's training at Kari-Keen's Leeds Airport, circa 1930.

Formation of the Kari-Keen Aircraft Company in 1928, a subsidiary of the Kari-Keen Manufacturing Company, launched Sioux City—albeit briefly—into the aircraft manufacturing industry. The firm's chief product was the Kari-Keen Coupe, a two-passenger, high-wing, wood and steel monoplane of which four different models, ranging from 60 to 175 horsepower, were built.

Between thirty and fifty airplanes were produced by the company at their Plymouth Street plant between 1928 and 1930, with testing carried out at the firm's own airport (shown above right) at 4320 Forty-first Street in Leeds. As an added inducement to potential customers, the company also offered a complete private pilot's instruction course for only $425. Room and board was also available.

A lawsuit resulting from the disastrous crash and death of a company test pilot at Sioux Falls, South Dakota, put the Kari-Keen Aircraft Company out of business in 1930. The Leeds Airport collapsed with the company's demise, and the hangar shown here was moved to the Tri-State (Rickenbacker) Airfield. *Photo courtesy of Woodworth Commercial Photos*

Ryans, Stearmans, and a host of other well-known flying machines of the period are rolled out for this company portrait of A. S. Hanford Jr.'s Tri-State Airlines at Rickenbacker Field, circa 1930.

Rickenbacker Field, in Stevens (now North Sioux City), South Dakota, emerged from the dust of that ace aviator's pre-World War I auto victories at the former Interstate Speedway site to become Sioux City's first airport. Founded in the late 1920s by the Spotts Flying Service, the tiny, forty-acre, dirt flying field was taken over by Sioux City aero enthusiast and auto dealer Ryal Miller in 1928, and later acquired, along with Miller's Tri-State commuter airline company, by creamery heir Arthur S. Hanford, Jr. Despite completion of the Sioux City Municipal Airport, at Sergeant Bluff, in 1940, Rickenbacker Field, later known as Graham Field, remained an operational center for local private and light commercial flying until the early 1970s. *Photo courtesy of Woodworth Commercial Photos*

Developer Frank Buckwalter created the quiet and affluent Country Club district in the rolling hills of the city's Northside during the 1920s. This northeasterly- *looking view from the late 1920s shows the 4500 block of Country Club Boulevard and a portion of Manor Circle. Photo courtesy of Woodworth Commercial Photos*

Nebraska Street north from Third Street looks markedly different in 1982 than in 1928: every structure as far north as midway between Fourth and Fifth streets has been removed. The West Hotel burned in 1953, and the Hotel Howard, later the Mayfair Hotel (right) was torn down in 1964. The primary occupants in the four large buildings at Fourth and Nebraska were the Toy National Bank (southwest corner), Security National Bank (northwest), T. S. Martin store (northeast), and the Anderson furniture store (southeast). Nebraska Street carried two-way traffic until 1960, and in 1928 diagonal parking was used. Photo courtesy of Woodworth Commercial Photos

The Shrine Mounted Patrol began operations in the early 1920s in an attempt to advertise Sioux City and provide funds for the Shriners' laudable program to assist crippled children. The original mounted patrol included several types of horses. By April 26, 1929, however, when this view in front of the Swift and Company plant was taken, all steeds were pure white Arabians.

The Abu-Bekr White Horse Patrol continues to be a vital force today. It is recognized nationally and has appeared at numerous large parades and festivals. Photo by N. N. Woodworth; courtesy of Sioux City Public Museum

The Sioux National Bank, located at the southeast corner of Fourth and Pierce, folded on December 6, 1930. This view tells the sad tale of many people, as these distraught and bewildered depositors mill around the old bank, uncertain of their next step. Eventually depositors received a portion of their investments in the Sioux National, which sat empty until all remaining assets were sold in a receiver's sale on February 14, 1936. Photo courtesy of Woodworth Commercial Photos

Chapter 7

Time of Turmoil

1930-1945

The Great Depression dominated virtually every aspect of Siouxland life, leaving an indelible imprint on the men, women, and children who struggled through it. It was a time of economic, political, and social transition for Sioux City. Seemingly-solid businesses suddenly failed, and several banks closed their doors overnight, never to reopen. There were exceptions. The *Sioux City Journal* heralded the reorganization and reopening of the First National Bank, the city's largest and longest-continuing financial institution, as the major local news story of 1931.

The Depression also struck a devastating blow to Siouxland's agricultural economy. Farmers were beset by falling prices and drought conditions in 1931 and 1932, and the large number of small-town bank failures added to the agrarians' woes. In 1932 Woodbury County had three times more farm foreclosure suits pending than any other Iowa county.

Desperate farmers finally banded together under the leadership of long-time rural activist Milo Reno and declared a strike. They refused to sell their goods at less than "the cost of production"—the main economic plank of Reno's campaign. The Iowa *Union Farmer*, expressing the rural sector's antipathy for Wall Street barons and seemingly-uncaring money lenders, championed the cause of Reno and his thousands of Siouxland followers, by declaring:

Let's call a Farmers' Holiday,
A Holiday let's hold.
We'll eat our wheat and ham and eggs,
And let them eat their gold.

Sioux City became the center of a regional agricultural revolt in 1932 and 1933. The Sioux City Milk Producers' Association, an organization of Siouxland dairy farmers, began the Sioux City "Milk War" on August 11, 1932. The disgruntled farmers used hay-bale barricades, nails, reaper blades, and clubs to stop Sioux City-bound milk trucks in an attempt to force dairies to meet the association's demand for higher prices. The Farmers' Holiday Association members soon joined the siege, adding other types of produce to the list of blockaded items. The rural activists even halted a livestock train and set loose its cargo.

The *Sioux City Tribune* sided editorially with the strikers, stating: "Agriculture is sinking, slowly but surely. Driven desperate, it promises to go down fighting, if it does not actually survive. They have an inherent right to fight for their homes and families." The *Sioux City Journal* agreed with its competitor, but questioned the farmers' methods.

Several Midwestern governors or their representatives met in September 1932 at Sioux City's Martin Hotel in an attempt to calm what had become a regionally-explosive situation. A protest parade of nearly 5,000 striking farmers and their sympathizers highlighted the first day of the meeting. After three days of sessions, the governors issued only a mild report to Congress and President Hoover. The governors took few steps at the state level, where they could wield power. The farmers, unimpressed with the conference's luke-warm results, voted to return to the barricades.

On September 29, 1932, Democratic presidential candidate Franklin D. Roosevelt spoke in Sioux City during a whirlwind campaign tour, and six days later President Herbert Hoover, a former Iowan, delivered his key agricultural speech in Des Moines. The Great Depression and rural unrest caused a complete reversal in traditional local politics. Woodbury County, a Republican party stronghold since 1860, voted Democratic by a large margin in the 1932 election. The entire Democratic slate of candidates defeated their Republican opponents. The Republican-inclined *Sioux City Journal* summed up Roosevelt's landslide as, "merely a protest of an overwhelming majority of the electorate against the conditions of the times."

The Farmers' Holiday Movement continued after Roosevelt's victory. By early 1933 the "penny auction" was making headlines. Through this method, friends of a farmer facing foreclosure joined ranks and made ridiculously low bids for their neighbor's personal property, only to return it to the original owner. Woe to anyone who attempted to bid higher. Creditors received only a small percentage of actual values for livestock and farm machinery, causing the banks and insurance companies to institute their own moratorium on personal property foreclosure suits.

The Siouxland-centered revolt lost support, however, when a more-radical element entered the scene, causing the original leaders to lose control over events. The near-lynching of District Court Judge Charles C. Bradley of LeMars, on April 27, 1933, turned public opinion against the movement and doomed the cause. The last picketing in the Sioux City area took place in November 1933. While the Farmers' Holiday Movement failed to change the existing price structure significantly, it graphically advertised agriculture's

plight and sent a message to the federal government that staid, conservative, Republican northwest Iowans demanded action—and fast!

Sioux City and the nation welcomed Roosevelt's election as a mandate for prohibition repeal. On the evening of April 17, 1933, in a specially-called session of the city council, Sioux City became Iowa's first municipality to legalize 3.2-percent beer. The enactment of the Twenty-first Amendment on November 7, 1933, made national prohibition a thing of the past. Sioux City, still a wide-open workingman's town, did not adapt well to the state restrictions enforced by the Iowa Liquor Control Commission. Graft and protection rackets flourished, much to the city's embarrassment.

On April 2, 1935, former Sioux Cityan Verne Marshall, the crusading editor of the *Cedar Rapids Gazette,* attempted to link the payment of protection money by Sioux City saloonkeepers to state government officials. He announced before a legislative committee that, "although Sioux City has never been known as a model city from a moral viewpoint, I am telling you on indisputable evidence that conditions there have never been as sordid as since repeal came to Iowa and the crooks and grafters organized themselves in that place." "Poor old Sioux City," replied the *Sioux City Journal* to Marshall's brickbats, "the goat for the rest of the state again! Of course, no such wickedness exists in other cities in Iowa—that is, not much!"

A massive graft investigation that ensued made front-page headlines for over a year. The exposé resulted in the resignations of County Attorney Max Duckworth and Commissioner of Public Safety Henry C. Kuhlmann, a shake-up in the Sioux City Police Department, and the trial of Iowa Attorney General Edward L. O'Connor in Sioux City. More than forty persons were indicted, but the acquittal of O'Connor in his January 1936 retrial and legal technicalities led to the dismissal of the remaining cases. The stigma of public maladministration gave impetus to a movement to adopt the council/manager form of government. In a 1939 special election, however, voters opted to retain the commission plan.

Roosevelt's declaration of a "bank holiday" on his third day in office (March 6, 1933) allowed Sioux City's badly-battered financial institutions to stabilize, or fade from the scene entirely. The Roosevelt administration also instituted many agencies designed to create employment, reform alleged financial abuses, and speed the nation's recovery. Many believe that the billions of dollars disbursed by Sioux City-born, New Deal administrator Harry Hopkins helped avert an unemployment crisis bordering on social revolution.

Sioux City felt the impact of FDR's relief and recovery agencies as thousands of job-hungry men and women were put to work. Projects ranged from creating the Sioux City Art Center to improving the Floyd River, from financing a historical records program to widening, surfacing, and providing badly-needed storm sewers for Sioux City's streets. A massive Civilian Conservation Corps project at Stone Park offered unemployed youth the dignity of productive labor while creating a beautiful park and nature setting.

Tenuous labor/management relations marked the 1930s both nationally and locally. On September 29, 1938, a sit-down strike was engineered by CIO organizers at Sioux City's Swift and Company packing plant. When violence erupted, on October 18, 1938, Iowa's governor dispatched the Iowa National Guard to the strike scene. By the time the strike was settled, after 119 days, the Swift strike had become the nation's longest meatpacking labor dispute to that time.

Despite the efforts of business and government, poor economic conditions remained until the late 1930s. At that time, however, Roosevelt's "Dr. Win-the-War" replaced "Dr. New Deal" as the nation geared up its military. The December 7, 1941, attack on Pearl Harbor plunged the nation into World War II. Sioux Cityans reacted instantly, and thousands marched off to war. World War II replaced farm strikes, prohibition, graft, and economic difficulties as the community's foremost concern from 1941 to 1945. Hardly a week went by without the announcement of yet another Siouxlander's final commitment to the nation. Nearly 400 Woodbury County men lost their lives.

In 1942 Sioux City's brand-new municipal airport, which until recently had existed only as a little-known and lightly-used sod airstrip, became the Sioux City Army Air Base. Between 1942 and 1945, thousands of pilots, navigators, gunners, and bombardiers received their training here in the intricacies of flying the world-famous B-17 Flying Fortress, B-24 Liberator, and B-29 Super Fortress, the most powerful aircraft of the Second World War.

The local residents joined with business, labor, government, and private organizations in supporting the nation at war. Rationing, War Bond drives, Victory Gardens, and the collection of scrap metal, grease, paper, and other items became common practices in the early 1940s. The food industries produced vast amounts of meat, dried eggs, and dried milk products for the war effort. The Wincharger Corporation, the world's largest wind-generator manufacturer, became the area's foremost defense plant, producing radio components, aircraft dynamotors, and giant wind machines designed to teach novice army glider pilots how to fly. Albertson and Company (later Sioux Tools) also played a significant role.

After years of growing anxiety, Sioux Cityans reacted to Japan's surrender on August 14, 1945, more with relief than with wildness. Crowds gathered at downtown street corners, but there was little confetti thrown. Sioux City's Polish-American community, joyful at the close of hostilities which had so harmed "the old country," held an impromptu and sincere celebration at South Westcott and Marshall Street, with residents dancing to accordion music. The next day, a large but rather restrained victory party was held at the Grandview Park Bandshell. Siouxlanders looked forward to beating their swords into plowshares.

Federal, state, and local governments attempted to counteract the vast economic problems of the Great Depression through various relief and recovery agencies. This photograph of hundreds of people lined up in front of the Social Agencies Building, at 315 Sixth Street, graphically depicts the plight of a sizable part of the populace throughout the early 1930s.

The building had been built as a residence and had served as the city detention hospital (1904-1913) and the police headquarters (1916-1924). On the right is the old City Hall, at the northwest corner of Sixth and Douglas. Photo courtesy of Sioux City Public Museum

The old Peavey Grand Opera House is on its last legs in this October 1930 photograph. It then housed the less-than-pretentious Grand Hotel, while Harry Zanfes' seven-booth cafe occupied the former site of the Iowa State National Bank. An even sadder note is that the once-ornate stage area had been relegated to serve as Hans Esperson's auto repair garage. The building burned on November 5, 1931. Photo courtesy of Woodworth Commercial Photos

Prior to 1929, only briar patches covered this 175-foot hill above Thirty-third and Rebecca streets. By the spring of 1930, however, when this photo was taken, it was well on its way to becoming a college.

Briar Cliff was founded as a women's college in 1929 by the Sisters of St. Francis, a Dubuque-based order, in conjunction with the Catholic Diocese of Sioux City and a funding committee of Sioux City business leaders. It opened as a two-year liberal arts college in 1930, with a total enrollment of twenty-four students and thirteen faculty members. It expanded to a four-year program in 1937 and became co-educational in 1966.

This photograph shows Heelan Hall under construction while grading crews with horse-drawn "frezno" scrapers whittle away at the nearby hilltops. Photo courtesy of Briar Cliff College

The Most Reverend Edmund Heelan, bishop of Sioux City, presides over the March 30, 1930, cornerstone laying of Heelan Hall, Briar Cliff College's first building. The photo also shows that suburban development is well under way in the Perry Creek Valley below. Photo courtesy of Briar Cliff College

Whether they were arriving or departing campus, Briar Cliff College students of 1936 faced an invigorating climb both ways. Shown here are Lois Dolan, Rose Marie Viet, Helen Hurley, and Mary Ellen "Mickey" Donahue. Photo courtesy of Helen Hurley Hurlburt

171

A contingent of Sioux City firemen pose with their rigs for this circa 1930 photograph north of Sixth Street along Douglas Street. George M. Kellogg (standing left of center between the pumper and the chief's car) was in his forty-first year as Sioux City's fire chief. He retired on November 15, 1939.

City Hall is on the left, with the Brooks-Pillar used car dealership, the Wetmore Automobile Company, the Auditorium, and the Warnock (later Benson) Building in the background. On the right is the Federal Building (foreground) and the Woodbury County Courthouse. Photo courtesy of Woodworth Commercial Photos

This 1930 view, looking south from Fifth and Jackson streets, shows the E&W (Ennanga and Walker) Clothing House occupying the ground floor of the Metropolitan Block (on the left), while a host of retailers are on the right.

A sign on the just-completed Badgerow Building advertises that new office spaces are available. B. E. Short's contracting firm had constructed the twelve-story, light-colored structure in 1929-30 for a trio of Sioux City businessmen—A. M. Seff, Herman Galinsky, and Egbert Badgerow. One person who evidently read the sign was the photographer of this image, Norman N. Woodworth. "Woody" moved his studio to the Badgerow Building in 1931. Photo courtesy of Woodworth Commercial Photos

One thousand men, women, and children, representing every Sioux City branch of organized labor, participate in this gala Labor Day parade through the business district on September 1, 1930. The parade, considered one of the largest in the city's history at that time, was witnessed by the thousands of people who gathered along the downtown streets and atop numerous buildings. This vantage point is the newly-completed Badgerow Building, at the southwest corner of Fourth and Jackson streets, looking west on Fourth Street. Photo courtesy of Russell Parmenter, San Antonio, Texas

The Roberts Sanitary Dairy Company was located at 809 Douglas at the time of this 1923 view. The company's slogan was Our Wagon Passes Your Door.

Nine years later, at their new location at West Fourteenth and Omaha streets, the city's largest milk dealer was at the center of the Sioux City Milk Strike. Roberts and most other dairies then paid farmers one dollar per hundred-weight for 3.5 percent butterfat milk. Embittered dairy farmers organized the Sioux City Milk Producers' Association on August 9, 1932, rallied behind Milo Reno's basic tenet of "cost of production" prices, and demanded $2.17 per hundred-weight for their goods. The farmers threatened to withhold their produce if their figure was not met. When J. R. Roberts, president of Roberts Dairy, scoffed at the ultimatum, the "milk war" began.

Farmers took to the road, blockaded highways, stopped and searched trucks, and dumped milk destined for Sioux City dairies. The agrarians also distributed free milk at seven city locations, preferring to give the product away rather than sell below cost.

The short-lived strike proved beneficial to area farmers, for on August 20, 1932, local dairies offered a compromise price of $1.80 per hundred-weight. The producers accepted. I. W. Reck, president of the Sioux City Milk Producers' Association, stated that the strike succeeded because of the free milk program, the support of the Farmers' Holiday Association, and the sympathy of Sioux City residents. Regional agricultural problems persisted, however, because non-dairy farmers, armed with pitchforks, had stormed Siouxland's highways on August 15, 1932, protesting market prices for other produce. Photo courtesy of Woodworth Commercial Photos

Truck Caravan Arrives Under Escort of Sheriff Here

Woodbury County Sheriff William R. Tice and his deputies pause in Greenville while escorting a caravan of fourteen livestock-carrying trucks from Cushing, Iowa to the Sioux City stockyards on November 8, 1933. According to Ralph E. Rippey, Plymouth County sheriff from 1931 to 1937, the near hanging of LeMars District Court Judge Charles C. Bradley, who had refused to stop farm foreclosure proceedings, broke the back of the Farmers' Holiday movement. While most agreed that the agrarian sector needed economic help, they would not tolerate the lynching of judges.

The last vestiges of picketing occurred in November 1933. Sheriff Tice described the protesters as "reds from Sioux City." Most area farmers had abandoned the movement because it was apparent that the holiday embargo was not affecting other Midwest markets and because they had lost faith in the venture. Many of those who had instigated the farm protest in 1932 were playing leading roles in Law and Order leagues, organizations designed to squelch the picketing. An extensive poll conducted by the Des Moines Register revealed that 77.15 percent of those farmers surveyed opposed the continuation of the farm strike, and 72.42 percent of them approved of the measures adopted by President Roosevelt. The Farmers' Holiday movement had ended. Photo from Sioux City Tribune; courtesy of Sioux City Public Museum

For more than a decade, Oscar M. Hartzell perpetuated a preposterous fraud on thousands of Americans, especially Siouxlanders, by promoting and selling shares in the mythical estate of legendary buccaneer Sir Francis Drake. Hartzell began the hoax in 1922, while in London, when he contacted people in America and claimed that he had become acquainted with the sole heir of the illegitimate son of Sir Francis Drake. Hartzell further disclosed that the heir had charged him with restoring the multi-billion dollar estate to its correct status and legal owner. The promoter's lieutenants intimated to their followers that Hartzell would return $5,000 for each dollar they invested. The results were amazing, and Hartzell lived well for ten years off his weekly take of $2,500. Finally, in 1932, England deported Hartzell as an "undesirable alien," and the United States government brought charges against him for using the U.S. mails to defraud.

A federal grand jury indicted Hartzell, and he stood trial in Sioux City at the old Federal Building, present-day City Hall. Flamboyant local attorney Carlos W. Goltz served as his chief defense attorney. Hartzell had so completely bamboozled the investors that, even after they were forced to admit that they had invested heavily and had not received anything in return, the contributors willingly testified as character witnesses for the defense. Even more amazingly, a group of original "shareholders" paid Hartzell's legal expenses and his bond, and continued to send him $2,500 a week.

The prosecution ultimately convinced the jury that the Drake estate promotion was fraudulant, and Hartzell was convicted on November 15, 1933. Federal Judge George C. Scott sentenced the schemer to a ten-year term in the Leavenworth, Kansas, penitentiary and levied a $10,000 fine on the defendant.

As a sidelight to the case, Oscar Hartzell complained about the quality of the photographs used by the newspapers in reporting the trial. He even had photos taken by Youngberg Studio and delivered to the press. Little did he suspect, however, that the Sioux City Tribune would doctor one of these likenesses following the verdict by adding cell bars. Photo by Youngberg Studio; courtesy of Sioux City Journal

Asks Resignation

F. Price Smith, a virtual unknown before being elected county treasurer in the Democratic landslide of 1932, served a stormy tenure of less than two years. Investigations and scandals characterized Smith's time in office. Routine audits generally revealed discrepancies and cash shortages, resulting from Smith's habit of exchanging his worthless checks for county funds. F. Price Smith was suspended from office on November 22, 1933, but later reinstated. The board of supervisors appealed the case to the Iowa Supreme Court.

The Democratic party naturally considered Smith to be a political liability in 1934 and selected Ray L. Duggan as its candidate for county treasurer. The Republicans chose Van W. Hammerstrom. The election was extremely close, with Duggan receiving 13,741 votes, Hammerstrom tallying 13,903, and Smith, running as an independent, garnering 737 votes. Smith likely swung the election to the Republicans by attracting disgruntled Democrats, and Hammerstrom began his forty-one-year tenure as county treasurer.

One week after the 1934 general election, the Iowa Supreme Court reversed the lower court decision and ordered the removal of Smith from office. F. Price did not go willingly. He dipped into county moneys one last time, took $2,000, and fled. Sheriff William R. Tice spread a dragnet for the former treasurer, and, the next day, two deputies captured F. Price Smith hiding in a chicken coop near Pender, Nebraska. Photo from the Sioux City Tribune; courtesy of Sioux City Public Museum

The staff of the County Recorder's Office pose for this December 1934 photograph. They are (sitting) Lewis B. Lunde, recorder John F. "Jack" Wilson, Frank A. Lynch; (standing) Olive Call, Bonita Williamson, and Fayola Hendrickson. Ragna E. Wold, standing on the far right, was the principal of Floyd Elementary School.

Prior to 1932, the Democratic party was a negligible factor in county politics. County recorder candidate Jack Wilson and his Democratic running mates swept to victory, however, in the FDR landslide of 1932. The party remained competitive throughout the 1930s, which led to an increased turnout of voters on election day. Wilson remained in office until his death on March 28, 1941. By 1942 the Republican party had regained almost complete control. Photo courtesy of Sioux City Public Museum

Soon after the repeal of prohibition in 1933, a new management resurrected the Sioux City Brewing Company in the former Interstate Brewing Company plant at the southeast corner of West First and Isabella streets (circa 1935). The new firm manufactured Heidel Brau and Western Brew brands of beer. The Sioux City Brewing Company operated until 1958, and a series of bars and discotheques have since occupied the main structure. Photo courtesy of Woodworth Commercial Photos

County Attorney Max E. Duckworth resigned from office less than three months after Cedar Rapids Gazette editor Verne Marshall undertook to show that part of the liquor and gambling payoffs in Sioux City ultimately found its way into the pockets of state officials. Marshall had announced publicly that Duckworth was a ringleader in the local crime circle.

The board of supervisors selected twenty-eight-year-old Maurice E. Rawlings (shown bottom) as the new county attorney on May 21, 1935. Rawlings (1906-1982), an Onawa, Iowa native, had served as an assistant to Duckworth during 1933-34, before resigning over an ethical dispute with the county attorney. The supervisors evidently presumed that such a problem would undoubtedly be an asset for Rawlings.

The remaining graft cases consumed a large part of Rawlings' time in 1935, yet he actively pursued a course of ridding Sioux City of its Little Chicago atmosphere. Former District Judge Ralph W. Crary, who served as an assistant county attorney under Rawlings in 1937, described Rawlings's efforts and the local crime scene: "I know he was very active, and really took out after graft and corruption. He was very successful, and closed up a lot of places around town. And it was a bad situation. The underworld had a lot of things going for it in those days."

Rawlings was county attorney for seven-and-a-half years, until Edward L. Moran defeated him in the 1942 general election. Rawlings later served as regional director of the Office of Price Administration during World War II, legal advisor to the city council, president of the Sioux City Board of Education, and district court judge. He climaxed his fine legal career by serving on the Iowa Supreme Court from 1965 to 1978. Photo courtesy of Maurice E. Rawlings

Most of the large number of southern and eastern European immigrants who came to Sioux City to work in the packinghouses lived in the Floyd River "bottoms" south and east of downtown. This is a rather typical residential scene of the region in 1934, showing Lafayette Street. Photo courtesy of Woodworth Commercial Photos

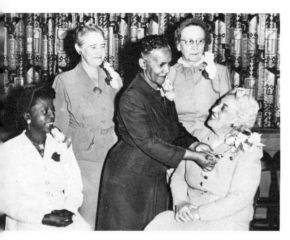

The Booker T. Washington Community Center opened in 1933 at 722½ West Seventh under the administration of Lena N. Thomas. The organization moved in 1944 to 912½ West Seventh and in 1951 to 1700 Geneva Street, into a building whose construction had been financed by Sioux City philanthropists Arthur and Stella Sanford. Renamed the Sanford Community Center, it remains today as an integral part of the city's Westside.

These five long-term leaders and advisors of the Sanford Community Center gathered for the organization's twentieth anniversary celebration on October 23, 1953. All were original board members and had played significant roles in the development of the institution. Beulah Webb is shown pinning a jeweled gift on the lapel of Mary J. Treglia, while Elzona B. Trosper (seated), Mabel Hoyt (standing left), and Caroline Kriege look on. Photo courtesy of Sioux City Journal

The Community House was organized in 1921 and had its headquarters on the second floor of Edwards and Browne Lumber Company's office at 1604 Fourth Street. The primary goal of the institution was to assist in "Americanizing" the new residents—teaching English, offering classes in citizenship, and helping the immigrants adjust socially and economically—while still maintaining the flavor of the old country culture.

The Fourth Street location soon proved inadequate for the growing needs of the organization, and groundbreaking ceremonies for a new building at 513 Morgan Street were held on February 26, 1933. Shown here in 1934, the year of its opening, this $37,000 structure received the wholehearted support of the community and actually cost only $8,000, the remaining materials and labor being donated. The

Community House operated from this building for twenty-nine years, finally moving to 900 Jennings Street in 1963, when the Floyd River rechannelization project swept away the Morgan Street building.

Dorothy Anderson served as the Community House's first director, succeeded in 1926 by Mary J. Treglia. Herself the daughter of Italian immigrants, Treglia (1897-1959) is one of the most interesting personalities in the city's history. A gifted athlete, Mary Treglia played for the all-female Bloomer Girls baseball team and appeared in several silent motion pictures before assuming the directorship of the Community House. She administered the agency for thirty-three years. The institution was renamed the Mary J. Treglia Community House in her honor. Photo courtesy of Woodworth Commercial Photos

In 1926-27, Arthur Sanford's Frances Building Corporation constructed the $1,750,000 Frances-Orpheum Theatre, at the southeast corner of Sixth and Pierce. The lavishly-decorated, 2,600-seat New Orpheum Theatre opened on December 19, 1927, and became Sioux City's center for "high class vaudeville and the best feature photoplays."

In this mid-1930s summer view, signs advise residents who are considering seeing Douglas Fairbanks in Reaching For the Moon that "It's Refreshingly Cool Inside Sioux City's Own Summer Resort."

A four-story addition to the New Orpheum was completed by March 1949. The Sioux City Gas and Electric Company and its descendant, Iowa Public Service Company, occupied much of the building from 1949 to 1980. Photo courtesy of Woodworth Commercial Photos

One of the members of FDR's brain trust was former New York social worker Harry L. Hopkins, who was born in this house, at 512 Tenth Street, on August 17, 1890.

Hopkins held a succession of important positions in the Roosevelt administration. He began as head of the Federal Emergency Relief Administration (FERA) in May 1933, and added the duties of the Civil Works Administration (CWA) the following November. Hopkins became chief of the Works Progress Administration (WPA) in 1935 and secretary of commerce in 1938. Illness caused Hopkins to relinquish his Commerce Department duties in 1940, but he continued as one of Roosevelt's chief lieutenants during World War II.

Hopkins administered the spending of nearly $9 billion in national work relief programs during the 1930s, providing employment for many Siouxlanders. According to historian John N. Schacht, Hopkins worked under a simple philosophy that "if people need work, it should be made available to them....Afterwards his friends and foes agreed on at least one point: not a penny ever stuck to Hopkins' fingers." Photo courtesy of Julie Goodson

The Sioux City Public Schools purchased, according to long-time board secretary H. C. Roberts, "a very uninviting tract of sixteen acres between Vine and Peters Avenues and South Rustin and South Cecelia Streets" for $10,000 in 1925. In the hopes of providing East High School with an athletic field, an engineer drew plans for a football stadium, complete with a quarter-mile track and bleachers on both sides. The plans sat in a vault for eight years due to a lack of construction funds.

In the winter of 1933, however, the Civil Works Administration, one of Franklin Roosevelt's New Deal agencies, allocated money to local governments for the creation of jobs to combat massive unemployment. Sioux City received an allocation large enough to employ 4,000 able-bodied men for three months. Roberts recalled: "The Stadium plans were dusted off and 1,800 men were working with wheelbarrows and shovels within a week." The men were divided into two shifts, each working five hours a day.

These two photographs, taken by K. B. White, document the huge undertaking and the accomplishments made in just eleven days. In the view (on the left), taken at 12:20 p.m. on December 11, 1933, and looking northeast from the corner of South Irene Street and Peters Avenue, a large number of men are just beginning the process of leveling the rolling hills at the northwest corner of the tract and filling in the low spots. They are using horses to cut down the hills and nearly fifty trucks to haul the dirt. No work has started on the east end, where the stadium was to be built.

In the view on the right, the western portion has been changed drastically, and fully half of the men are busy performing a similar task on the eastern portion. There are also fewer trucks involved; two days earlier, the CWA had ruled that all of its projects should become more labor-intensive.

Building engineer K. B. White demonstrates the precision of his profession in his description of this view: "Taken Friday, December 22, 1933, from the edge of the bank on the west side of the sidewalk twelve feet south of Peters Avenue on the southwest corner of South Rustin Street and Peters Avenue, facing northeast at 11:35 a.m."

Work continued on the project for six years: preparing the football field with its underground watering system, erecting the bleachers, installing the lights, and much more. Roberts Stadium, named in honor of H. C. Roberts, has been the principal field for Morningside College and the Sioux City school system since the 1940s. (H. C. Roberts, The Public Schools of Sioux City, Iowa). Photo courtesy of the K. B. White family

Sioux City's largest WPA project was the Floyd River Improvement project, employing over 300 workers and lasting five years. The attempt to tame the potentially-dangerous Floyd began on November 22, 1935, when previously-jobless men began widening the channel from Grand Avenue north to Twenty-eighth Street. The second stage, constructing a concrete channel on the lower mile, commenced on December 8, 1937, and was still in progress in 1940, when this photograph, looking upriver, was taken. These men worked a thirty-hour week and received an hourly wage from thirty-seven to fifty-four cents. Photo courtesy of Division of the State Historical Society, Iowa City, Iowa

Improving local roads was another project funded by the WPA. These men are widening Military Road in 1936. Photo courtesy of Division of the State Historical Society, Iowa City, Iowa

The Monahan Post Band began an active campaign for a music shell in Grandview Park in 1930, but for several years little progress resulted because of a lack of money during the first years of the Great Depression.

Roosevelt's New Deal provided the financing, however, and local architect Henry L. Kamphoefner's award-winning plans, along with hundreds of unemployed persons, were put to work. The project began on May 5, 1934, sponsored by the Civil Works Administration (CWA), and later under the umbrella of the Federal Emergency Relief Administration (FERA). The Iowa Emergency Relief Administration and the city government also contributed funds. Kamphoefner served as architectural inspector, and engineer K. B. White supervised construction.

The labor-intensive project concluded on May 24, 1935, and two days later the Grandview Music Pavilion was dedicated. Iowa Governor Clyde L. Herring gave an address and the justly-proud Monahan Post Band provided the music.

The dedication program aptly summarizes the project and the famous band shell, "Out of the chaos of the worldwide depression Sioux City emerges with a temple to music and beauty which will be an inspiration as long as the Grandview Music Pavilion stands." Today it continues to function as the summer home of the Municipal Band, the descendant of the Monahan Post Band. Photo courtesy of Woodworth Commercial Photos

WPA workmen hand weave a giant revetment mattress of green willow saplings around wooden river pilings during the first stages of construction of Gordon Drive, in 1941.

Prior to 1949, highway travel between downtown Sioux City and Riverside was limited to a circuitous and often congested route along West Fourth Street via the Bruguier Bridge, with heavy truck traffic restricted to an equally treacherous Military Road. Gordon Drive was the solution to that problem. Begun in 1939 and completed ten years later, the three-and-a-half-mile river road was constructed throughout much of its distance from the river itself, utilizing pilings, stone rip-rap, and willow mattresswork as shown above, with sand dredged from both the Missouri and Big Sioux rivers as a foundation. The eighty-foot-wide highway project, named in honor of pioneer Sioux City builder and promoter William Gordon, opened in 1949 and linked the city with South Dakota Highway 77 at

Riverside. A decade later it was widened and raised and became part of Interstate 29.

Photo courtesy of Division of the State Historical Society, Iowa City, Iowa

This horde of WPA employees is cutting down part of a hill overlooking Half Moon Lake and landscaping the area in 1935. This project provided for a new roadway and allowed the creation of Pulaski Park, which was developed into a large-scale youth baseball complex in the late 1970s. The Cudahy and Company plant is in the background. Photo courtesy of Division of the State Historical Society, Iowa City, Iowa

Among the numerous WPA projects in Sioux City during the 1930s and early 1940s were two sewing programs. The County Sewing Room (shown here) was in the basement of the Woodbury County Court-house. The project began on December 18, 1933. By July 1940, it employed twenty-seven women. In addition to providing much-needed employment, the program had a second purpose. The clothing and other materials manufactured by these workers were distributed to the "one-third of the nation" that President Roosevelt described in his 1937 inaugural address as "ill-clad." Photo courtesy of Division of the State Historical Society, Iowa City, Iowa

The Post Office and Federal Building, fronting on the south side of Sixth Street between Pearl and Douglas streets, is depicted in this 1934 photo. Construction began in late 1932, at the height of both local farm unrest and the presidential campaign. Federal offices began operation in this structure on January 2, 1934, after vacating the old Federal Building (later City Hall).

The Sioux City Journal *offered this comment on the 317-by-150-foot building, "Born as it was, in the midst of an economic disturbance, this magnificent structure stands as a monument to public confidence and prosperity." Photo courtesy of Woodworth Commercial Photos*

Mount Sinai Temple, at the southeast corner of Fourteenth and Nebraska, shown here in 1939, served Sioux City's followers of Reform Judaism for fifty-five years and one day.

Although the congregation had been formed in 1895, it was in November 1898 that plans were completed for a permanent meeting place. The Sioux City Journal, on November 29, 1898, described one unique fund-raising plan for the structure: "Mount Sinai Congregation . . . has started the 'endless chain' of letters . . . . Each person who receives a letter is expected to contribute 10 cents and ask two friends to do the same. Each of these friends in turn asks contributions from two more, and so on without limits."

Speakers, music, and flowers highlighted the building's dedication on September 1, 1901. In the 1950s the members decided to build a new house of worship, and ground-breaking ceremonies for the present edifice took place on August 10, 1955. The old Mount Sinai Temple closed on September 2, 1956, but the building soon became the United Orthodox Synagogue. Photo courtesy of Sioux City Journal

The giant Wincharger Corporation was born in this farm building near Cherokee, Iowa, in the early 1930s. This circa 1934 photo shows brothers John and Gearhard Albers working with their father on one of their earliest propellors.

The brothers moved to Sioux City and began the Wincharger Corporation in 1935 in the old Hawkeye Truck Company plant at 2700 Hawkeye Drive. In 1937 the company required more space and moved to the old Kari-Keen Manufacturing Company plant at 2201 East Seventh Street.

Zenith Corporation purchased Wincharger in the 1930s (although the Wincharger name was retained for many years). The firm eventually started making radios and other electrical products. Wincharger (Zenith) moved to a new plant in the Tri-View industrial area in 1967. Photo courtesy of Sioux City Public Museum

The generators produced by the Albers brothers and their employees were a familiar sight on American farms prior to rural electrification; thousands of Winchargers were manufactured annually during the late 1930s.

A new 110-volt direct drive unit, called the "Streamliner" in this advertisement, reached the market about 1940. The company informed local farmers that electric lights would increase egg production and urged the agrarians to "let free electricity milk your cows" and bring you "new worlds of radio enjoyment."

Ronald Patnaud, a Wincharger employee for over forty years, is shown in this advertisement. Patnaud frequently was featured in sales brochures because he was "handsome in the Clark Gable tradition." Photo courtesy of Sioux City Public Museum

Central High students organized the International Relations Club in the spring of 1934, originally to improve their understanding of the League of Nations, but later to discuss current world affairs.

In 1935 the members posed for this club photo with the Castle on the Hill in the background. Shown here top row, are: Marjorie Howard, June Blake, Katherine Hampe, Rosanna Dikel, Sadie Taxer, Miriam Barish, and Anthe Keriakedes. Middle row: Margaret Pederson, Elizabeth Miller, Vida Nemesio, Esther "Eppie" Friedman (described as "Peppy and cute"), Pauline "Po-Po" Friedman ("Cute and Peppy"), and Betty Lou Mangold. Bottom row: Olga Keriakedes, Elsie Aspland, advisor Miss Nora Nelson, Mary Ellen Ault, Ernest Jenkinson, Sidney Kalin, and _____ Lee. From the 1935 Central High School annual; courtesy of Sioux City Public Museum

The Central High School class of 1936 held its fortieth reunion in 1976. The Friedman twins, "Eppie" and "Po-Po," were among those who attended. After graduating from Central, each had attended Morningside College as journalism majors, had written for the Collegiate Reporter, and, in the mid-1950s, had become widely-read "advisors to the lovelorn," with each of their columns syndicated nationally.

On the left is Pauline Esther "Po-Po" Friedman, who writes under the name of "Abigail Van Buren" or "Dear Abby." Esther Pauline "Eppie" Friedman, on the right, is better known to millions as "Ann Landers." Photo courtesy of the Sioux City Journal

This circa 1937 view from the Floyd Cemetery shows the weaving Floyd River and the Grand Avenue Viaduct.

The new viaduct, constructed under the mayoral term of W. D. Hayes, became a political issue in the 1938 municipal election. Mayor Hayes, running for an unprecedented fifth two-year term, was challenged by local attorney David F. Loepp. Loepp claimed that the bridge "began nowhere and ended nowhere" and used the viaduct as an example of waste in government.

The voters elected Loepp, but they have used Hayes' creation for decades. Photo courtesy of Woodworth Commercial Photos

Sleek racehorses glistening in the rain—two east-bound Milwaukee Road Hiawatha locomotives pause at the railroad's Second and Pierce Street station for this rare twin-portrait of steam's finest hour.

Sioux City's only streamliners operated on the Milwaukee Road's "crack" daily- and nightly-passenger trains through Sioux City from Mitchell and Sioux Falls, South Dakota, to Chicago during the final days of steam passenger service in the late 1930s and 1940s. Milwaukee Road passenger service through Sioux City ended in 1965, followed by the abandonment of the line's freight service in 1980. Photo courtesy of the Spaghetti Depot

"Big bands" rose to prominence in the 1930s and 1940s, and nightclubs and dancehalls were an important part of Sioux City's recreational scene.

On April 30, 1939, Watertown, South Dakotan Lawrence Welk brought his band and this female singer to the Skylon Ballroom, located atop the Commerce Building. "The patrons of the Skylon are assured of an evening of the finest entertainment and dance music," ballroom manager Mark Scobel announced prior to the event, for "after an absence of two years, Lawrence brings back his famous music which so popularized him in the east. He no doubt is well on his way to national fame." Photo courtesy of Woodworth Commercial Photos

Teenagers congregate in what is presently called Ravine Park, located along the south side of Lincoln Way in Morningside, circa 1940. The park, which also has been known as Garretson Park, Quick Park, and South Ravine Park, has been the setting for recreation and reflection since the 1890s.

August Williges informed the members of the Woodbury County Pioneer Club on December 12, 1931, that the proper name for the area was "Quick Park," because Williges' close friend J. Herbert Quick walked these hills and there received the inspiration for his first production—Fairyland. Photo courtesy of Division of the State Historical Society, Iowa City, Iowa

American Pop Corn Company president
Howard C. Smith, circa 1940.
Cloid H. Smith and his son Howard
began shelling, cleaning, and packaging
popcorn in 1914 in the family's home at
2727 Nebraska Street. The American Pop
Corn Company built its first corncrib in
Leeds later that year and added facilities in
Schaller, Iowa, in 1918. Both plants have
grown tremendously; the maker of Jolly
Times has become the world's largest
popcorn company. Photo courtesy of
American Pop Corn Company.

"Eat More Jolly Time Pop Corn." Two
teenagers successfully hawk their product in
1942 in front of Toller's Drug Store, located
in the old Krummann Block at the northeast corner of Fourth and Court streets.
People's department store is visible across
the street. Photo by N. N. Woodworth;
courtesy of American Pop Corn Company

This aerial view of the city's Northside features St. Joseph's Hospital, located north and west of Twenty-first and Court streets. The photo, taken in May 1943, marked the opening of a new $500,000 hospital addition. The medical complex's prior capacity of 200 beds increased to 300 beds through the new wing and the remodeling of older structures. Another massive expansion took place in 1952.

Reverend Superior Agatha and the Sisters of Mercy started St. Joseph's Hospital in 1890 at the northeast corner of Twenty-eighth and Jennings streets, in a house that promoter John Peirce had built as a wedding present for one of his daughters. The marriage plans, however, had fallen through. It became apparent almost at once that the hospital needed more space, and the sisters purchased John Peirce's personal residence, called Ingleside, and the surrounding acreage. Several sizable buildings were added in the ensuing years.

The rolling hills in the background later were subdivided into lots and became the Indian Hills area. Photo courtesy of Woodworth Commercial Photos

The lights from the 1941 Christmas display on Fourth Street reflect off the newly-fallen snow and the parked cars. This view looks west towards Nebraska Street; the T. S. Martin store is on the right, and a series of furniture and clothing stores are on the left. The tranquility of this scene belies the actual situation, however, for this was the December of Pearl Harbor. Photo courtesy of Sioux City Public Museum

Sioux City Municipal Airport came into existence in 1938, when the city purchased 240 acres of farmland and a small airstrip near Sergeant Bluff. It was dedicated on October 27, 1940. The airfield, after a WPA-supported improvement program, boasted two 3,200-foot runways and one 3,900-foot runway, as well as a modern terminal building for passenger and flight operations, making it the region's most modern air facility.

The U.S. Army, at the outbreak of World War II, leased the Sioux City Municipal Airport, together with an adjoining 1,020 acres, as a training base for bomber crews. It was a massive community of buildings and people. On September 30, 1943, at the peak of operations, 943 officers, 5,180 enlisted men, and 52 WACs were stationed at the Sioux City Army Air Base, en route for assignments in the European, North African, or Pacific war theaters. Among the thousands of men and women who trained here were such notable figures as the brother of U.S. Army General "Hap" Arnold, and Hollywood actor Jimmy Stewart, who arrived as a lieutenant and left as a captain. The end of hostilities brought a halt to bomber-training activities at the Sioux City Air Base and a brief role as a U.S. Army separation center for returning soldiers.

Since 1945 a succession of closings and recommissionings have colored Sioux City Municipal's military career. These events included the airport's reactivation as a training center for the 174th Fighter Squadron of the Air National Guard in 1950 and for the 2470th Air Reserve in 1962. The U.S. Air Force selected the Sioux City Air Base as one of twenty-one national defense sector centers and constructed a $52-million, semi-automatic-ground environment (SAGE) complex at the base for the Air Force's Thirtieth Air Division.

The Sioux City Municipal Airport, deactivated by the air force for the final time in 1969, retains its military traditions as home to the 185th Tactical Fighter Group of the Iowa Air National Guard.

Excitement abounds on August 1, 1944, as civilians are allowed on the grounds of the Sioux City Army Air Base for the first time since its opening. The B-17G (shown here), the latest example of military technology, draws spectators like a magnet.

The banner proclaims the city's success in the Fourth National Bond Sale. Raising money to help the war effort was a major responsibility of those on the homefront, and Siouxlanders rose to each and every occasion. Photo courtesy of Sioux City Public Museum

Grading and paving crews extend the runways on the Sioux City Municipal Airport—later U.S. Army Air Base—near Sergeant Bluff in 1941. Although Sioux Cityans approved four separate bond issues to finance these improvements. Works Progress Administration funds from Roosevelt's New Deal programs absorbed the largest share of the project's labor costs. Photo courtesy of Division of the State Historical Society, Iowa City, Iowa

An unidentified air corps weatherman trainee checks out equipment atop the wooden weather tower at Sioux City's Army Air Base in 1944, as his colleagues inside track an outgoing flight of B-17 Flying Fortresses en route for one of many practice bombing fields in the area. A foursome of shiny-new P-51 fighters also await missions on this cold winter's morning.

This photo was taken from the base's original control tower. Photo courtesy of Sioux City Public Museum

In 1944 Crew No. 4100 of the 244th Army Air Force's Base Unit, Combat Crew Training School at Sioux City pose with their "bird" for the unit's yearbook prior to departing for Europe. Shown here, kneeling, are: Sergeant W. F. Otto, Watertown, Wisconsin; Sergeant C. M. Ryan, Seminole, Oklahoma; Sergeant L. A. Harris, Idaho; Sergeant W. H. Parks, New Springfield, Ohio. Standing: Staff Sergeant M. N. Maizel, New York City, Second Lieutenant G. Tomea, Clifton, New Jersey; Second Lieutenant H. P. Sperber, Bronx, New York; Second Lieutenant J. W. Henry, Brooklyn, New York; and Staff Sergeant R. H. Lull, Coulee Dam, Wisconsin.

"Beside us," intoned the editors of the air base's first and only World War II yearbook, "are our 'chutes, fleece-lined flying clothes, sextants, cameras and guns. In our planes there are bombsights, gun turrets, and the engines and controls to fly them. We've learned to use all of these, and we've learned teamwork to perfection. Soon we're 'going across' to meet our opponents, and we know we're ready!" Photo from Final Approaches a yearbook of the 224th A.A.A. Base Unit, Combat Training School, 1944; courtesy of Jim Henry.

In 1947, the Wincharger Corporation erected a massive FM transmission tower on Prospect Hill for KSCJ radio station. The next year, Wincharger employee Ronald Patnaud scaled the tower and took this and the three following views of Sioux City's Westside, downtown, and riverfront districts. All four images provide fantastic documentation of the houses on Prospect Hill.

Bluff Street is in the foreground of this northwesterly-looking image. The open area on the left is the old Dr. John K. Cook Park, and St. Boniface Catholic Church is beyond the park. The large building in the center then housed the Pepsi-Cola Bottling Company of Sioux City. Photo by Ronald Patnaud; courtesy of Sioux City Public Museum

Chapter 8
All-American Challenges, All-American Solutions
1945-1962

A roller coaster-like spirit of abundant joy and bitter disillusionment characterized the first decade of the post-World War II era in Sioux City. The euphoria shown locally over V-E (Victory in Europe) Day in May 1945 and V-J (Victory in Japan) Day in September of that same year was tempered by the shutdown of Sioux City's bomber base and a mild recession that invariably follows any war. But World War II—*The War* to a generation of Sioux Cityans—mercifully was over. Loved ones would at last be coming home.

The era opened with vitality as Sioux City's voting populace, their ranks now swollen with thousands of progressive young vets of Guadalcanal and "the Bulge," pushed to completion several major civic improvements delayed by the war, as well as a number of new endeavors. Construction of the new Municipal Auditorium, which had been halted in 1943, resumed, and the completed structure opened in September 1950. Other public and private buildings sprang up rapidly when post-war shortages of materials and labor allowed. The city government moved into its "new" home in the remodeled former Federal Building on October 28, 1948, and launched a flurry of substantial street and road projects. The largest of these was the completion of the long-awaited Gordon Drive "river road" between downtown Sioux City and Riverside.

During this period the city also resumed ownership of the former Sioux City Army Air Base as the Municipal Airport. This sprawling former bomber base, with its small city of giant aircraft hangars, barracks, and other facilities, soon was recognized as a mixed blessing. Some viewed the takeover of the base's high operating costs as a burden that post-war Sioux City could ill afford.

The northern downtown area is seen in this view to the northeast. Bekins Van and Storage Company, at Fifth and Wesley Way, is in the center. In the background, Central High School appears to look over the city in much the manner of a feudal castle.

Fourth Street highlights this easterly-looking photograph, with the Battery Building visible at Fourth and Water streets. The old Judge Zuver residence, at the "southwest" corner of West Second and Kansas streets, had lost most of its once-elegant appearance by 1948.

The Combination Bridge dominates this view to the southeast. The bridge's northern (Iowa-side) turning span is totally above dry land. Within ten years this span would be removed.

On the Iowa side, the outlet for Perry Creek is just beyond the bridge. On the Nebraska side, a cluster of cottages and small homes occupy the future site of the Marina Inn. Photos by Ronald Patnaud; courtesy of Sioux City Public Museum

Such economic problems combined with a series of natural and man-made tragedies in the early 1950s to sink Sioux City morale to one of the lowest points in its history—in some ways a bleaker time than the great crash of 1893.

On August 28, 1951, local and national indignation erupted against Sioux City when Memorial Park Cemetery refused burial to Korean War casualty Sergeant First Class John R. Rice because he was part-Indian. The act drew outrage and heated criticism from the U.S. Senate and President Truman. Although municipal officials and the majority of Sioux Cityans opposed the terrible injustice done to Sergeant Rice and his family, Sioux Cityans—at least to the outside world—appeared powerless or unwilling to act. Eight days later, John R. Rice was laid to rest with soldiers' honors in Arlington National Cemetery. The incident dramatized the racial discrimination found both locally and nationally, and caused Sioux Cityans great embarrassment.

A nationwide polio epidemic in the late 1940s and early 1950s struck Sioux City and the Siouxland area with special vengeance. In 1952, the worst year of the onslaught, local hospitals were overcrowded with 923 victims of the dreaded paralysis. Swimming pools and other public places thought to harbor the disease were avoided, and parents fearfully sent their children to school. In the end, despite mass inoculations and other preventive measures, hundreds were left crippled.

During that same year, 1952, the Missouri River swelled far beyond its banks, wreaking monumental damage to Sioux City, South Sioux City, and hundreds of neighboring Missouri Valley communities. As if to aggravate an already-devastating situation, the Floyd River in 1953 smote the city with its most disastrous flood on record, driving thousands from their homes and businesses and leaving millions of dollars in property damage in its wake.

Gross dissatisfaction with local government's apparent impotence in the face of these and other troubles led advocates of the council/manager plan in 1953 to attempt to change the form of Sioux City's government. Supporters argued that, not only was the old commission system unable to cope effectively with many of the city's problems, but that it also suffered from a lack of checks and balances and was riddled with maladministration. As one pro-manager campaign pamphlet summed up, "Taxes have reached an all-time high, and confidence in our public officials has reached an all-time low." Council/manager promoters further reasoned that a part-time council could both create policy and direct a professional city manager with far greater efficiency—and honesty—than could be had by the old commission system.

In a landmark election held April 28, 1953, Sioux City voters cast their ballots in favor of the new system that would take effect in January 1954. Ironically, in November 1953, a Woodbury County grand jury indicted Public Safety Commissioner Nicholas P. O'Millinuk, Parks Commissioner Drew H. Fletcher, and Finance Commissioner Clem A. Evans on a variety of graft and bribery charges. Fletcher and Evans pleaded guilty to lesser charges and resigned their posts. City purchasing agent Frank Bennett also resigned under pressure. The commission form of government, thus, had faded from the city scene by the end of 1953. Since that time, the council/manager system has been challenged at the polls on five occasions (1959, 1963, 1970, 1975, and 1979), but the voters have sustained the plan each time.

Sioux City's first city council under the new plan—George Young, Carl J. Wolle, C. Fred Stilwell, Paul Beck, and Harold O. Benson—selected Robert Hoisington of Springfield, Ohio, as the community's first city manager. During Hoisington's stay, the machinery upon which future council/manager administrations were to function was set firmly into motion.

With hard times behind them, the community was in a mood to celebrate. The opportunity came in July 1954, as Sioux City, now 100 years old, rejoiced in its centennial. Men grew beards; women donned calico dresses and bonnets; wagons and buggies of grandpa's day were fetched out of hiding and harnessed. A week-long birthday party replete with parades, athletic contests, and a 282-page historical supplement to the *Sioux City Journal* highlighted the event. The largest production of the centennial was the Sioux City *Centurama,* a ninety-minute historical pageant boasting a cast of 2,000 Sioux Cityans. Performed at the Public School (later Roberts) Stadium, the *Centurama* played to enthusiastic audiences for seven nights from July 24 through 31. Wally W. Wilson, who later became mayor, served as chairman of the week-long festival.

A change of leaders and a birthday celebration seemed only a temporary respite for a city plagued by half-a-decade of reverses. The prevailing optimism quickly evaporated when the Cudahy Packing Company, the city's largest meatpacking plant in terms of employees, announced on September 27, 1954, that it would be shutting down its Sioux City plant, thus leaving 1,700 wage earners without jobs. Cudahy officials cited chronic financial losses stemming from outmoded facilities and competitor pressure as the cause, but recurring Floyd River flood damage could not have helped the situation.

Once again, dedicated Sioux City leaders banded together to tackle this and other problems face-to-face. In 1956 an eight-week long Sioux City Study, funded in part by the Ford Foundation and chaired by adult education coordinator John F. Schmidt, brought together nearly 600 Sioux Cityans from all walks of life to discuss the city and its problems and to propose remedies. Individual suggestions varied, but the group reached a consensus on the projects of highest priority: flood control, an expanded industrial base, improved transportation systems, business district renovation, upgraded health and sanitation services, and overall civic beautification. Paramount to achieving these goals was a renewed sense of civic pride. Backed by this list of challenges and a supportive media, the entire community set to work.

The Sioux City Industrial Development Council, an offshoot of a revitalized local chamber of commerce, took the lead in 1957 with the announcement of its plans to develop the mile-long riverfront dumping grounds and hobo jungle west of the Combination Bridge into the city's first industrial park. By the end of the decade, several large plants employing a growing number of Siouxland laborers had become firmly established at the Tri-View site.

Expansion also took place in other areas as positive attitudes and favorable economic conditions took root. Sunset Plaza—Sioux City's first shopping center—sprang up during the late 1950s and early 1960s to serve the rapidly-growing Westside and Northside suburbs. Briar Cliff and Morningside colleges added new buildings to their expanding campuses, and the passage of a $2.2-million bond issue allowed the Sioux City school system to construct several new structures.

In 1958 Cornelius "Conny" Bodine, Jr., became Sioux City's second city manager. Under his youthful and farsighted leadership, the city developed and implemented long-range planning and, with the aid of other governmental branches, mobilized its resources toward the completion of several large-scale projects. Construction of Interstate Highway 29 along Sioux City's under-utilized riverfront during the late 1950s—part of a multi-billion dollar national highway network—was one of the highlights of Bodine's administration. Inter-governmental planning and cooperation resulted in the local pace of highway construction exceeding state and national averages.

The ever-present threat of the Floyd River's periodic ravages, however, continued to haunt the city. The Floyd River Valley contained the entire stockyards region, miles of railroad trackage, and thousands of homes. Firms situated in the flood-prone area employed fully half of the city's work force. Even the slightest rise of the unpredictable Floyd signaled economic and human disaster, and the fear of flooding stagnated the basin area. As early as 1892, the cry had been raised to "fix the Floyd." A series of attempts, including the WPA-sponsored Floyd River Improvement project of the 1930s and 1940s, had failed to solve the problem, as the 1953 flood demonstrated. The time had come for action.

Beginning in the late 1950s, federal, state, and local officials, with the support of the community at large, set into motion the massive Floyd River Rechannelization project. Northwest Iowa Congressman Charles Hoeven spearheaded the measure through Congress. Even though much of the project's actual work would not take place until the following decade, the groundwork played a major role in boosting the city's industrial, economic, and social morale.

Evidence of an economic upturn also was reflected in the city's population figures as the number of residents grew from 83,991 in 1950 to 89,159 in 1960, providing a modest, yet heartening, increase. The new look, the new blood, and the fresh ideas of a youthful generation of leaders already were taking effect.

Under the leadership of Marjorie Howe, community leaders worked diligently to secure for Sioux City the All-America City status which had barely eluded the town's grasp in 1959. Their efforts paid off. The nation recognized Sioux City's work, resilience, and unusual fortitude on March 14, 1962, when *Look* magazine and the National Municipal League selected the Iowa river community as one of only eleven American cities to wear the coveted All-America crown. Sioux City was the first city in Iowa to achieve this honor.

It was a fitting reward for a decade of hard work. The city still was far from perfect, but as noted pollster George H. Gallup, foreman of *Look*'s All-America City jury pointed out: "The awards are given for citizen teamwork rather than for municipal perfection. To be selected an 'All-America City,' a community must show noteworthy accomplishments through alert, continuing citizen participation."

The popularity of the hit tune "Sioux City Sue" led the chamber of commerce to conduct its own Sioux City Sue contest: girls without red hair and blue eyes need not apply. Of the ninety girls who responded, local civic clubs sponsored twenty-three finalists. Before a gathering of thousands at the Grandview Park Bandshell on August 11, 1946, Dick Thomas, co-composer of the song, selected nineteen-year-old Gayle Jean Hofstad to be Sioux City Sue.

Gayle, born in Elk Point, South Dakota, and graduated from Central High School in 1945, was an employee in the Junior Miss department of Davidson Brothers store. In addition to winning a new fall wardrobe, the Sioux City Journal stated that she received a free trip to Hollywood, a tour of the studios, a chance to meet many stars, and "best of all if it turns out right—the promise of a screen test and possibly a contract with the Republic studios."

Sioux City Sue was heard to say, "I never dreamed that this would happen to me." Photo by George Newman; courtesy of Sioux City Public Museum

This October 21, 1946, Sioux City Symphony concert at the Orpheum Theatre was a special event in the local social life. The Sioux City Music Association had secured renowned soprano Frances Greer (standing right of center), a veteran of forty-eight performances at the Metropolitan in just four years, as the featured soloist. In addition, this Monday evening concert marked the return of the Maestro, Leo Kucinski (standing left of center), after three years in the armed services.

Kucinski and music have been synonymous in Siouxland since the 1920s. He accepted a teaching position at Morningside College in 1923 and immediately became concertmaster for the Morningside College Symphony, which grew to become the Sioux City Symphony. Kucinski became director in 1926 and retained the position, except for

the World War II period, until 1977. Starting with a group of less than twenty people, the Polish-born conductor helped build the organization's membership and attendance; sixty-nine instrumentalists are shown in this 1946 view. Kucinski also led the Monahan Post Band and its successor, the Municipal Band, from 1929 until the late 1970s, although he was not a member of the post until 1946. In addition, he directed other regional musical units and worked with the community school. Siouxland has been fortunate to have such a "music-man."

The Sioux City Concert Course and the Sioux City Symphony, now under the direction of Thomas Lewis, remain vital parts of the community's cultural life. Photo courtesy of Woodworth Commercial Photos

A mood of expansion engulfs this July 1947 Sunday noon aerial shot of Morningside College. The A. W. Jones Hall of Science, started the preceding year, is taking shape, with building materials sitting in wait. Eight other major structures would be built in the twenty-seven years following this photograph, as the college spilled north across Peters Avenue and southwest towards and across Sioux Trail.

In the background, left, are found Roberts' Stadium, a portion of Lewis Park, including the tennis courts, and Lillian E. Dimmitt Hall, the women's dormitory. Two years later, ground would be broken just east of Dimmitt Hall for Allee Gymnasium.

In the center are the college's three oldest extant buildings. Charles City Hall, earlier called the Conservatory of Music, the oldest structure, is on the right, with Lewis Hall (earlier Main Hall) in the center. On the left, directly behind the construction site, is the old gymnasium. It later served for three years as a student activity and art center, and since 1956 has been the college library.

In the left foreground is Grace Methodist Church, with members of the congregation enjoying pleasant conversation after the service. This church building, dedicated in 1908, was the third home of Morningside's oldest congregation. It burned on January 31, 1957, and was replaced by a new church building. Photo courtesy of Morningside College Library

The old Municipal Auditorium, at the southwest corner of Seventh and Douglas, was deemed inadequate by the late 1930s, and efforts were made to obtain a building capable of matching the needs and wants of the community. After defeating two earlier bond issues, city voters approved a $590,000 auditorium construction measure on November 8, 1938. They also unofficially selected the riverfront location between Pierce and Pearl streets as the building site, choosing it over nine other locations.

The project moved slowly as city officials tried unsuccessfully to secure federal aid for the auditorium's construction. Finally, in April 1941, the city council issued the bonds and selected the plans of local architect K. E. Westerlind, a former associate of William L. Steele's. Work stopped on the project in 1943, though, because of the pressing war needs. At that time, only the basement had been dug, pilings had been driven, and concrete footings had been poured.

On May 20, 1947, voters approved a $975,000 bond issue, and the project was revived. Problems and cost overruns,

however, continued to haunt the auditorium. In this 1948 view, the building's shell was taking shape, but much remained to be done, and the funds were dwindling. To complete the project, Sioux Cityans overwhelmingly supported a whopping $1,140,000 bond issue on April 26, 1949. Photo courtesy of Woodworth Commercial Photos

Sioux City's Municipal Auditorium on September 9, 1950. This was opening day, an event nearly twelve years in the making. Through delays, post-war inflated prices, and other problems, the $590,000 auditorium of 1938 ultimately cost $2,705,000 by 1950. Despite the expense, however, the community could now look with pride at their Municipal Auditorium. Photo courtesy of Sioux City Public Museum

Tragedy struck Sioux City's stockyards district on December 14, 1949, when a sudden blast ripped through five floors of the Swift and Company packing plant at 11:33 a.m. killing twenty employees and one truck driver, and injuring ninety-one more. In this photo, taken minutes after the disaster, Swift employees join firemen and volunteer rescue workers searching for victims among the debris. An undetected natural gas leak was thought to be the cause of the city's worst industrial accident. Photo courtesy of Sioux City Public Museum

Sioux City's United Packinghouse Local members joined civic and church groups to aid Swift plant explosion victims and their families. Photo courtesy of Division of the State Historical Society, Iowa City, Iowa

Through much of the twentieth century, Sioux City's stockyards district was serviced by its own railroad line, the Sioux City Terminal Railroad. Although this mid-city railroad, founded in 1907, operated in just a one-square-mile area, it provided a vital interchange between the city's five major railroads and an estimated twenty-five track-miles of cattle unloading docks, packinghouses, and private industrial spurs in the district. During the line's peak years of operation, in the 1920s, SCTR crews shipped and received an estimated 600 cars of livestock, meat products, fertilizer, hay, feed, and fuel daily, employing as many as eleven locomotives around the clock.

Sioux City Terminal Railroad officers and staff, shown here at the company's receiving yard in 1951, are celebrating the arrival of the railroad's first diesel-electric locomotives. Packing plant shutdowns and farm-to-market trucking brought about the abandonment of the SCTR in 1970. Stockyards industries today are served by the Burlington Northern Railroad. Photo courtesy of Sioux City Stock Yards Company

In the late 1940s and early 1950s, the nation suffered through severe polio epidemics, which hit the Siouxland region more forcefully than almost anywhere else. While the dreaded disease had claimed some victims in the 1930s and early 1940s, it was in 1946 that a significant rise in numbers was noted, with 188 cases treated in Sioux City, primarily by two main treatment centers—St. Joseph's and St. Vincent's hospitals. Eleven deaths were reported. After a decline in 1947, the total shot up to 274 persons afflicted in 1948, resulting in twenty-one deaths. The period from 1949 to 1951 was quieter, but the worst outbreak hit in 1952. In that year, local hospitals treated 923 cases, 53 of these fatal, in the bleakest point in the city's medical history. The polio epidemic peaked the same year as the massive Missouri River flood, and the double-barreled disasters captured headlines across the nation and focused attention and sympathy on the Sioux City area.

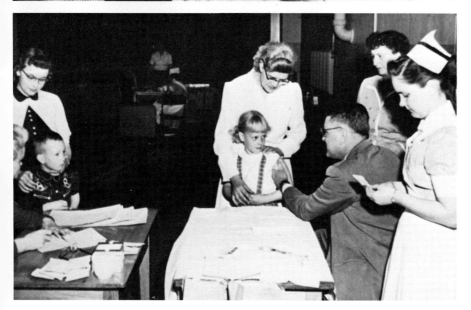

United community action, augmented by national health agencies, gallantly attempted to stem the tide of suffering in 1952. A twenty-one-member team of doctors and nurses arrived in July to establish treatment sites for the inoculation of 16,500 Woodbury County and Dakota County, Nebraska, children with gamma globulin, a blood derivative. Also, under the joint direction of Dr. and Mrs. J. H. Humphrey, many iron lungs were flown to Sioux City by Sioux City Air Base personnel for use in treating those already afflicted. This view (above), taken on November 30, 1952, shows one such respirator en route to a Sioux City hospital. Photo courtesy of Sioux City Public Museum

Comedian and goodwill ambassador Bob Hope journeyed to Sioux City during the height of the 1952 epidemic to head a polio benefit show sponsored by the junior chamber of commerce. After the show, he visited hospital polio wards and lifted the spirits of the afflicted. These four unfortunate youngsters seem both awed and pleased by Hope's presence and heartfelt good wishes. Photo courtesy of Sioux City Public Museum

The locally-severe 1952 polio epidemic resulted in Sioux City's being selected as one of the nation's first testing spots for Dr. Jonas Salk's vaccine. Medical personnel, school officials, and volunteers pooled their efforts to make real progress against the much-feared disease. On May 4, 1954, at Smith Elementary School, Dr. Donald B. Blume prepares to inoculate six-year-olds Frances Cook and Michael Delaney with the first of three scheduled injections. Photo courtesy of Sioux City Journal

Rapid thaws after heavy snows in the spring of 1952 caused massive flooding in Siouxland and the entire Midwest. In late March, the Floyd and Big Sioux rivers left their banks, serving only as a portent of things to come. On April 13, 1952, the Missouri River swelled beyond flood stage, causing multi-million dollar damage for communities and farmsteads from lower South Dakota to Missouri and Kansas. Low-lying South Sioux City, Nebraska, was especially hard hit, with fully half the town under water. Photo by George Newman; courtesy of Sioux City Public Museum

A scene from Prospect Hill shows part of the throngs that gathered to get a cross-country view of the raging Missouri River. On the left, dikes protect the water-encircled Municipal Auditorium.

CBS news analyst Edward R. Murrow overlooked a similar scene on the Missouri River and filed this report:

> *I'd like to offer you some impressions. There is being waged on both sides of the Missouri River a grim and grinding battle. Fatigue and determination mark the faces of men and women. The white men crowded the river too closely, but they're determined not to retreat. The people don't seem to hate the river. They're too busy trying to control it. They may win or they may lose. Whatever the outcome may be, these people have already met the big test. The people who live along the Missouri have gained a certain dignity from this fight with the river and they've set an example of fortitude and hard work. Somehow, we shall eliminate these recurring battles with our rivers, the terrible waste of property and energy. Tonight, those who've left their homes along the Missouri have done what they can, and now they can only wait. If the whole Congress could see this, something surely would be done.*

Indeed, something was done. Massive expenditures of federal money financed the building of dams and the stabilization of the Missouri River, thus taming the "Mighty Mo." Photo courtesy of Sioux City Public Museum

The most severe Floyd River flood on record hit with a sudden fury on June 8, 1953, following 8-to-11-inch rains the preceding day in the Sheldon, Iowa area. At James, Iowa, just north of Sioux City, the river was estimated to be eleven-and-a-half feet above flood stage. Not a single county road bridge over the Floyd was left standing from Sheldon to Sioux City. The rampaging river knocked out dikes and rudely surprised Floyd Valley residents and workers in nearby industries.

The flood waters swept quickly through Sioux City, striking Leeds, Springdale, the stockyards, and the South and East bottoms. The disastrous flood resulted in the loss of fourteen lives and property damage measured in the tens of millions of dollars.

Leeds was hard hit by the 1953 flood, as was the case in all Floyd River overflows. This view, looking north along Floyd Boulevard from Forty-first Street, was taken on June 9, as the water began to recede. Young Byron Blackstone looks forelorn as he sweeps mud from in front of the Leeds Hardware, operated by his uncle, Byron D. Blackstone. Other merchants also were busy cleaning up in front of Michael Danese's confectionery and Wag's Hut restaurant. The Council Oak grocery store is in the foreground. Photo by George Newman; courtesy of Sioux City Public Museum

The rampaging Floyd reopened its pre-1904 channel to the Missouri River during the afternoon of June 8, 1953. This photograph reveals that the water bisected the railroad right-of-way, leaving the C & NW tracks at the west edge of the stockyards swinging in the air like a hanging footbridge. Railroad cars, a large portion of the Sioux City Terminal's rail yard, stock pens, and livestock all fell victim to the terrible force of this wall of water. Photo by George Newman; courtesy of Sioux City Public Museum

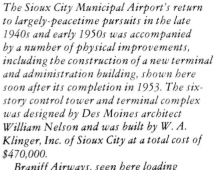

The Sioux City Municipal Airport's return to largely-peacetime pursuits in the late 1940s and early 1950s was accompanied by a number of physical improvements, including the construction of a new terminal and administration building, shown here soon after its completion in 1953. The six-story control tower and terminal complex was designed by Des Moines architect William Nelson and was built by W. A. Klinger, Inc. of Sioux City at a total cost of $470,000.

Braniff Airways, seen here loading passengers and mail in front of the terminal, had early Sioux City connections. It purchased Mid-Continent Airlines, the descendant of Sioux Cityan A. S. Hanford, Jr.'s Tri-State Airline Company, which had originated at Rickenbacker Field in 1928. Braniff ended service to Sioux City in 1967. Photo courtesy of Woodworth Commercial Photos

The construction of the $1-million Badgerow Building and $1.25-million Warrior Hotel, referred to in its beginning stages as the Fontenelle Hotel, significantly changed Sioux City's skyline in 1930. Designed by Kansas City architect Alonzo H. Gentry and built by the Blackstone Realty Company, the 300-room Warrior Hotel was first leased and later purchased by Omaha hotel magnate Eugene C. Eppley.

The Sheraton Corporation of America purchased the Warrior and Martin hotels from the Eppley Hotel Company and added the word "Sheraton" before each hotel's name on July 16, 1956. Since then the structure has had several owners, including Sioux City contractors Joseph and Frank Audino, who changed the hotel's name to the Aventino Motor Inn, as well as the Security National Bank and W. A. Klinger, Inc. Photo courtesy of Woodworth Commercial Photos

West Seventh Street has been the commercial avenue of Sioux City's Westside for decades. In this 1962 photograph, looking towards the "northwest" corner of West Seventh and Bluff streets, the Westside Hardware and Toy store occupies the corner building. Surrounding the hardware firm on two sides is the Miller-Kidder Chevrolet truck dealership, while on the far right, along Bluff Street, is the Hutton-Tufty used car lot. Photo courtesy of Woodworth Commercial Photos

Sioux City celebrated its centennial in late July of 1954. Wally W. Wilson, who later became mayor, chaired the week-long event; many other citizens supervised committees and organized activities. The community, beset with monumental problems, rallied with great energy to this up-beat celebration.

On Monday, July 26, 1954, at 10 a.m., the eleven-block-long Children's Centennial Parade began from the intersection of Seventh and Douglas. A photographer captures television station KVTV's filming of the event. Photo courtesy of KCAU-TV

Youngsters gape as Canyon Kid (right) interviews cowboy star Hoot Gibson (center) in 1953. Jim Henry's "Canyon Kid's Show" on KVTV (later KCAU) television station has entertained more than two generations of area children. Photo courtesy of Jim Henry

Early television personalities had to be flexible, well-rounded, and (hopefully) the possessors of fine senses of humor. KVTV (later KCAU) announcer, newscaster, and weatherman Ken Lawson is shown here as host of "The Little Rascals." He later served as news supervisor for KMEG-TV and, since 1971, has been director of the Siouxland Community Blood Bank.

City voters elected Lawson to the city council in November 1981. His victory was impressive in that he was the highest vote-getter, he won far more precincts than the other candidates combined, and he finished no lower than third in any precinct. The new city council selected him as Sioux City's mayor in January 1982. Photo courtesy of KCAU-TV

The city is buzzing with excitement. A huge interstate highway system is in various stages of construction, and Christmas of 1958 is fast approaching.

The old and the new come together in this image of Prospect Hill and the city's western downtown and residential areas. In the background, Briar Cliff College is on the left, and the Sunset Plaza Shopping Center is in the center. In the foreground, residents of the city's oldest section look down upon the new Combination Bridge cloverleaf. This I-29 interchange, opened on December 15, 1957, was the first section of interstate highway completed in Iowa. Photo courtesy of Sioux City Public Museum

The downtown core, appearing prosperous and established, with its Christmas decorations on display, would soon be embarking on a long and extensive renovation period which would alter the skyline significantly. The area east of the Municipal Auditorium would experience an almost complete overhauling, with motor lodges and grocery stores replacing railroad facilities, implement dealers, and seed companies. Central High School and St. Joseph's Hospital adorn the background. Photo courtesy of Sioux City Public Museum

This view of the stockyards region, taken in July 1957, depicts the prevailing hum of activity in Sioux City. The Raskin Packing Company, on the right, had helped to relieve the economic strain brought about by the closing of the Cudahy plant. The old Floyd River channel winds its way past Sioux City Cold Storage and Armour and Company. Despite the WPA project, the channel was still far from ideal.

Beyond the railroad bridge, construction is under way on Interstate-29, part of a gigantic, nationwide highway program. The bridge across the mouth of the Floyd River is being anchored to recently-removed sand from the Missouri River. The land had to be extended to allow sufficient room for the new thoroughfare along the river bank. On the left, a towboat pushes another load of rock to be placed along the shore line. Photo by George Newman; courtesy of Sioux City Public Museum

The construction of I-29 meant the destruction of many houses in the South Bottoms area. An even greater change was in store for the old neighborhood, however, for most of the remaining homes were right in the middle of the new Floyd River channel. On the left is the East Bottoms area, which virtually disappeared during the Mary Treglia urban renewal project. Two other residential neighborhoods—Greenville and Coles Addition—are in the background center and right. Many of the people in these homes worked in the grain elevators, rail yards, stockpens, and meatpacking plants shown here. Photo courtesy of Sioux City Public Museum

This view of Morningside, Greenville, and neighboring farmlands was obtained by looking east over the stockyards. Tenuous economic conditions afflicted the local meatpacking industry at the time as national companies closed older and supposedly less-efficient plants. Cudahy ceased its Sioux City operation in 1954, and the Sioux City Cold Storage Company now occupies part of the old plant. On the right is the Armour plant, which closed in 1963. Photo courtesy of Sioux City Public Museum

The Big Sioux River, forming the boundary between Iowa and South Dakota, meanders past Riverside Park towards its confluence with the Missouri River circa 1958. A footbridge connects the Sioux City Boat Club with its golf course in South Dakota. In the background, downtown Sioux City is on the left, and South Sioux City and Dakota County, Nebraska, are on the right.

Interstate 29, built in stages along Sioux City's riverfront, is under construction. The foreground portion already is paved, but the stretch between Riverside and downtown remains unfinished. The Gordon Twin Drive-In and the Riverside Boulevard interchange occupy the former site of the Interstate Fair grounds, and the old Bruguier Bridge is seen to the left of the eastern-most movie screen. Photo courtesy of Sioux City Public Museum

John Peirce's mansion had several occupants in the years following the infamous raffle of 1900. The best remembered owners were the T. S. Martin and J. Earle Martin families. Martha Zanfes, who lived there from 1948 to 1951, attempted to sell the residence through a second lottery in 1950, but law enforcement officials halted the project almost immediately. From 1951 to 1957 the structure served as a residence for Lutheran Hospital nursing students. Photo courtesy of Sioux City Public Museum

The Junior League of Sioux City purchased the Peirce mansion in 1958 for $10,000 for the purpose of providing the city with a cultural building. In this view, on April 23, 1959, during a formal dedication on the front porch, Mrs. Bernice L. Holtze, representing the Junior League, turns over the deed of the property to councilmember Carl J. Wolle, acting on behalf of Mayor Wally Wilson.

The Sioux City Public Museum, formerly housed in the Sioux City Public Library's main branch, opened at 2901 Jackson Street in 1961. Photo courtesy of Sioux City Public Museum

Sioux City Art Center instructor Joe Dailey works with a group of nine-to twelve-year-olds on December 4, 1959. During this Friday afternoon class, held on the fifth floor of the Commerce Building, the students evidently are decorating canisters with their watercolor creations, turning the containers into personalized wastebaskets.

The people on the outside of the tables are, clockwise from lower left, Mary Jo Wiedemeier, Pam Kass, Barbara Davey, Joe Dailey, Barton Levich, Eugene Kempers, Patty Scoblic, and Margaret Goode. Those on the inside of the tables, clockwise from lower left, are Shelly Hagan, Carol Wiedemeier, Virginia Hanlon, Julianna Haviland, and Diane Swanson.

The organization of the Sioux City Society of Fine Arts in 1914 signaled the beginning of the town's arts programming, with both exhibitions and classes offered. When WPA funds became available, the Sioux City Art Center was launched, formally opening on February 20, 1938, at 615 Pierce Street. The Sioux City Art Center was Iowa's only WPA-supported arts project to survive the cessation of federal funds. The art center later occupied space in the Commerce Building, a building at 617 Douglas, and since 1966, at its present site at 513 Nebraska Street. Photo courtesy of Sioux City Public Museum

Hundreds of people, young and not-so-young, flock to the old Leif Erickson swimming pool at Thirty-first and Court streets circa 1960. Although work began on the pool in late 1933, as a CWA project, the $90,000 pool was not completed and dedicated until June 8, 1941. A sand beach originally surrounded the pool, but it was replaced by concrete during the polio epidemic of the late 1940s and early 1950s because it was feared that the sand served as a transmitting agent for the disease. The city government built a new swimming pool in the same park in 1978.

In the background, to the east, one of the first buildings of the Valley Park Apartments is visible. Photo courtesy of Sioux City Public Museum

Remember, keep your racket extended! These dozen youngsters are taking tennis lessons at the Lewis Park courts circa 1960. The instructor is demonstrating to them the technique of serving.

The city began adding many leisure-time facilities and programs in the late 1950s. These tennis enthusiasts were among the fortunate ones who were accepted into the over-subscribed youth tennis classes. Photo courtesy of Sioux City Public Museum

The lights of downtown Sioux City illuminate this evening view from the railroad bridge in 1962. Interstate 29 from the Combination Bridge to the Bridgeport Industrial interchange formally opened in July 15, 1960, granting a greatly improved transportation system to the community. Photo by Woodworth Commercial Photos; courtesy of Sioux City Public Museum

Early warnings and massive citizen effort averted extensive damage along the lower Floyd River in the March 1962 flood. Military personnel, boy scouts, and residents filled and piled 450,000 sandbags along the river's dikes in just eighty-four hours, a rate of almost ninety per minute around the clock. A federal grant of $215,000 helped to offset the enormous flood prevention costs. Photo courtesy of Sioux City Public Museum

Mayor George Young and Marjorie Howe, chairperson of Sioux City's All-America Recognition committee, unfurl the All-America City flag on the steps of City Hall on March 15, 1962.

Look magazine and the National Municipal League named Sioux City an All-America City in 1962. The community also had been a finalist in the 1959 competition.

The award served as a fitting climax to a decade of monumental efforts designed to transform Sioux City from a flood-prone river town bogged down by a scandal-ridden government to a progressive, far-sighted city under able administration.

Sioux City Journal reporter Robert Gunsolley summed up the situation by writing, "Sioux City won All-America honors by facing up to its problems and taking action to solve them." The award

also served as a reminder, according to committee co-chairman David J. Albert, of how projects which lay ahead should be approached. Albert continued, "It is important that through this celebration Sioux Cityans can be sold on the idea of keeping Sioux City an All-America City for all time." Photo courtesy of Sioux City Public Museum

The Gateway Arch—symbolic of Sioux City's location at the juncture of three states—welcomes highway travelers and locals alike to the city's downtown business district. The $225,000 roadside park and reflecting pool, dedicated on April 24, 1981, was financed through donations from Sioux City civic organizations, businesses, and private individuals as the centerpiece of an ongoing downtown beautification project. Photo courtesy of DeWild, Grant, Reckert and Associates

The community that *Look* magazine had hailed as an All-America City in 1962 did not rest on its laurels. New goals were established and old projects were completed as Sioux Cityans confronted the challenges of the 1960s and 1970s.

The completion of the Floyd River Rechannelization Project in 1964 and the subsequent Mary J. Treglia Urban Renewal Program in 1969 set the tempo for civic undertakings during this period. Though hundreds of South and East bottoms families and businesses were forced to relocate, the rechannelization project freed the lower Floyd Valley from the catastrophic human and economic disasters of the past, and the urban renewal program transformed the blighted area into a modern wholesaling, retailing, and light manufacturing district. The site attracted new and existing Sioux City industries, resulting in a significant increase in the region's property values. Car dealerships and other businesses moved to locations along Sixth Street between Highway 75 and Morgan Street. Now popularly known as Auto Row, Sixth Street rests directly above the old channel.

The implementation of the Pick-Sloan Missouri River Flood Control Project, begun in 1944 by the U. S. Army Corps of Engineers, provided another economic and environmental boost to Sioux City. The Pick-Sloan project decreased the threat of brutal flooding to Sioux City and its Missouri Valley neighbors. The high point of the undertaking locally was the creation of a six-foot navigational channel (later increased to nine feet) between Sioux City and St. Louis in 1964. Sioux City again became a Missouri River shipping port. The upsurge of river barge traffic triggered the expansion of terminal grain facilities, as Siouxland grain reached international markets. The barge traffic bolstered the region's economy.

Despite these significant gains, many critical problems faced the city in the 1960s. The baby boom that followed World War II created serious problems for the school system, especially at the high school level, as older, crowded, and inefficient structures were forced to accommodate the city's largest-ever high school enrollment. As outlying shopping malls were becoming popular in the region, Sioux City's downtown retail district was experiencing difficulties in attracting and retaining customers. Part of Sioux City's retail trade area was being absorbed by Omaha and Sioux Falls.

The announcement in 1963 that Armour and Company would close its old and costly Sioux City operation sent shock waves through the stockyards and the entire community. A vigorous attempt by government, business, and labor failed to reverse Armour's decision, and the Sioux City plant closed its doors, throwing more than 1,000 people out of work.

The community, in dealing with these troubles, seemed to take stock of its assets. During its history, Sioux City had had an ever-increasing economic relationship with the surrounding territory. In the early 1960s, the emphasis expanded from the community of Sioux City to the region of Siouxland. Changes that occurred permitted local business leaders to take greater advantage of the forty-two-county retail marketing area. The opening of Interstate Highway 29 and the increased importance of Missouri River shipping allowed the construction of industrial districts within the region. The growth of nearby Nebraska communities also improved the economic outlook.

Iowa Beef Packers (later Iowa Beef Processors and, still later, IBP Inc.), the brainchild of Andy Anderson and one-time Swift and Company slaughterhouse laborer-turned-businessman Currier J. Holman, moved its base of operations in 1964 from its Denison, Iowa, plant to a new $12-million plant in Dakota City, Nebraska. IBP restructured the out-of-date beef packing industry and emerged as the world's largest producer of pre-packaged beef products. The opening of other locally-owned packing houses combined with the growth of IBP to soften the economic blow of the Armour pullout.

City planners and business leaders recognized that a diversified economy would lessen the impact of future plant closings. During the 1960s, Sioux City's Industrial Development Council attracted new firms and established Sioux City businesses to the new industrial parks. In 1964, Iowa Public Service Company (IPS) began operation of the Port Neal generating plant, located along the Missouri River near Salix, Iowa. Three years later, IPS disclosed that the power company would construct the first of three large additions to the Port Neal complex. That same year, Terra Chemicals International opened a multi-million-dollar plant in the Port Neal industrial district.

The Bridgeport Industrial Park, near Sioux City's southern border, began to take shape in the mid-1960s and attracted fifteen firms in less than ten years. Tri-View, the city's first industrial district, continued to expand, highlighted by the 1967 opening of the Zenith (Wincharger) Corporations's new plant.

Civic improvements and housing expansion accompanied the industrial growth of Sioux City's "post-Armour" years. The founding of Western Iowa Tech Community College in 1967, the passage of a citizen-spearheaded $13.5-million bond issue for three new high schools in 1969, construction of a new Mor-

ningside branch library, and the planning of two new Missouri River bridges were major elements in the city's growth. Corn fields, wood lots, orchards, and former landfills gave way to urban sprawl. The most remarkable conversion during the 1960s and 1970s occurred in the far-Northside and Morningside neighborhoods—areas that Boom Years promoters of the 1880s and 1890s had mapped out in anticipation of just such a trend.

Urban renewal plans, their successes and failures, dominated the 1960s and 1970s. Sioux City's downtown echoed the pulse of the wrecker's ball as many of its retail shops and theaters made way for new construction. The Mary J. Treglia project was the first of six massive, multi-million-dollar programs designed to improve portions of Sioux City. The districts renovated included: Central Business District (CBD)-East, CBD-West, Hamilton area, Mid-City area, and Prospect Hill. The demolitions did not receive universal acclaim, as many citizens, especially patrons of the stately T. S. Martin Department Store, questioned whether change necessarily meant progress. The changes caused the chamber of commerce to label Sioux City as A City on the Move.

The execution of the CBD-East Urban Renewal Program drastically altered the skyline of the downtown's east end. While the development of the area was not without severe problems, the finished product was the transformation of a badly-deteriorated shopping district into a healthy retail and business center. By the end of 1975, the Federal Plaza Office Building, the Riviera Theaters, the twelve-story Hilton Hotel, the new J. C. Penney Department Store, and two large municipal parking ramps stood on the site of earlier structures. Several new bank buildings were built adjoining the CBD-East area. Progress in CBD-West languished, however, as economic and developmental problems hindered growth in that region.

A controversy between those favoring downtown and those favoring outlying merchandising facilities sprang up in 1969. A group of developers had announced their intention to build a regional shopping mall—in South Morningside or on land south of the city limits. The issue was whether Sioux City could support simultaneous development of both regions or whether the result would be two inadequate shopping areas and the erosion of Sioux City's forty-two-county retail trade market. Advocates of downtown improvements, including a majority of the city council, fought to disallow the construction of the outlying mall. The ensuing eight-year campaign, described as one of the most divisive in recent city history, climaxed when the 1977 municipal election swung the city council in favor of the mall. The opening of the Southern Hills Mall in March 1980, and the earlier completion of the Highway 20 By-Pass and the Sergeant Floyd Memorial Bridge to Nebraska, enhanced Sioux City's retail trade.

Private construction downtown in the late 1970s and early 1980s included the IPS Building, the First

National Bank, the Marian Health Center hospital, the Terra/Northwestern Bank Building and the post office. These and other developments proved that the downtown was still vital and would continue to serve as the financial, professional, and governmental center of the city and play a major role as a retailing district.

Sioux City in the 1980s features attractive retail centers, first-rate medical facilities, a limited but important industrial base, and an enviable system of educational, religious, and cultural institutions.

The Boom Years philosophy of the Sioux City Way did not die in 1893. Rather, it is continually being redefined and reshaped to meet the changing needs of Sioux City's people. It is Sioux Cityans' resilience in the face of adversity that makes Sioux City's history exciting, but even those who left in disgust (or fled in disgrace) would agree with a story told by Stella Davis Gordon in 1929:

A Sioux City woman who was traveling abroad wanted to send a cable home. As she stood in the cable office trying to reduce her message to the fewest number of words possible, the clerk interrupted. "You can leave out the word Iowa," he suggested, "because there is only one Sioux City in the world."

Cornelius "Conny" Bodine, Jr., became Sioux City's second city manager, assuming the duties in January 1958. This was Bodine's sixth city manager position. He was not, however, the first Bodine in Sioux City's history, as relative Samuel T. Bodine, a Philadelphia resident, had served as general manager of the Sioux City Gas and the Sioux City Electric companies at the turn of the century.

The new city manager worked to improve personnel training and reporting and to secure a greater share of state and federal funds. The hallmark of Conny Bodine's managerial stint, though, was the further development of city government planning. He, his staff, and the city council created long-range goals for the community which carried the city ahead during the 1950s, 1960s, and 1970s. He also served a sufficiently-long tenure to enact many of these plans. Bodine's regime was a time of major projects—the construction of Interstate Highway 29, the rechannelization of the Floyd River, the Mary J. Treglia urban renewal project, and the groundwork of downtown urban renewal.

A series of controversies in 1966 and 1967, including the construction of a bitterly contested new Morningside Branch Library, the relocation of the Sioux City Art Center to its 513 Nebraska Street site, and the disapproval of some councilmembers with Bodine's public and private expressions of his views led to Bodine's forced resignation on March 21, 1967. The Sioux City Journal deemed the sudden ending of Bodine's nine-year tenure, far longer than the term of any other local city manager, to be the major news story of 1967.

James Burke, a former assistant to Bodine, reacted angrily to the ouster of Bodine: "For all of Mr. Bodine's faults, he was like a breath of spring to our town. For the first time in decades, the average guy can go out and find a job in Sioux City, factories are being built, new homes are being constructed, and there is no graft and corruption."

After his resignation, Bodine served as an executive of Iowa Beef Processors, Inc. and was business administrator for the city of Newark, New Jersey. He formed a consulting firm in 1978. Bodine was a member of the city government's Charter Commission in 1979, a body which reviewed the existing form of government and made recommendations on what changes, if any, should be made. The voters elected Conny Bodine to a four-year term on the city council in November 1979. Photo courtesy of KCAU-TV

The human price of progress. A near-Eastside renter, aided by a city-furnished truck and moving crew, begins the heart-rending task of moving to a new home in 1962 during the first stages of the Floyd River Rechannelization project. An estimated 550 families, many of them members of low-income minority groups, suffered the tragedy of forced relocation as homes as this one were razed to make way for such projects as Floyd Rechannelization, urban renewal, and I-29 construction. Their plight, compounded by a lack of consistent relocation policy in early years, helped awaken Sioux Cityans during the 1960s and 1970s to the need for low-income housing. Photo courtesy of Sioux City Public Museum

This aerial perspective, looking upstream on November 6, 1962, shows the construction of the new Floyd River channel (center), as well as the old channel (right). The Sioux City Soos ball park is in the upper left, and the Missouri Valley Steel Company's plant and the Terminal Grain Corporation's elevators are in the upper right. In evidence, to the left (west) of the new channel, is the grading of Hoeven Drive, named in honor of northwest Iowa Congressman Charles B. Hoeven; in the center, workers are in the early stages of building the Eleventh Street Bridge.

On March 14, 1964, Congressman Hoeven, Governor Harold Hughes, Senator Jack Miller, and others sat upon the completed Eleventh Street Bridge and witnessed Sioux City reaching a milestone, when the Floyd was diverted into its new channel. Even the failure of sticks of dynamite to function properly and open the earthen dam holding the Floyd from its new home did not dampen the spirits or mar the day. An enterprising bulldozer operator reacted quickly, mounted his machine, and cleared the path.

Journal reporter Helen Benedict

described the day's events, including a jam-packed tour of the area: "There were memories of times when a streak of lightning brought tension, and a heavy rain brought fear to anyone in the Floyd valley. There were memories of death and destruction and hardship—of hastily-moved household goods—of hundreds of persons huddled hopelessly in shelters, awaiting the word that they could return to their damaged homes....It was a day to look backward—and also to look forward, when the now improved drive will be one of scenic beauty—where the grazing cattle and great industries will have nothing to fear from their former major enemy, the Floyd River. At the conclusion of the festivities, hundreds happily munched free hot dogs and decided that it was indeed a proud day for Sioux Cityans." Photo by the U.S. Corps of Engineers; courtesy of Sioux City Public Museum

On May 26, 1969, the city of Sioux City entered into a contractual agreement with Woodbury Development Corporation for the development of CBD-East, a three-square block portion of downtown. Jack Dowd, chairman of Central City Committee, a group of business leaders advocating a resurgence of activity in the downtown area, hailed the signing "as the culmination of five years of planning and execution."

The plans called for the demolishment of all buildings in an area bordered by Fourth, Fifth, Nebraska, and Jones streets, as well as the structures on the block south of Fourth Street between Jackson and Jones streets.

These two photographs show a part of the CBD-East area prior to the massive razing of structures during the early months of 1970.

In this view, the east side of Jackson Street between Fourth and Fifth streets is the main focus. The Hotel Jackson, put up in 1912 and once considered one of the city's finest hotels, is on the left. To the right is the Hollywood Theatre, which opened as the Princess Theatre in 1914. Next to the theater is the old Metropolitan Block, less than a shadow of its former splendor. The top three floors had been removed in 1955, and by this time only the ground floor was considered safe. The Hilton Hotel and a parking ramp now occupy this site. Photo courtesy of Sioux City Journal

In the bottom of view, the east side of Nebraska Street between Fourth and Fifth streets, a crowd braves the winter weather and moves slowly past the Rathskeller on its way to the Capitol Theatre to see Sidney Poitier "at his all time best" in the motion picture To Sir With Love. *The Capitol Theatre building opened in 1912 as the Isis Theatre and later housed the U.S.A. Theatre and the Orpheum Vaudeville Theatre.*

Many Sioux Cityans were angry or disappointed over the razing of the T.S. Martin store soon after this photo was snapped. In addition to those who simply hated to lose the fine buildings and store, many others argued against demolition prior to final commitment by a major tenant to reoccupy the site. The store came down, however, in early February 1970. The J. C. Penney Company's large department store now occupies this site. Photo courtsy of Sioux City Journal

This view from the fall of 1971 documents the activity taking place in the CBD-East region. Looking east from the Lytle Building, traffic is seen routed around Fifth Street east of Nebraska Street while workers lay new sewer pipes. On the right is the site of the soon-to-be-built J. C. Penney store, which opened on January 1, 1975.

This image (above), taken from St. Vincent's Hospital, reveals the project area and the order of construction. To the left of the Badgerow Building (with the weatherball on the roof), are the Riviera Theaters and Parking Ramp A. In front of the theaters is the site of the Hilton Hotel and Parking Ramp B.

Private investment was also taking place downtown. The Northwestern National Bank building is under construction at the northeast corner of Fifth and Jackson. Upon completion of the Terra/Northwestern Bank building in 1983, the "old" structure will become the Central Medical Office building for Marian Health Center. Photos courtesy of Sioux City Journal

The construction and occupancy of the twelve-story Hilton Hotel, shown here on June 13, 1974, was considered a bench mark of success for the CBD-East urban renewal program. It opened in January 1975. Photo courtesy of Woodworth Commercial Photos

Several Sioux City banks built new downtown structures during the 1970s, which greatly changed the city's appearance. In the spring of 1973, the old Toy National Bank, located at the southwest corner of Fourth and Nebraska, was torn down. The construction of the bank's new building went quickly, and the present Toy National Bank (shown here), occupying the same site, opened on November 16, 1974. Photo courtesy of Toy National Bank

The Hamilton Area urban renewal program, encompassing a thirty-two-block section of the city's Westside between Wesley Way and Hamilton Boulevard and "south" of West Seventh Street, entered the planning stage in 1969, and a Policy Advisory Committee (PAC) of interested area citizens was organized that same year. Execution of the residential improvement project started in 1971.

The Sioux City Chamber of Commerce played a leading role in the development of the West Park Apartments, a fifty-one-unit, subsidized complex for the elderly. Shown at the September 1975 groundbreaking are (left to right): William F. Turner, president of the chamber of commerce; Robert Gleeson, president of W. A. Klinger, Inc. Construction Company; Earlena Bobier, PAC officer; and Mayor George Cole.

The dedication of the relocated Dr. John K. Cook Park, on July 4, 1981, climaxed the Hamilton project. The urban renewal program successfully upgraded the area while retaining its predominantly-residential identity. Photo courtesy of Sioux City Public Museum

The air force mobilized the 860 members of the 185th Tactical Fighter Group at the Sioux City Air Base on January 27, 1968. Commanding officer Colonel (later General) Donald Forney theorized that the "Pueblo incident" was the cause of the sudden mustering to activity duty. The group fought gallantly in the Vietnam War.

The homecoming of the 185th brought a vast crowd to the air base in May 1969. These four women express emotions ranging from glad-heartedness to anxiety as they peer into the sun to catch a glimpse of their loved ones. In the background, a "Welcome Home" sign greets the 185th in general and Captain Robert Anderson in particular. Photo courtesy of Sioux City Journal

A youngster gnaws on his hand while he awaits his father's return. Photo courtesy of Sioux City Journal

215

Long a familiar figure at the corner of Fourth and Pierce, Sioux City policeman Efren Bata directs traffic on a summer afternoon in 1962. Photo courtesy of Sioux City Public Museum

Stanley Greigg, a graduate of East High School and Morningside College, returned to Morningside as dean of men after completing graduate school at Syracuse University. In 1961, at age thirty, he was selected to the city council and two years later became Sioux City's youngest mayor.

With the retirement of eleven-term Congressman Charles Hoeven, the seat was left wide open in 1964. Running on the Democratic ticket headed by President Lyndon B. Johnson, thirty-three-year-old Stanley Greigg emerged as this district's youngest congressman. He served one term and was defeated in his try for reelection. He remained in Washington, D.C., however, after receiving a judicial appointment by President Johnson. Photo courtesy of the Sioux City Journal

Local attorney Wiley Mayne emerged as the Republican party's nominee for U.S. Congress in 1966 and defeated his Democratic opponent, incumbent Stanley Greigg. Mayne served four terms and became a nationally-recognized figure during the impeachment proceedings of President Nixon. Political observer Theodore H. White, a classmate of Mayne's at Harvard University, notes in his book In Search of History (Harper & Row, Publishers) that, "wrestling with his conscience on whether to impeach or not, he [Mayne] seemed to be perhaps the most sensitive and human member of the Judiciary Committee."

On October 31, 1974, President Gerald R. Ford campaigned at the Municipal Airport in support of Mayne's bid for reelection, an event that drew a large crowd. The backlash against Watergate, including Mayne's support of President Nixon, coupled with Ford's pardoning of the former president, combined to hinder Mayne's chances. On election day just twelve days later, Democratic candidate, Berkley Bedell, a Spirit Lake, Iowa businessman, reversed a 1972 loss at the hands of Mayne and became Northwest Iowa's representative in Congress. Photo courtesy of Sioux City Journal

Project S, a movement to upgrade the Sioux City Public Schools, began in January 1968. Under the direction of Lloyd D. Fark, this dedicated committee of volunteers, working with school board members, superintendent William Anderson, administrators, and teachers, raised funds, created a speakers' bureau, and advertised the need for a new elementary school and three new high schools. The bond issue for the elementary school passed overwhelmingly in May 1968, allowing construction of Nodland Elementary School.

All efforts then turned to the high school levy. On election day, February 18, 1969, Project S received more than the 60 percent approval required, and the $13.5 million bond election passed.

The graduating class of 1972 marked the passing of four schools from the high school scene. East, Leeds, and Riverside high schools were converted into junior highs, while Central High School, the Castle on the Hill, closed altogether. In the fall of 1972, the three new high schools opened.

North High School, 4200 Cheyenne Boulevard.

West High School, 2001 Casselman street.

East High School, 5011 Mayhew Avenue. Photos courtesy of Woodworth Commercial Photos

Tri-View, circa 1972—the city's first industrial district.

A group of local business leaders, incorporated as the Industrial Development Expansion Association (I.D.E.A.), obtained a mile-long stretch of riverfront in June 1957 and began developing the Tri-View industrial district. I.D.E.A., working closely with the chamber of commerce, the Industrial Development Council, and the municipal government, improved the acreage and secured tenants. By 1962, when Sioux City received its All-America City recognition, ten new buildings had been constructed in the Tri-View area.

In March 1966 Wincharger Corporation announced that it would build a $3-million manufacturing plant in the district. This provided two major benefits to the city— more jobs and an increase in assessed valuation. This aerial photograph, looking east, shows the large, square Wincharger (Zenith) plant, in the center, and a number of other business concerns. In the background, upriver from the Combination Bridge, is the Cimmarina.

The closing of the Zenith plant in the late 1970s greatly hindered the local economy and adversely affected many people. The plant later reopened as the Rochester Products Division of General Motors. Photo courtesy of Woodworth Commercial Photos

A fireman winds up the last of his hose during cleanup operations at Sioux City's Bartlett Grain Company elevator, May 1, 1974. A massive grain dust explosion at the giant Leeds facility the day before left four men dead and one seriously injured in what has been termed Sioux City's worst industrial mishap since 1949. Walter Beggs photo; courtesy of American Pop Corn Company

A 1981 aerial view of the Sioux Honey Association's Sioux City plant—the makers of Sue Bee Honey.

Edward G. Brown, Clarence Kautz, and three local beekeepers incorporated the Sioux Honey Association on December 31, 1921. The company processes, packages, markets, and distributes honey products for its membership. The first "plant" was a 25- by 40-foot basement portion of the Morningside Masonic Temple. The association moved in 1937 to the old Kari-Keen trunk (later the Kari-Keen airplane) building at 509 Plymouth Street. Many additions have been constructed since then, and the company also has plants in several other cities throughout the south and west.

The Sioux Honey Association has become the world's largest honey marketing organization. From a retail sales level in 1922 of 20,000 pounds of honey, the association now boasts an annual capacity of 30 million pounds. Photo courtesy of Sioux Honey Association

The Big Soo Terminal is headquarters for Sioux City's international river transportation system.

Although steamboats had churned up the Missouri River since the 1830s, the river's speed, rapid rate of descent, and constantly-changing course had made boat transportation a very hazardous profession. In the early 1900s, George C. Call, A. B. Beall, John C. Kelly, and others helped initiate a program to improve the river and thereby benefit upper Missouri shipping. Their advice and work did not gain a measurable foothold, but it laid the seed for later growth. The U.S. Army Corps of Engineers began massive improvements to the Missouri River in the 1930s.

The Sioux City and New Orleans Barge Lines started in January 1940 and presided over by George R. Call (son of George C.), brought its first shipment to Sioux City on June 27, 1940. The arrival of these upriver goods for the wholesale hardware firm of Knapp and Spencer marked the opening of Sioux City to barge traffic. Sioux City's Terminal Grain Corporation, headed by Edward C. Palmer, another long-time river improvement advocate, shipped 300 tons of grain to the port of Memphis, Tennessee, on the maiden return trip. Still, many betterments were required before Sioux City could be considered a true river port. During the 1940s, 1950s, and 1960s, further improvements were made to the Missouri River, stabilizing the banks and increasing the river's navigational depth. Finally, in 1964, a six-foot channel was secured the entire distance from Sioux City to the mouth of the Missouri River.

Terminal Grain Corporation organized the Big Soo Terminal Company as a subsidiary and constructed a public terminal in 1963. Sioux City Journal reporter Robert Gunsolley then wrote that the terminal "will include a 35- by 300-foot dock, mooring space for four or five barges, loading and unloading equipment, and storage facilities for grain, bulk liquids, and other commodities." An estimated eighty barges arrived in 1964, when Sioux City first became a significant port. The Big Soo Terminal remains an important economic factor for grain merchants, farmers, livestock byproduct companies, and the community. Photo courtesy of Big Soo Terminal

River-Cade was organized in 1964 to commemorate the Missouri River's channelization with a six-foot navigational depth. The main objective was to focus attention on the new port of Sioux City as a gateway to worldwide shipments of Siouxland's agricultural goods. River-Cade also was created to demonstrate recreational and industrial river safety.

The annual attraction provides something for everyone—a carnival midway, parade, sky diving, athletics, fireworks, hot-air balloons, a queen coronation, and much more.

These Siouxlanders and visitors gather at Chris Larsen Park during the 1976 River-Cade celebration. The Combination Bridge is in the background. Photo courtesy of Robert Chapman

Sioux City Community Theatre cast members perform their parts in the December 1964 production of Damn Yankees.

Although the conditions of the organization's playhouse at 615 Fifth Street were far from ideal, the structure was filled with history. It opened in 1906 as the Lyric Theatre and the following year became the Orpheum, the city's first full-time vaudeville house. Later, the building was known as the Gayety, Rialto, and Victory theatres. It became the home of the Community Theatre in 1956.

Shore Acres Ballroom closed because of a lack of attendance just seven months after this 1964 production. Shortly thereafter, the Community Theatre acquired the old boat club/dancehall, located along the Big Sioux River. It remains the home of Sioux City's theater group. Photo by Edward S. Wood; courtesy of Jim Henry

Noted actor Macdonald Carey, the son of Charles and Elizabeth Carey and the nephew of former Sioux City Journal *editor John W. Carey, grew up on Sioux City's Northside in the family's home at 2711 Jones Street. He graduated from Central High School and briefly attended Morningside College before matriculating at the University of Iowa.*

Carey quickly rose to prominence in the entertainment field, appearing in many movies and plays before specializing on the "small screeen." He joined the cast of the daytime television show "Days of Our Lives" in 1965 and has received two Emmy awards for his role as Dr. Tom Horton. Photo courtesy of Sioux City Journal

The Sioux City Musketeers, under the direction of Gary Lipshutz, joined the United States Hockey League in 1972. The team compiled only a 16-26 record in its initial season but ended on a strong note. Management staged an awards night for the final game, on March 17, 1973, and a photographer captured Muskie goalie Keith Hall receiving the Most Valuable Player award from Sioux City Mayor Paul Berger. Some of the 1,738 spectators are in the background. The largest crowd of the

season saw the Musketeers' best game of the year, a commanding 8-0 shutout of a highly-touted Marquette team.

The most successful season for the Sioux City Musketeers was in 1981-82. In a dramatic turn-around, the Muskies rose from last place in 1980-81 and became the champions of the U.S.H.L. during both the regular season and the playoffs. The team then journeyed to Detroit for a national tournament and took second place honors. Photo courtesy of Gary Lipshutz

College forwards Mark Faber of Morningside and Rolando Frazer of Briar Cliff leap high for a rebound in this December 6, 1979, game at the Sioux City Auditorium. Briar Cliff emerged with a 69-59 victory, their seventh straight triumph over the Chiefs. Morningside broke the spell twelve days later, however, with a stunning upset of the highly-ranked Chargers by a score of 82-78.

Rolando Frazer fired in thirty-seven points in the first game and forty-four in the rematch. The Panama native's 3,078 career point total at Briar Cliff stands as the record for all Iowa collegiate basketball players. Photo courtesy of Briar Cliff College

Until the 1960s, vocational education in the Siouxland area was limited to on-the-job training. In August 1966, however, the Iowa State Board of Education accepted a plan submitted by the counties of Ida, Monona, Plymouth, and Woodbury for the creation of an area vocational-technical school.

Instructional activity for the new technical school—now known as Western Iowa Tech—began on January 27, 1967, with two technical and one post-high school vocational programs. By August 1967 the school boasted seventeen full-time training programs in classes conducted on the former seminary campus of Trinity College and in rented stores and shop buildings in Siouxland.

Today's Western Iowa Tech Community College, shown here on its modern hillside campus at 4647 Stone Avenue, reflects the community's growing emphasis on formal vocational-educational training. Over 14,000 full- and part-time students, both youth and adult, presently are enrolled in fifty-four specialized programs, including agricultural technology, engineering, solar technology, nursing, data processing, electronics, and communications. The campus also is home to radio station KWIT-FM—Siouxlands public broadcasting station. Photo courtesy of Western Iowa Tech Community College

The I-29 bridge, which connects the Morningside area and the southern edge of South Sioux City, Nebraska, opened on November 22, 1976, seventeen years after the planning began for the thoroughfare. The appropriation of interstate highway funds in 1968 spurred development and vanquished the idea of making it a toll bridge. With severe problems affecting the newer Siouxland Veterans' Memorial Bridge in 1982, this $30 million structure, known locally as the Sergeant Floyd Bridge, has proved a lifesaver to the region.

In this aerial view, looking south, Highway 75 and Interstate-29 are on the left, and the Big Soo Terminal, the Bridgeport industrial district, and the Municipal Airport are in the background. Photo courtesy of Sioux City Public Museum

The groundbreaking ceremony for the replacement to the Combination Bridge was held on November 22, 1976, the same day that the Sergeant Floyd Memorial Bridge was dedicated. In this summer of 1980 view, taken from the Nebraska side, the 425-foot main span is being constructed.

The nearly $30-million Siouxland Veterans' Memorial Bridge, named in honor of area residents who have been in military service, was dedicated on July 22, 1981. Less than ten months later, the Iowa Department of Transportation closed the bridge because of structural deficiencies. Repair work on the bridge began in late 1982. Photo courtesy of Sioux City Public Museum

End of a landmark. A Sioux City Journal photographer captures the demolition of the Combination Bridge's northern fixed span on February 23, 1981—eighty-five years and thirty-three days after the span was dedicated.

Beyond the puffs of smoke is the Siouxland Veterans' Memorial Bridge. Photo courtesy of Sioux City Journal

On December 4, 1981, an old era ended and a new one began with the crossing of this Burlington Northern unit grain train over Sioux City's new Missouri River railroad bridge. Constructed at a cost of $14 million, the new bridge replaced the original Missouri River Railroad Bridge (shown right) almost ninety-three years to the day after it opened. The replacement signaled Sioux City's revival as a major Midwestern rail-grain shipping terminus. Photo courtesy of Burlington Northern Railroad

The central building of St. Luke's Regional Medical Center opened in 1972, followed three years later by a three-story addition to the structure. In 1979 a five-story patient wing was dedicated. The complex, located between Twenty-seventh and Twenty-ninth streets and Pierce and Douglas streets, forms part of a regional health care system of which all of Siouxland justly is proud.

The merger of two established Sioux City institutions, the Methodist and Lutheran hospitals, formed St. Luke's Medical Center in 1966. ("Regional" was added to the name later.) The Methodist Hospital had been in its Twenty-ninth and Douglas streets building since 1925. The Lutheran Hospital (called the German Lutheran Hospital until World War I) had started in 1901 at the northeast corner of Twenty-seventh and Pierce streets. The Lutheran Hospital constructed numerous additions in the decades that followed, the largest being a $1.25-million venture in 1951-53, which provided fifty-five new beds. Photo courtesy of St. Luke's Regional Medical Center

St. Joseph's and St. Vincent's hospitals combined in 1977 to form Marian Health Center. In order to centralize services, Marian Health Center began building this large, new hospital in September 1979. The hospital site occupies the entire block bordered by Fifth, Sixth, Jones, and Jennings streets; a skywalk connects the St. Vincent's unit with the new structure. The new hospital, one of the largest projects ever undertaken in Sioux City's downtown, opened in 1982. Photo courtesy of Marian Health Center

The Southern Hills Mall, at South Lakeport and the Highway 20 Bypass, is the result of years of effort and struggle.

The push for a regional shopping center in South Morningside began in 1969, when developer Carl A. Johnson announced his intention to build Lincolnshire Mall. In the early 1970s, Martin Bucksbaum, board chairman of General Growth Development, Inc., of Des Moines, one of the nation's biggest shopping center developers, stated that his company also planned to create a mall just south of the city limits. Vigorous discussions ensued concerning the outlying mall's potential impact on the downtown's revitalization scheme. At the end of 1977, however, three of the five city council members supported the construction of the suburban mall.

Construction began in 1978, and the Southern Hills Mall opened on March 5, 1980. Sears, Younkers, and Target stores anchor the massive complex, while approximately 100 other retailers strive to serve the consumer. Photo by B. Paul Chicoine

Shoppers explore the Clock Court of the Southern Hills Mall, Sioux City's first fully-enclosed retail shopping complex. Photo courtesy of General Growth Corporation, Des Moines, Iowa

The Iowa Public Service building stimulated growth to the downtown's west end.

The second phase of downtown urban renewal, called CBD-West, was to include a major department store, a covered mall, retail shops, and, perhaps, a civic/cultural building. CBD-West has not developed according to plans, however, because of financial uncertainties and related problems.

Iowa Public Service Company, which had been located in the Orpheum Building since January 1949, needed additional and improved quarters by the mid-1970s. After

initially turning down the offer, West End Developers, the successors to Metro Center as the developer of CBD-West, approved the location of IPS on a site originally earmarked for a shopping center.

IPS selected Rossetti Associates of Detroit and FEH Associates of Sioux City as the architects and W. A. Klinger of Sioux City as the general contractor. The ground-breaking for the $13.3 million IPS system control center and corporate headquarters was held on November 29, 1978. Utilizing a joint design-build process, the structure rose quickly and opened on December 22, 1980.

In explaining the ultra-modern structure, architects Gino Rossetti and James Cruthis wrote: "The IPS headquarters was conceived as a dramatic enhancement to the urban environment of Sioux City. The downtown site was deliberately chosen in the hope that this project would provide an economic and environmental renaissance for the downtown area." Photo courtesy of Iowa Public Service Company

Inside Iowa Public Service's downtown corporate headquarters, engineers and dispatchers forecast and coordinate daily electric load and natural gas transmission for the utility company's multi-state customer service area. Photo courtesy of Iowa Public Service Company

The new First National Bank building at Fifth and Pierce streets exemplifies the new look being imparted on Sioux City's skyline by the progressive business builders of the eighties. Begun in 1980 and finished two years later, the monolithic brick and glass structure replaced the bank's earlier home on the same site. Designers for the project were FEH Associates, with construction by W. A. Klinger. Photo by Grant Jensen; courtesy of First National Bank

Sioux City's new Terra Building rises from the ruins of "Lake Brandeis."

The problems encountered in developing Block 70 of the CBD-East project, bordered by Third, Fourth, Nebraska, and Jackson streets, were a sore spot in the city's revitalization program for many years. The failure to secure the Brandeis department store, after leveling all existing structures in the block except the Badgerow Building, led many people to call the hole "Lake Brandeis."

Monumental efforts and good faith in the early 1980s, however, changed this prevailing attitude. The Northwestern National Bank (Banco Properties, Inc.) and Terra Chemicals International announced on December 18, 1980, that they would construct and occupy Sioux City's tallest building, shown here in an architectural drawing. The complex, located in Block 70, would also include a series of small, retail shops. It was a day for rejoicing for city planners and area construction workers.

The groundbreaking ceremony for the $18 million structure was held on April 6, 1982, and the magnificent glass-clad ediface is scheduled for completion in late 1983. Photo courtesy of Terra Chemicals International

The new post office building, shown here in an architectural rendering, will relieve overcrowded conditions in the 1934-vintage Federal Building and allow more stream-lined mail processing. Its construction will also provide a vital shot-in-the-arm to Sioux City's economy.

Work began on the $8.5-million project in 1982 on a site between Second and Third streets and east of Jackson Street. It is scheduled to open late in 1983. Photo courtesy of U.S. Post Office

225

The 1922-vintage War Eagle Monument, honoring the noted Native American leader from the area's frontier days, had grown unsightly by the early 1970s because of vandalism and age. Contractor Byron J. Brower spearheaded a movement of local individuals and companies to secure funds for a new monument, and the Woodbury County Conservation Board instituted a competition among area artists to design a new structure. The contest's judges selected a Sioux City resident Donald T. Willson's rendition of a peace pipe imbedded in stone. Willson's plan, though, was revised by Peter Rudokas of Middleton, Ohio, who also created the sculpture.

The completed War Eagle Monument (shown here) is thirty-one feet tall, the base measuring eighteen feet in height and the sculpture reaching up an additional thirteen feet. Joe Rockboy, a Dakota Indian, wrote the text for the plaques. The monument, dedicated on July 4, 1975, overlooks the states of Iowa, South Dakota, and Nebraska and is a recognizable feature for those traveling along Interstate Highway 29. It also served as a fitting reminder of the community's heritage and culture. Photo courtesy of Woodworth Commercial Photos

Bibliography

The primary sources of information used in the preparation of this book are cited here. Other sources included photographs, maps, collections of personal papers and local government records, city directories, newspaper clippings, manuscripts written by local residents, transcribed oral history collections, and selected artifacts. These catalogued archival holdings, as well as the sources listed below, are available to the public through the Sioux City Public Museum.

BOOKS

Adams, John D. *Three Quarters of a Century of Progress.* Sioux City: Verstegen Printing Company, 1923.

Allen, Arthur Francis, ed. *Northwestern Iowa: Its History and Traditions.* 3 vols. Chicago: S. J. Clarke Publishing Company, 1927.

Andreas, Alfred T. *Illustrated Atlas of the State of Iowa.* Chicago: Andreas Atlas Company, 1875.

Biddle, Nicholas, ed. *The Journals of the Expedition Under the Command of Captains Lewis and Clark.* New York: The Heritage Press, 1962; reprint ed.

Brigham, Johnson. *Iowa: Its History and Its Foremost Citizens.* 3 vols. Chicago: S. J. Clarke Publishing Company, 1915.

Clark, Will Leach et al. *History of the Counties of Woodbury and Plymouth, Iowa.* Chicago: A. Warner and Company, 1890-1891.

Gue, Benjamin F. *History of Iowa.* 4 vols. New York: The Century History Company, 1903.

Hanson, Joseph Mills. *The Conquest of the Missouri: Being the Story of the Life and Exploits of Captain Grant Marsh.* Chicago: A. C. McClure and Company, 1909.

Harlan, Edgar R. *A Narrative History of the People of Iowa.* 5 vols. Chicago: The American Historical Society, 1931.

Heizer, E. P., ed. *Sioux City Illustrated.* Sioux City and Omaha: D. C. Dunbar and Company, 1888.

History of Western Iowa. Sioux City: Western Publishing Company, 1882.

Holman, Albert M. and Constant R. Marks. *Pioneering in the Northwest.* Sioux City: Deitch and Lamar Company, 1924.

Koerselman, Jon David. "The Origins of Sioux City, Iowa, 1850-1870." M.A. thesis, University of South Dakota, 1975.

Lass, William E. *A History of Steamboating on the Upper Missouri River.* Lincoln, Nebraska: University of Nebraska Press, 1962.

Lokken, Roscoe L. *Iowa Public Land Disposal.* Iowa City, Iowa: State Historical Society of Iowa, 1942.

Marks, Constant R. "Autobiography of Louis D. Letellier." In *South Dakota Historical Collections,* pp. 215-254. Compiled by Doane Robinson, South Dakota State Historical Society. Sioux Falls, South Dakota: Mark D. Scott, 1908.

Marks, Constant R. "Pioneers of Sioux City and South Dakota." In *South Dakota Historical Collections,* pp. 255-274. Compiled by Doane Robinson, South Dakota State Historical Society. Sioux Falls, South Dakota: Mark D. Scott, 1908.

Marks, Constant R., ed. *Past and Present of Sioux City and Woodbury County, Iowa.* Chicago: S. J. Clarke Publishing Company, 1904.

O'Neil, Paul. *The Rivermen.* New York: Time-Life Books, 1975.

Rees, Ida Mae. "Sioux City as a Steamboat Port, 1856-1873.'" M.A. thesis, University of South Dakota, 1967.

Roberts, H. C. *The Public Schools of Sioux City, Iowa.* Sioux City: Board of Education, 1954.

Schmidt, John F. *A Historical Profile of Sioux City.* Sioux City: Sioux City Stationery Company, 1969.

Shambaugh, Benjamin F. *The Constitutions of Iowa.* Iowa City, Iowa: State Historical Society of Iowa, 1934.

Short, Mary. *Just One American.* Sioux City: By the Author, 1943.

Shover, John L. *Cornbelt Rebellion: The Farmers' Holiday Association.* Urbana, Illinois: University of Illinois Press, 1965.

Shuman, Bernard. *A History of the Sioux City Jewish Community.* Sioux City: Jewish Federation, 1969.

Silag, William. "City, Town, and Countryside: Northwest Iowa and the Ecology of Urbanization." Ph.D. dissertation, University of Iowa, 1979.

Sorensen, Scott Alan. "Law Enforcement During the 1930s in Sioux City, Iowa." M.A. thesis, University of South Dakota, 1976.

Wilson, Richard Guy and Sidney K. Robinson. *The Prairie School in Iowa.* Ames, Iowa: Iowa State University Press, 1977.

PERIODICALS

Allen, Leola. "Anti-German Sentiment in Iowa During World War I." *The Annals of Iowa* (Fall 1974): 418-429.

Briggs, John Ely. "The Sioux City Corn Palaces." *Palimpsest* (December 1963): 549-562.

Chicoine, B. Paul. "From Armor Plate to Roustabouts." *The Iowan* (Winter 1981): 34-39, 52-53.

Chicoine, B. Paul. "Rails Across the Sky." *The Iowan* (Spring 1980): 45-45, 53-54.

Clark, Dan Elbert. "Frontier Defense in Iowa, 1850-1865." *The Iowa Journal of History and Politics* (July 1918): 315-386.

Clark, Dan Elbert. "The History of Liquor Legislation in Iowa, 1878-1908." *The Iowa Journal of History and Politics* (October 1908): 503-608.

Cumberland, William H. "Plain Honesty: Wallace Short and the I.W.W." *Palimpsest* (September/October 1980): 146-160.

DiLeva, Frank D. "Attempt to Hang an Iowa Judge." *The Annals of Iowa* (July 1954): 337-364.

Donavon, Frank P., Jr. "The Great Northern in Iowa." *Palimpsest* (April 1965): 193-208.

Donavon, Frank P., Jr. "The Illinois Central in Iowa." *Palimpsest* (June 1962): 265-304.

Eriksson, Erik M. "Sioux City and the Black Hills Gold Rush, 1874-1877." *The Iowa Journal of History and Politics* (July 1922): 319-347.

Garver, Frank H. "The Settlement of Woodbury County." *The Iowa Journal of History and Politics* (July 1911): 359-384.

Ingham, W. H. "Iowa Northern Brigade." *The Annals of Iowa* (October 1902): 481-523.

Johnson, J. R. "Covington, Nebraska's Sinful City." *Nebraska History* (Autumn 1968): 269-282.

Lee, Robert Edson. "Politics and Society in Sioux City, 1859." *Iowa Journal of History* (April 1956): 117-130.

Merrill, Pauline Skorunka. "Pioneer Iowa Bohemians." *The Annals of Iowa* (April 1945): 261-274.

Petersen, Peter L. "Language and Loyalty: Governor Harding and Iowa's Danish-Americans During World War I." *The Annals of Iowa* (Fall 1974): 404-417.

Petersen, William J. "Abu-Bekr Temple." *Palimpsest* (May 1963): 207-217.

Petersen, William J. "Steamboating on the Missouri River." *Iowa Journal of History* (April 1955): 97-120.

Reed, C. A. "Sioux City and the Frontier." *Palimpsest* (December 1954): 511-518.

Sioux City Spirit of Progress. Chamber of Commerce publication. (1921-1926, 1928-1930).

Snyder, Charles E. "Unitarianism in Iowa." *Palimpsest* (November 1949): 355-374.

NEWSPAPERS

Sioux City Eagle (Weekly)
Sioux City Journal (Daily and Weekly)
Sioux City Journal-Tribune (Daily)
Sioux City Register (Weekly)
Sioux City Times (Daily and Weekly)
Sioux City Tribune (Daily and Weekly)
Unionist and Public Forum (Weekly)

INDEX